THE AFRO-AMERICAN EXPERIENCE:
A Cultural History Through Emancipation

THE AFRO-AMERICAN EXPERIENCE:
A Cultural History Through Emancipation

JAMES H. DORMON
ROBERT R. JONES

John Wiley & Sons, Inc.
New York · London · Sydney · Toronto

Library of Congress Cataloging in Publication Data:

Dormon, James H.
  The Afro-American experience.

  Includes bibliographies.
  1. Negroes—History—To 1863.   I. Jones,
Robert Rivers, 1934—   joint author.   II. Title.

E185.D65   1974   917.3′06′96073   73-16475
ISBN 0-471-21913-4
ISBN 0-471-21914-2 (pbk.)

Printed in the United States of America

10 9 8 7 6 5 4 3 2 1

PREFACE

Despite the fact that Afro-America has existed since the discovery and development of the New World, and despite the fact that Afro-Americans have participated in almost every aspect of the total American experience, Afro-American history as an academic discipline is relatively new. Prior to 1950, there were few professional historians specializing in the field; indeed, the reigning historical "Establishment" recognized no Afro-American field. This does not mean that notable scholars did not write, and write very well, on black history subjects. Important contributions were made by such eminent black scholars as Carter G. Woodson, E. Franklin Frazier, John Hope Franklin, W. E. B. DuBois, and others. But when DuBois, one of the most perceptive of the early interpreters of Afro-America, wrote a black-centered version of post-Civil War reconstruction, his work was ignored by the Establishment, written off as a form of special pleading or condemned for its "Marxist" leanings. This important work came out in 1935. Establishment historians, mostly white and mostly imbued with traditional white racial assumptions about blacks, were neither ready nor able to rethink America's past and give the black experience its proper place and perspective.

Since 1950, however, there has been a flood of Afro-American materials as amateur and professional scholars have taken a long second look at the record and have recognized the richness, variety, and overriding historical significance of black America. It probably was inevitable that the ensuing vogue of "black studies" would produce (in the rush to publish) considerable work of questionable scholarly value. Yet, along with the indifferent material, there has also been considerable good work and some that is outstanding. As time has passed, the good work has come to outweigh the mediocre, and there is now a large and growing body of monographic and interpretative literature treating various aspects of the black experience.*

As is usually the case, however, the new, original, provocative scholarship of the last decade has not yet filtered down to popular publications or to the history and social studies textbooks used in American schools. Most of the textbooks designed for standard survey courses, despite superficial and largely ineffective efforts to "integrate" their contents, remain essentially white oriented, assuming that white behavior and white values constitute the desirable norm. Consequently, the nonspecialist—student, teacher, or interested layman—cannot gain much real awareness of the nature of the Afro-American experience and cannot learn of black America in its formative years by going to a standard textbook or a popular history. A readily available, brief volume that incorporates the best of the recent scholarship on early Afro-American history and culture has simply not been available. We have attempted to write such a book, one that "synthesizes" the most important work in the field; by referring to this single volume, one can explore what current scholarship has to say about the black experience through the period of emancipation.

We have tried to accomplish this synthesis within a general framework of culture theory and have thus employed an interdisciplinary approach to provide an ordering principal for our story. Chapter 1 introduces the reader to the crucial but complex concepts of culture and race and provides some intellectual tools for use in the remainder of the book.

*The most recent and now indispensable guide to black studies literature is James M. McPherson, Laurence B. Holland, et. al., Blacks in America. Bibliographical Essays (N. Y.: Doubleday, 1971; Anchor Books edition, 1972).

Whenever possible we have used primary materials from black sources in order to evoke black ideas, feelings, and sensibilities, and to emphasize that in the history of Afro-America, black people themselves were the active historical ingredients. However, the book claims little in the way of originality of research. We have tried for a fresh approach and — an impossible dream — comprehensive use of the best secondary materials to come out in recent years. We have also attempted to stimulate further interest on the part of the student, hoping to encourage him to read more widely and deeply. For this reason, there are extensive comments on the pertinent literature at the end of each chapter. Text footnotes elaborate on the many more important scholarly controversies that are germane to our discussion. However, if the reader prefers a straightforward narrative, he should feel free to skip the notes and move on with the story.

Because this book is synthetic in nature and interdisciplinary in approach, we have incurred obligations to other scholars that are more extensive than usual. Without the time, effort, and thought of J. V. Guillotte, Ted Kibbe, Robert Butler, Walter Craddock, W. Magruder Drake, Allen Begnaud, and others who read and criticized parts of the manuscript, there could have been no book. John Cameron, Gloria Fiero, and Lawrence Rice lent able assistance in the final stages of the book's preparation. Our students over the past six years have also helped us by providing many of the right questions and some of the answers, too. Our editors and the publisher's readers have been enormously helpful.

However, we feel that we owe most to those who have made Afro-American history and culture a viable and challenging field of study, even as they participated in the shaping of that history. We refer to those countless hundreds of people, mostly young and mostly black, who have determined to create an atmosphere in the United States in which black people might live in dignity, comfort, and with pride in their heritage. In their determination, these history makers have fought on many fronts: in courthouses and state houses, in the streets, on buses and trains, in schools and churches and, often enough, in jail. They have made an ongoing revolution. In a woefully inadequate gesture of respect and appreciation, this book is dedicated to them.

James H. Dormon

Robert R. Jones

CONTENTS

Chapter 1

CULTURE AND RACE

*"What really binds men together is their culture—the
ideas and the standards they have in common."* Ruth
Benedict, *Patterns of Culture*

Of all the great historical developments of the past decade or so, none has had more profound impact on the
Afro-American experience than the emergence of black consciousness. Beginning with the civil rights movement of the
late 1950s and gaining in intensity over the years, the sense
of black identity, self-awareness, and solidarity has given
birth to a nation. Black Americans, particularly the younger
black Americans, have determined to look on themselves as
beautiful, capable, proud, and powerful. As their sense of
identity and worth has grown, it has created the need for
symbolic recognition of that identity, demonstrated in the
use of slogans ("black is beautiful"), special "Afro" styles
of appearance (the natural haircut, the *dashiki*), in-group
gestures (the power salute, dapping), and a defining descriptive terminology: the term Afro-American itself.

The idea of an African-American nationality status is
actually an *old* one. Black emigrants to the New World
recognized it from the beginning, and by the late nineteenth
century the term Afro-American had come into use. The
prefixes "Afro" or "African" have long been attached to a
variety of black organizations and institutions. However,
"Afro-American" is also a *new* concept; only in the recent

Note. Footnotes for this chapter are located on pages 22-23.

past have numbers of young black Americans, seeking the roots of their national and cultural heritage, begun to insist on Afro-American as the only acceptable description of their ethnonational status and, indeed, of their very identity. The term is charged with special meaning for our own times.

The concept "Afro-American" is both old and new, historic and immediately relevant; it is also quite precise and, at the same time, almost mystical in its connotations and implications. Its precision is that of any descriptive hyphenate: an Afro-American is an American whose old country forebears were from Africa. Yet the term suggests so much more than this. It suggests that an Afro-American is a special kind of American, one whose historical experience is different from that of other Americans, even other hyphenate-Americans. It suggests, in addition to differences in historical experience, a difference in race. The majority of the Afro-American's conationalists are of western European derivation and form something of a massive ethnoracial unit that stands in clear distinction, and often in high relief, apart from Afro-America. Finally, the use of the term Afro-American suggests a sense of pride in historical, national, cultural, ethnic, and racial differences. And if all these differences could be boiled down to their essentials, those essentials would be "culture" and "race." Consequently, in order to appreciate the distinctiveness of the Afro-American experience, it is necessary to understand something of the nature of culture and race.

"Culture" is a fundamental anthropological concept; some would argue that it is the *central* concept of anthropology and the most important contribution of that discipline to the social studies. It is also a relatively new concept.[1] One of the founding fathers of anthropological science, Edward B. Tylor, provided the starting point for the study of culture in 1871 by suggesting a definition of the term. "Culture," Tylor wrote, "is that complex whole which includes knowledge, belief, art, morals, law, custom, and any other capabilities and habits acquired by man as a member of society." In the years that followed, other scholars came to question certain aspects of the Tylor definition, adding something here, qualifying a bit there. Inevitably, they often disagreed as a new field of study— cultural anthropology—slowly and sometimes painfully developed.

Even today there would probably be great difficulty in achieving complete agreement on a definition of culture, but by now most anthropologists could agree on certain essentials of a definition, if not on all details. Construed broadly, culture is the way of life of a group of people: the sum total of all the values, customs, mores, habits, institutions, and traditions, as well as the sanctioned modes of behavior and appearance that the individual must learn in order to become an acceptable member of his society. Moreover, all of these ingredients (and many others) form a fairly well-integrated pattern or system, the parts of which are interrelated and often interdependent in their structure.

To clarify further, we should reiterate and amplify some of the essentials of a working definition of culture. First, we must be dealing with a group of people—a "society" of some sort—reasonably well circumscribed, reasonably well-defined and delineated. The second essential aspect of culture is its nonbiological transmission. It is passed from one generation to the next. It must be *learned;* it cannot be inherited genetically. And if culture must be learned, the "teachers" must have some sort of symbol system available that can be employed in transmitting the culture material. This is a third essential of culture, one that makes culture the great human achievement that it is. Although other animals, especially the higher primates, seem to have an incipient form of culture, they lack the capacity to communicate their experiences symbolically; without symbols there can be no real culture. For example, the most important of the symbol systems employed in culture transmission is language. Through language virtually every aspect of culture comes to be symbolically identified; hence, it may then be symbolically transmitted from the old members of the group to the new. One major result of this process of symbolic identification and transmission is that the very way in which the people of a given culture perceive reality—how they view and understand the world in which they live—is shaped and formed by the system of symbols employed in that culture.

It should be perfectly apparent that culture is a powerful force constantly operating on the individual from the moment of his birth. As a person grows and develops in his culture, he experiences a process of "enculturation," whereby he is shaped into a desirable, or at least acceptable, part of his group. His enculturation process will also give him his value system and his sets of priorities. Leslie White, an influential cultural anthropologist (he calls himself a "culturologist"), argues persuasively for a kind of cultural determinism. Consider, he suggests, the case of a baby born into any cultural milieu. That infant's culture "will determine how he will think, feel, and act. It will determine what language he will speak, what clothes if any he will wear, what gods he will believe in, and how he will marry, select and prepare his foods, treat the sick, and dispose of the dead." Moreover, White argues, ". . . it is not 'we' who control our culture [;] . . . our culture controls us." Whether or not we go as far as White does in the direction of cultural determinism, we must agree that culture is the force that, except for our genetically inherited characteristics, makes us what we are, by providing us with our values, our customs, and, generally speaking, the rules and sanctions by which we live.[2] Culture is *a* primary, if not *the* primary, human dimension.

Granting the enormous influence exercised by culture on the individual and the group, it should come as no surprise to find that cultures tend to maintain powerful continuity. Culture material, particularly values, mores, kinship systems, language, and religion, is stable stuff. It is stable because of the great value placed on it by its recipients. But even though it is stable and pervasive, culture is never static. It grows. It "develops." It experiences modifications, deviations, variations of all sorts, as people discover or are taught new and different ways of doing things. It is constantly in process and experiencing change.[3]

According to most authorities there are two general categories of culture change: "internal" and "external." Internal change ordinarily comes about through innovation occurring within the culture. Such development frequently accompanies technological improvements or innovations in techniques of subsistence as, for example, when people whose livelihood depends on hunting and gathering discover or improve on plant cultivation or animal domestication. They are then capable of stable planting or herding; hence, they may settle in a single limited area on a more permanent basis. The culture change accompanying such innovation is, of course, enormous. Usually the change is not so dramatic or profound; relatively small innovations in subsistence techniques can and do carry with them the probability of culture change. Another sort of internal change comes in the form of so-called "growth change:" the gradual accretion of small modifications in values or ways of thinking that lead eventually to new religions or value systems or to institutional reconstruction of some sort. There are still other forms that internal change may take, but the key to the understanding of the concept lies in the designation "internal." Change occurs from *within* a society without reference to external matters or to contacts with other, foreign cultures.

External change is more important for the purposes of Afro-American culture history. Again, the anthropologists have fought over the nature of external change for years without agreeing on all details. Basically, however, external change occurs by at least one of three theoretical processes: "diffusion," "acculturation," or "assimilation." All three involve change brought about in one culture by varying degrees of contact with elements of other cultures; all three involve change brought from *without* the system. Diffusion is the process whereby culture elements spread from one culture to another on the basis of only limited contact; it is a kind of cultural borrowing of selected culture materials. Such borrowing, of course, leads to a greater complexity in the culture of the borrower, and is consequently a primary means whereby cultures "grow." But diffusion implies only limited change. The borrowing culture borrows only selectively and utilizes the borrowed material within the framework of its existing culture system.[4]

Acculturation and assimilation are different matters altogether. In acculturation we find one culture—the "acculturating" one—undergoing substantial, even drastic, change by way of conforming to another culture. Here the borrowing occurs on a massive basis; it can happen only in the case of contact of culture wholes. Modifications are drastic in the acculturating society, but vast as they may be (as, for example, in the case of the contact of western Europeans and the aboriginal population of the New World), the changes are not sufficient to destroy the identity of the original culture. As one anthropologist has stated, the acculturating society "becomes adjusted to, but not assimilated in, the dominant society."

This leads quite naturally to the third and rarest form of culture change, assimilation. In this process, one culture incorporates all of another culture. The second group loses its individual cultural identity completely; it becomes a part of the dominant group. In view of what has been said regarding the stability of culture, it should be clear why assimilation is so rare. Individuals do not readily give up their own cultures to identify fully with the ways and traditions of different cultures. Moreover, dominant groups are rarely willing to incorporate foreign culture elements. And because assimilation is so rare, diffusion and acculturation remain the most influential processes in culture dynamics.

Up to this point, most of what has been said about culture and culture change has pertained to relatively small, "primitive" societies. In overwhelmingly complex modern nations, culture considerations are comparably complex. We may, however, speak with some meaning of "total national cultures," as one anthropologist has phrased it, if we keep in mind that there are degrees of cultural integration and cohesion that provide the possibility of considerable variety at the subsocietal levels. To state it differently, today there are certain broad, dominant national culture patterns that coincide generally with the nations themselves, but within these national patterns there are diverse variables, which relate usually to ethnic, economic, class, or caste considerations, or to some combination of such considerations. These subgroups (or "subcultures") frequently exhibit many of the characteristics of individualized cultures. They exhibit patterns peculiar to themselves. Although they are part of the broad national culture, they manifest distinctive qualities and experience their own particular culture imperatives. Subcultures share in the total national culture—the government, legal system, economic institutions, possibly the state religion—but may differ from the *dominant* culture system in a great variety of ways, including modes of behavior and appearance, dietary habits, customs, and values. Consequently, everything said about culture imperatives up to this point may be applied to subcultures existing in the complex modern culture systems.

One final concept that should be mentioned in any brief introduction to culture theory is that of "cultural relativism." Anthropologists consider this concept among their greatest contributions to the social sciences. The term describes a way of thinking and a method of approaching the evaluation of cultures that are foreign to one's own. Basically, the concept of cultural relativism suggests that since all cultural facts are relative to the culture producing them, the individual should avoid judging other cultures by the standards of his own. The concept implies that any custom, however strange or even "barbaric," is perfectly "normal" to its practitioners and thus perfectly acceptable in terms of its cultural setting. To understand a foreign culture, the observer must maintain detachment, strive for real empathy, and employ his imagination in his attempt to see another people as they see themselves.

Obviously, there are certain problems inherent in an extreme interpretation of the principle of cultural relativism. Granted, one may accept the *validity* of any custom sanctioned by the culture manifesting it, but must he admit its *acceptability?* Cultural relativism could well involve cer-

tain ethical and moral relativisms objectionable to many
persons, but the solution to this dilemma (one that has long
plagued the relativists) lies in establishing one's reason for
considering a foreign culture at all. One might well reject
as unacceptable, for example, certain bloody puberty rites,
while at the same time he could (and should) understand
that the objectionable practice is part of a whole structure
that is quite acceptable to those living in it. Only by doing
so can the foreigner hope to *understand* the people he is considering.

If not carried to its extreme, cultural relativism in the
broad sense is a worthy ideal for all people in forming
their opinions of people of other cultures (or subcultures).
The concept simply suggests that we must divest ourselves
of the notion that our way is the best way for everyone.
We should, to use the more technical expression, avoid
"ethnocentric" judgments. We should attempt to view
other cultures as equally valid to their culture bearers as
ours is to us. We should be able to accept the fact that a
person of another culture behaves and appears as he does
because his culture sanctions such behavior and appearance.
The essence of ethnocentrism is the uncritical judgment of
other people by the standards established in one's own culture, a foolish and dangerous practice. It all too frequently
gives rise to fear, distrust, and even hatred of anything or
anyone "foreign." Consequently, ethnocentrism is the
force behind much of man's inability to live in peace with
man. Cultural relativism is a concept that, if widely accepted, might counter that force. This is why the anthropologists consider it such an important contribution of their
discipline.

As important and simple as it is, the concept of cultural
relativism was a long time in coming; in fact, it is a product of twentieth-century thought. And the basic, fundamental reason it took so long in coming was a confusion
that has confounded and plagued mankind since time im-
memorial, the confusion of culture and race. Before beginning our consideration of race, we should establish
clearly and indelibly that culture and race are mutually exclu-

sive by definition. Whatever else may be said of culture, one thing is perfectly clear: it is *learned*. Therefore, it *is not and cannot be* genetically transmitted. And whatever else may be said of race, this much is perfectly clear: it is inherited biologically. Therefore it is and *must necessarily be* genetically transmitted.

If the anthropologists have had their differences of opinion on the question of culture, the "race question" has been a battle royal. One of the deans of American Cultural Anthropology, Franz Boas, lamented in 1936, "We talk all the time glibly of races and nobody can give us a definite answer to the question What constitutes a race." There is some doubt whether anyone even now can provide a definite answer, and no doubt whatever that there would be no more than minimal agreement on any definition offered. The problems inherent in the concept of race transcend not only the boundaries of several scholarly disciplines, but also scholarship itself. The average layman "knows" and always has known what constitutes race, and his "knowing" makes the specialist's job more difficult than ever.

Perhaps the best way to approach an introduction to the concept of race is to examine the nature of the controversy surrounding the subject at the scientific level. First, race is a subject claimed as the special province of many disciplines, among them human biology, population genetics, evolutionary biology, zoology, and, of course, physical anthropology. Each of these specialties claims a particular concern for race studies; each assumes a different perspective and different postulates in its approach to race. The human biologist, more specifically the "taxonomist"—the specialist in classification of biological phenomena—would probably argue that "race" is merely a convenient taxonomic unit, a convenient category (or set of categories) into which mankind may be divided. But his definition of race would very likely differ from that of the geneticist, who is interested in differences in gene-group frequencies, however small; or from that of the anthropologist, who might be more concerned with finding distinctive combinations of physical traits in an effort to account for evolutionary functions and processes.

A second source of controversy is the matter of the origins of human differentiation. Assuming that there are certain differences in man, differences of a broad, morphological type, how did those differences come about? Most would agree that they had something to do with the process of evolution, but evolution itself is a terribly controversial matter. We simply do not know enough about many of the mechanical processes that produce genetic variants to do more than theorize about the nature of evolutionary function and its possible racial implications. There have been numerous theories propounded, some of them contradictory. All of them have been argued with great scholarly persuasiveness, but they are still only theories. It is generally agreed that man is a single species of the genus Homo (genus—Homo, species—Sapiens). But two questions immediately arise. First, what is the nature of human variation exhibited at the *sub*specific level (assuming there is a subspecific level)? Second, did the differences (if there are any) come about before or after the speciation process? In other words, did the differences in man occur before or after Homo erectus became Homo sapiens? It is on these seemingly abstruse and highly technical questions that most of the scholarly controversy surrounding the concept of race has raged.

There is, of course, still no solution to the controversy, and certainly none will be attempted here. We might, however, construct some order from the chaos if we separate the problem of race into some of its component questions, then consider them individually. We should first ask, "why deal with the concept of race at all?" If the subject is so loaded with scientific difficulties and an incredible emotional charge, why not discard it altogether and replace it with some term or set of terms that have more precise meanings? Of course, this very solution has been suggested by the specialists themselves, and in answering it they divide into two fairly distinct schools of thought. On the one hand, there are those who say that the concept of race should be maintained because it *is* a convenient taxonomic unit. On the other hand, there are those who contend that the concept should be abandoned as, in the words of one prominent scholar, "man's most dangerous myth."

In the opinion of the first school, which we might call the "race-is-useful" school, "race" is a term with considerable meaning and, although plagued by some imprecision, still serves a useful function. A race, argue members of the race-is-useful persuasion, is a group of people (or, in the case of nonhuman life, a group of organisms) that share in common a proportion of their genes statistically sufficient to produce genetic similarity of a greater or lesser degree. The genetic similarity may be great enough to produce a broad morphological "type" whose members manifest a distinct combination of physical traits, or small enough that they differ from other people only in the statistical frequency of the appearance of a single gene. But a race must be a breeding population and must have lived for some time in relative isolation from other breeding populations. In other works, it must be the product of inbreeding, for only through inbreeding may genetic similarities occur with sufficient frequency to constitute a race. Once these postulates are accepted, the taxonomist may classify man (or any organism), describing the distinctive genetic qualities of each classification and assigning to that classification (or subspecies or "race") a special name and a special place on the classification list of types of man.

The obvious question to ask a representative of the race-is-useful school is "Just how many races are there?" However, considering the lack of precision in defining the term race, the questioner should be prepared for a vague answer. The biologist, geneticist, or physical anthropologist would most likely reply, "That depends." He would then elaborate, observing that it depends on the degree of genetic similarity insisted on in establishing a race. The number of races of man could range from six or seven to countless hundreds. It all depends on whether the taxonomist involved is a "lumper" or a "splitter," i.e., on the criteria he employs to differentiate the races. Most agree that race should be divided into several varieties, and current taxonomic usage settles on three: geographical races, local races, and microgeographical races. Geographical races comprise the populations of large, clearly defined land areas, frequently continental in scope, where the genetic similarities of the people are broadly (but by no means precisely) manifested in certain morphological similarities. Most taxonomists agree that there are six to eight such races identified with such land masses as (1) Europe and western Asia (roughly analogous to the older classification "Caucasoid"), (2) Africa (analogous to the older "Negroid"), (3) northern and eastern Asia (analogous to "Mongoloid"), (4) India, (5) Micronesia and Melanesia, (6) Polynesia, and (7) the Americas (the original inhabitants were formerly termed "Amerinds"), although there is still controversy over whether North and South America should be separated. The geographical races are generally those that the classifiers refer to when they speak of the human taxonomic unit directly beneath species.

By "local races" the taxonomists mean smaller units of classification, composed of the actual breeding populations within the larger geographical areas. One physical anthropologist has referred to local races as "human islands" where people exhibit some measurable genetic trait frequency, albeit possibly small, that is the result of relatively tight inbreeding brought about by isolation, physical or cultural. (It is noteworthy that by this definition Afro-Americans could justifiably be designated a local race.) The term "microgeographical races" suggests a still smaller breeding unit, differing only quantitatively from local races. But how many local races are there, and how many are microgeographical? Once again it depends on whether you lump or split. As one race specialist puts it, the ennumeration "depends on the minimum size of the population units we wish to consider (in the case of local races) and on the minimum degree of difference we choose to emphasize (in respect to microgeographical races.)" Still, it all seems somehow vague. And indeed, the lack of precision is the chief argument used against race as the basis of a taxonomic system involving man.

In support of the race-is-useful school, the specialists are getting ever further away from broad morphological characteristics—the so-called "phenotype"—and moving more to "pure" genetics in establishing their criteria for genetic differentiation. Such characteristics as head shape, cranial capacity, nose shape, and body type are practically obsolete as taxonomic differentials. The most important distinguishing characteristic has become the serological factor: blood group frequencies. On the basis of one of several possible blood-group classifications, the modern geneticist can actually measure the frequency of appearance of a given blood group or factor. This approach is useful because it is most empirical, most "scientific." It is thus far more precise than crude measurements or simple phenotypic appearance in distinguishing human variety. Establishing a "genotype" is infinitely more accurate than observing a phenotype.

Establishing a genotype is also more difficult. In fact, human taxonomy is a highly technical business that should be left to trained specialists. Unfortunately, this is not possible because, as we have noted, everyone "knows" what race is, including politicians who have all too often made political use of their "knowledge." One well-known (and controversial) physical anthropologist, Carleton S. Coon, has suggested that even though this is true, it is of no concern to the specialist. "It is not our business," he said, "to worry about what politicians will do with our data." Other scholars, however, are far more concerned over the uses and misuses of their science, which brings us to the second school of scholarly attitudes toward race: those who view race as a dangerous myth.

Although there are many representatives of the race-as-myth school, including Franz Boas and Ruth Benedict, the name of M. F. Ashley Montagu stands out. Montagu argues that, granted the existence of technical differences in man based on gene frequency peculiarity, why should the specialists in genetics and physical anthropology continue to use the crude, imprecise designation "race" to express these differences? Populations should be described, according to Montagu, "in terms of their gene frequency differences," without any reference to that value-laden term "race."[5] We should, then eliminate the term and replace it with something more specific and precise, and thereby deprive the much abused concept of its scientific sanction. To describe and classify a certain genotype, why not refer to a genotype (or genogroup) instead of a "race"? If we bring in cultural factors along with genetic factors (as many of those who misuse the concept of race do), why not refer to an "ethnic group" instead of a race? That way, over time, the term "race" would lose its academic status and ultimately perhaps its popular currency.

Other supporters of the race-as-myth viewpoint attack the concept of race as devoid of empirical meaning. Again, admitting subspecific genetic variation, they argue that, in the words of one anthropologist, "this variability does not conform to the discrete packages labelled races. . . ."[6] Similarly, a well-known taxonomist, Jean Hiernaux, concluded a study of the concept of race and human taxonomy with these words: "From whatever viewpoint one approaches the question of the applicability of the concept of race to mankind, the modalities of human variability appear so far from those required for a coherent classification that the concept must be considered as of very limited use." Another taxonomist, in rejecting race as a viable basis for human classification, notes that there exist 150 *named* subspecies (i.e., "races") of the pocket-gopher *Thomomys bottae*. The implications of such "splitting" when applied to the number of races of man are staggering. But perhaps it was anthropologist Paul Bohannan who summed up the race-as-myth view most succinctly in one chapter of his *Social Anthropology* entitled "The Chimera of Race." The Chimera was a mythical beast who sported three heads (each of which breathed fire), the body of a goat, and a serpent for a tail. Even in mythology he is depicted as a most distasteful fellow.

Thus the scholarly battle continues, with the interested

student perhaps more frustrated than informed should he pursue the elusive matter of race very far. Even the most outspoken of the race-is-useful school admit that the concept is quite vague in many ways (and imprecision is the *bête noire* of the scientist), while the staunchest of the race-as-myth supporters readily admit genetic variability and the validity of a taxonomy based on gene frequency grouping. The problem of race (as distinguished from the "race problem") exists, and little would be served in pretending that it does not. Perhaps we might look again for the common denominator, certain areas of agreement among the specialists in the field, and attempt to draw some tentative conclusions about racial differences among *Homo sapiens.*

It might be useful to reiterate that so far as science is concerned, race is essentially a taxonomic concept—a unit of classification—and as such is concerned only with hereditary genetic qualities. If it is meaningful as a concept, it is only so as a tool or guide to human subspecific variability based on highly technical genetic criteria for differentiation, not on broad morphological characteristics (however certain the layman might be that he can readily identify the members of a given "race"). Moreover, the concept is essentially relative in nature. Nobody would argue that every member of a given population is genetically alike, even in the frequency of appearance of one gene. Stated differently, there are no "pure" races. Racial differentiation is statistical; it refers only to the *relative* frequency of certain genetic similarities. Hence it is necessarily imprecise, referring to averages or modalities.

Because race is a taxonomic unit based on genetics, "racial characteristics" must be hereditary characteristics, passed on from parents to child in the chromosomal-genetic structure of the child. The process of genetic inheritance has nothing to do with blood. The genes carried in the chromosomes are the sole means of determining biological hereditary. Nor does race have anything to do with religion (there is no "Jewish race"), language (there is no "Semitic race," no "Hamitic race"), or nationality (no

"German race"). All of these incorrect uses of the concept of race have come about because of widespread popular misunderstanding of race, frequently aided and abetted by the scientists (or pseudoscientists) themselves. None of these factors is racial, because they are all cultural; they are all learned, not genetically inherited. Nor have these factors been the only ones about which serious error has occurred, based on the confusion of culture and race.[7] Frightful problems have plagued mankind because we have not been able to separate racial considerations from cultural considerations with regard to differences in behavior, character, achievement, and capacity. These latter difficulties have frequently been the root of the most horrendous injustices perpetrated by man upon man, especially in the modern world.

Before considering the thorny problem of functional racial differences, real or imagined, one final point should be made about the hereditary nature of genetic differences. It relates to human variability and the evolutionary process, and is, of course, very much in the realm of theory. Physical anthropologists generally agree that the most prominent and apparent of "racial" differences, the broad morphological characteristics that are sometimes termed "cluster traits" (referring to complex "clusters" of genes required to produce them) came about by a process of evolutionary adaptation. Thus, dark skin is believed to have had some sort of adaptive advantage, which in the evolutionary process helped dark-skinned people in their fight for survival. The advantage of black skin derives from its high melanin content. Melanin is the pigment that produces dark skin; the higher the melanin content, the darker the skin. High melanin content apparently served a vital function, by protecting dark-skinned humans from the dangerous actinic rays of the sun in the largely nonforested regions where black people originally lived. Thus, black was not only beautiful, it was also extremely useful to those people of the Old World tropics living within 10 to 20 degrees of the equator.

Similarly, there seems to be a connection (albeit one that

is not fully understood) between climate and body type: tall, thin people with relatively large skin areas tend to be associated with hot, dry climates, where the greater skin area promoted body cooling by providing more sweat glands and thus more moisture. Small, stocky people, on the other hand, generally live (or once lived) in cold, wet climates, where their more compact bodies supply the adaptive advantage. Another adaptive factor seems to have been involved in producing differing nose shapes: broad noses are generally associated with breathing in high temperatures, narrow, thin, long noses with breathing in lower temperatures. Three other physical traits frequently termed "racial" characteristics—hair form, eyelid shape (the presence or absence of the "epicanthic fold"), and degree of lip eversion (thin lips versus full lips)—have not yet had their adaptive functions clearly established, although there are several theories.[8] Clearly, then, it is absurd to think in terms of broad "racial" superiority or inferiority in any overt physical sense. Whatever physical differences there are in human beings very probably came to be because they provided improvements in the equipment a given population had to cope with its environment.

A more difficult area of the "race question" is "racial difference" in character, behavior, and capacity, especially "intellectual capacity." What about the relationship of "race" and temperament? Are some "races" more passionate than others? More fun loving? More given to aggressive behavior? More indolent? The difficulties inherent in these questions are multifold. If we cannot adequately define "race" or settle on a system of classification of the "races" of man, how are we to inquire as to their characterological and behaviorial characteristics? Nevertheless, judgments on these matters *are* made, and no consideration of the concept of race should fail to include them. Once again, it should be noted that most such judgments result from the confusion of racial and cultural factors. Character and personality relate ultimately to value systems, and value systems are cultural, not genetic, in nature. On the basis of what is now known about genetic processes, supposed "racial" differences in character, temperament, and behavior come about because of culture, not "race." One of the foremost modern authorities on evolutionary genetics, Stanley Garn (a foremost representative of the race-is-useful school), concludes, "So far, there is no evidence for racial differences in character and temperament, other than those due to cultural conditioning. The same may be said for behavior in general." Practically all of Garn's colleagues would agree with this appraisal.

No area of disagreement has generated more heat on the matter of racial difference than has inherent intellectual capacity. Are some "races" inherently more intelligent than others? Conversely, are some less so? Theoretically, it is possible that some genogroup *could* possess some minor variation in brain structure that might produce a functional advantage not present in genogroups not favored with the variable. It should be emphasized, however, that this is only theoretical. There is no evidence that such brain structure variations do, in fact, exist. Similarly, the seemingly endless controversy over "racial" I.Q. differentials is likely to go on unabated, each side convinced that it has the absolute truth. Since World War I, when I.Q. testing became popular, psychologists have tirelessly attempted to determine whether I.Q. differences among the "races" do exist. And what, after all those tests and all the related rhetoric, do we know now? We know little more now than we knew at the outset. Otto Klineberg, who spent the greater part of his scholarly lifetime studying I.Q. differentials, published the first results of his work in 1933, after surveying all of the testing up to that point. He concluded, "If intellectual differences between racial and social groups do exist (and this point is still debatable) the testing technique is nevertheless incapable of proving their existence." Three decades and thousands of tests later, these findings were unchanged. In 1964, another scholar, Thomas F. Pettigrew, concluded that theories of innate racial I.Q. differences are "simply not supported by the empirical findings of the biological and social sciences."

The problem involved in attempting to measure I.Q. differences is at least threefold. First, how does one establish a "race," especially in the United States, where the Afro-American population is, genetically speaking, about one-third European? Second, how does one perfect a test that is capable of measuring "innate" intelligence or prepare a "culture-free" intelligence test? Third, how does one establish criteria for interpreting the results of those tests when administered to groups of people with different cultural backgrounds? These problems are still unsolved, but two factors consistently appear in the results of the testing done until now. There is so much statistical overlapping that the majority of all ethnic groups test out as being of comparable I.Q.. And the closer any two groups are matched in terms of their cultural backgrounds, the closer they test out in terms of average I.Q. scores. At this point we must accept the answer that satisfies neither those who believe that there are racial differences in measured I.Q. scores nor those who believe that there are no such differences; as of now we do not know. If there are genetic variants that affect man's ability to learn, to know, or to perform, they are certainly not in the sum and total of what we call intelligence, but instead they lie in certain specifics or details. Stanley Garn suggests, as an "informed guess," that "race differences may exist in form-discrimination, color-sense, tonal-memory, mechanical reasoning, abstract reasoning and with other special (rather than general) aspects of intelligence." But this, too, remains to be proved or disproved.

Considering the above, what can we conclude about racial differences? Once again, "race" is a crude term, not a precise or specific one, when used to designate the varieties of man. Moreover, there exists greater overall variety *within* a so-called "race" than exists *among* the "races." Thus, the term should probably be replaced by other terms that may be applied with greater precision to the specific variable or variables involved. But there is little likelihood that this will happen, partly because there are numerous specialists in several disciplines who find the concept useful and employ it in their work. There is, however, another, much better reason that the concept of race is likely to prevail. Race is useful to a second group, not scientists, but laymen, who not only believe in the existence of race, but also attach great value to "racial" considerations and are often guided in their dealings with other people by such considerations. This large second group is comprised of "racists," who have long abused the concept of race by combining it with countless irrelevant culture considerations, then basing their judgment of men on "race." They are likely to continue to do so, no matter what the scientists tell them. Certain categories of people designated "races" in common usage are a cultural fact of our time. It must be clearly established that when we speak of a "race" in this context, we are not talking about race at all, but rather what the racists call race.

Racism undoubtedly involves an exceedingly complex psychic mechanism, so complex that social psychologists still cannot account for it satisfactorily. Basically, a racist is one who *believes dogmatically* that one race is innately superior to another; superior in intelligence, genius, "morality," or any other attributes. The superior race is usually the one in which the racist claims membership. The essence of racism, as Ruth Benedict once observed, can be summed up in five words: "I belong to the elect." It is a most useful concept, especially if one group of people needs a rationalization for exploiting another group, or, as in the case of the more virulent racist politicians, one group needs a scapegoat on which to blame all social ills. Racist dogma reached its height in Nazi Germany, where "pro-Aryan" polemics and antisemitic scapegoating pointed ultimately to genocide. "Semites," in fact, are not a race at all, except in some sort of nominalist rationale that concludes that a race is a race because I call it a race.

Naturally, there are varying degrees of racism. Some forms are more malignant than others. They range in intensity from a vague "race consciousness," which implies only a slight perjorative, to the mania and the Nazi or the Klansman who make a veritable fetish out of their race hatred. Whatever its degree, racism prevails as one of the more important functions of culture in much of the modern world. It persists because it is frequently inherent in the value system of a society. Again, racism can be so useful that it may be used to the advantage of any group and, as Bohannan has observed, "Since it has no basis in fact, no claim is too extravagant to make for it." Thus racism is particularly susceptible to the "big lie" political technique. Racism, however, rarely has anything to do with race and the concepts can and usually do function separately. The racist and the taxonomist do not mean the same thing when the former refers with absolute conviction to a given "race" and the latter speaks of the high frequency of the *Rhesus Gene Ro* or of blood type AB in a given population. The study of race in its technical sense belongs to the biological sciences; the study of racism belongs to the social sciences, particularly cultural history.

Which, after a considerable circumlocution, brings us back to the original topic under consideration: the concept of Afro-American and its implications. And in view of all that has been said of culture and race, it would seem that, even with its built-in ambiguities, the term "Afro-American" is still useful and even rather precisely descriptive. For "Afro-American," considered both denotatively and connotatively, from the standpoint of cultural considerations and those of "race" (or genogroup), carries great meaning when applied to black Americans and to their historical experience.

The prefix "Afro," of course, points back historically to Africa, the point at which any discussion of the Afro-American experience must begin. Equipped with some of the conceptual baggage introduced in this discussion, we now can consider that huge, much misunderstood, myth-ridden, infinitely complex, and variable continent out of which the ancestors of most black Americans came.

NOTES

[1] There are, of course, several ways that the term culture may be used that are not directly related to its anthropological usage. One may speak of *soil* culture in the sense of plant cultivation; biologists often refer to "a culture," meaning a growth of microorganisms; some people are termed "cultured," with the implication that they are highly developed in an intellectual and aesthetic sense, or with reference to the life-style of certain social classes. Our concern in the present chapter is with culture in the much broader sense of *human* culture.

[2] Although cultural determinism has fallen into some disrepute among many of the younger anthropologists, a relatively recent and increasingly significant concept of culture called "structuralism" seems to lend new credence to the determinists. Led by the French anthropologist Claude Levi-Straus, the structuralists argue that any culture contains a general ordering structure as well as an enormous complexity of substructures that are closely interrelated that collectively determine virtually every aspect of the society's existence.

[3] Frequently, the people in a given society are not aware of culture change as it occurs among them. The change is usually subtle, and even as the change is in process, at any specific moment in time, the individuals making up the society possess a culture. The structuralists stress that culture may be simultaneously stable and dynamic.

[4] The new culture elements do not have to be *thought* of as new, and frequently, they are not. Through a process known as "reinterpretation," old values or meanings are simply applied to the new elements and the new elements are accepted within the framework of the old ways. One common form of reinterpretation is "syncretism," where-

by the new and the old are combined and thereby reconciled, as, for example, in the case of large-scale acceptance of a new religion. A striking example of religious syncretism is New World Voodoo, a combination of Roman Catholicism and traditional African religious practices.

[5] In what is perhaps the strongest statement of the race-as-myth position, Montagu, writing in 1941, argued that "the concept of race is nothing but a whited sepulchre, a conception which in light of modern experimental genetics is utterly erroneous and meaningless. . . . [It] should therefore be dropped from the vocabulary of the anthropologist, for it has done an infinite amount of harm and no good at all." The date is noteworthy.

[6] The author of this statement, the distinguished anthropologist Frank B. Livingstone, chose to entitle the article from which it is quoted "On the Non-existence of Human Races."

[7] This is not to say that culture plays *no* role in the process of subspecific variation. Theoretically it could, but *only* in terms of evolutionary time. For example, diet factors could relate in some causal manner to an adaptive advantage in some dental mutation, which might produce a variation in dentition. But it would require quite a long period of time.

[8] Some have suggested that hair form relates to climate by providing protection against the sun, but it may also have served as a sort of built-in helmet. A rich, thick head of hair could provide protection for the skull and brain. The epicanthic fold may have provided protection for the eyes, especially in cold climates. As for lip eversion, the zoologist Desmond Morris suggests a fascinating evolutionary possibility in his best-seller, *The Naked Ape.* He theorizes that lip eversion came about as a response to a need for new secondary sexual characteristics. As hominids became humans, lips came to serve as a more important means of attracting and holding a mate; thus lip eversion became an adaptive advantage, not only in perpetuating mankind, but also in contributing to the development of pair-bond mating.

SUGGESTIONS FOR FURTHER READING

The concepts of culture and race claim a vast literature ranging from the detached to the polemical and from the superb to the ridiculous. Both are legitimately within the province of anthropology, however, so a good beginning point would be an elementary introduction to that field. Ernest L. Shusky and T. Patrick Culbert have written a useful brief survey in *Introducing Culture* (Englewood Cliffs, N.J.: Prentice-Hall, 1967). Somewhat more detailed but still basic (and quite readable) is Paul Bohannan, *Social Anthropology* (New York: Holt, Rinehart and Winston, 1963).

Alfred L. Kroeber wrote the work that should provide the point of departure for the study of culture in his book *The Nature of Culture* (Chicago: University of Chicago Press, 1952). Melville J. Herskovits, *Cultural Dynamics* (New York: Knopf, 1964), is an abridgement of the great scholar's *Cultural Anthropology*, originally published in 1947. It provides an excellent introduction to culture change, a subject treated more fully (and from a very different perspective) in Julian H. Steward, *Theory of Culture Change* (Urbana, Ill.: University of Illinois Press, 1955). Chapters 3 and 4, "Levels of Sociocultural Integration: An Operational Concept" and "National Sociocultural Systems," are especially pertinent. Two provocative journal articles that take different views on cultural determinism are Leslie A. White, "Man's Control Over Civilization: An Anthropocentric Illusion," *The Scientific Monthly*, 1948, 66:235-247, and Morris E. Opler, "The Human Being in Culture Theory," *American Anthropologist*, 1964, 66:507-528. Both essays are included in Morton H. Fried, ed., *Readings in Anthropology*, 2nd. edition, 2 volumes (New

York: Crowell, 1968), a suberb collection of readings ranging over the entire field of cultural and physical anthropology. A brief introduction to Levi-Strauss and the structuralists may be gained through the introduction to Richard and Fernande De George, *The Structuralists From Marx to Levi-Strauss* (Garden City, N. Y.: Anchor Books, 1972).

A black biologist, Richard A. Goldsby of Yale University, has recently published a short, clear, objective study entitled *Race and Races* (New York: Macmillan, 1971). Stanley M. Garn, *Human Races*, 2nd edition (Springfield, Ill.: Charles C. Thomas, 1965) gives a brief summary by a noted taxonomist of the "race-is-useful" persuasion. Garn has also published provocative articles entitled "Race and Evolution," *American Anthropologist*, 1957, *59*:218-224, and, in collaboration with Carleton S. Coon, "On the Number of Races of Mankind," *American Anthropologist*, 1955, *57*:996-1001. Coon caused considerable controversy within (and without) the profession with the publication of his *The Origin of Races* (New York: Knopf, 1962), which argues theoretically for a presapient raciation of man, a point of view not generally accepted by his peers.

M. F. Ashley Montagu, *Man's Most Dangerous Myth: The Fallacy of Race*, 4th ed., (New York: World Publishing, 1964) provides a clear statement of the race-as-myth position, while Montagu, ed., *The Concept of Race* (New York: Free Press of Glencoe, 1964) is a collection of readings that attacks the race concept from the point of view of several different disciplines. Two of Montagu's own essays are included: his extreme 1941 antirace statement "The Concept of Race in the Human Species in the Light of Genetics," (originally called "The Meaninglessness of the Anthropological Conception of Race") and a more moderate statement of the same argument, "The Concept of Race."

An investigation of the complex phenomenon called racism might well begin with Gordon W. Allport, *The Nature of Prejudice*, abridged edition (New York: Doubleday Anchor, 1958). A useful, older study is Ruth Benedict's *Race: Science and Politics*, originally published in 1940, but updated and provided with an introduction by Margaret Mead in 1959 (New York: Viking Press, 1959). The Viking edition also includes a notable essay by Benedict and Gene Weltfish, "The Races of Mankind." Perhaps the best of the recent theoretical studies of both race and racism is Pierre L. van den Berghe, *Race and Racism: A Comparative Perspective* (New York: Wiley, 1967). Joel Kovel, *White Racism. A Psychohistory* (New York: Vintage Books, 1971) is another recent and provocative study of the psychic bases of white racism. The nature and effects of antiblack racism in early America are treated brilliantly in Winthrop D. Jordan's prize-winning *White Over Black: American Attitudes Toward The Negro*, 1550-1812 (Chapel Hill: The University of North Carolina Press, 1968). John Hope Franklin, ed., *Color and Race* (Boston: Beacon Press, 1969) is a collection of readings on racial attitudes, largely contemporary, outside the United States. By placing racism in a world context, this collection pinpoints the near-universality of color consciousness and/or discrimination based on "race" and color.

CHAPTER 2

THE AFRICAN BACKGROUND: CONSIDERATIONS

Until recently, the history of Africa has been partially or completely hidden from the eyes and consciousness of the West. Scholars and laymen alike have viewed this vast continent through a veil of mythology so pervasive that even otherwise enlightened people hold the stereotyped image of a "Dark Continent," a teeming jungle inhabited by vicious wild animals and neolithic black savages. The individual myths are numberless. We just noted four of the most prominent ones: The myth of the jungle, the myth of the beast in the jungle, the myth of the savage, and the all-encompassing myth of the Dark Continent. To these we might add two others, equally pervasive and powerful in their tendency toward masking and distorting the African past: (1) the myth of uniformity—the notion that all of Africa is essentially the same—and (2) the myth of cultural sterility—the belief that Africa has contributed nothing to the course of human "civilization." All of these myths, are related and interwoven (and these are only the more conspicuous ones). It is the nature of complex mythologies that the component myths be related and mutually reinforcing. But the myths of Africa also interrelate because they have grown and developed out of the same set of western attitudes, assumptions, and premises about black men and their homeland.

African history has been hidden behind a shroud of

Note. Footnotes for this chapter are located on pages 54-56.

mythology because until recently African history and African studies in general have been confined to the very people who made the myths. Edgar Rice Burroughs, creator of "Tarzan of the Apes," has been a key figure in the perpetuation of African stereotypes, but he did not invent them. He simply based his immensely popular series on prevailing European attitudes, attitudes created by ignorance, prejudice, and ethnocentrism. The eminent British Imperial historian, A. P. Newton, in an address to the African Society of London in 1923, expressed a typical attitude. Africa south of the Sahara had "no history," he insisted, "before the coming of the Europeans." Hugh Trevor-Roper, another notable historian went even farther. African history, he said, consists largely of "the unrewarding gyrations of barbarous tribes in picturesque but irrelevant corners of the globe." Here we have ethnocentrism with a vengeance. These opinions voiced by reputable scholars suggest that Africa and Africans have traditionally been linked in the European mind with notions of inferiority and servility. Racism has reinforced ethnocentrism in the development of European attitudes toward Africa. Black Africa—"barbaric" Africa—was simply not worthy of the historian's serious attention.

It seems incredible that these attitudes and false assumptions have persisted for so long. They are most easily refuted. An elementary knowledge of African geography destroys the myth of the jungle. Only about 5% of the continent is occupied by tropical rain forest or "jungle," and that is restricted to narrow coastal fringes and the Congo River basin. By far the largest land area is "savanna," vast rolling grasslands marked by only scattered trees and intermittent bush. Both north and south of the great savanna regions lie deserts—the Kalahari to the south and the Sahara to the north— where vegetation is even more sparse. Similarly, the beast in the jungle, especially as symbolized by the lion, is totally out of accord with reality. Lions do not live in jungles, nor do elephants, zebras, or giraffes. They live out in the grasslands. Tigers do not live in Africa at all. So much for the first two myths.

The myth of uniformity is also refuted when it is tested against reality. Instead of uniformity, enormous diversity is most characteristic of the African continent. Africa claims more cultural and ethnic diversity than any other continent. There are, for example, over 800 indigenous languages spoken there. The precise number of African cultural units has not been determined, but anthropologist George P. Murdock has attempted to name and catalogue as many as he could establish. His list of names (in four-column format) requires *31 pages* of a large volume. Alphabetically, the names run from Aandonga to Zungwa. African political organization prior to the coming of the Europeans ranged in complexity from the simplest hunting–gathering bands without formal leadership or obvious structure, to great states with complex bureaucracies and governing hierarchies. Subsistence techniques were equally diverse, ranging from hunting to sophisticated agriculture and herding, and to the mining and fabricating of iron. Finally, African history is as diverse and complex as these cultural considerations might suggest. It is frequently forgotten that ancient Egypt was African, as were the Berber states of the Mediterranean coast that were part of the Roman Empire, and the rulers of ancient Kush on the upper Nile once controlled pharonic Egypt. One has only to consider these facts to appreciate the great sweep of African history.

And what of the myth of cultural sterility? What *has* Africa contributed to world progress? Evidence is now just about conclusive that the primary contribution of Africa to the civilization of mankind was man himself. No less an authority than Charles Darwin had surmised that the first "hominids" or protohumans had appeared in the tropics, probably in Africa, and recent discoveries in the southeastern part of the continent have apparently verified Darwin's informed guess. In the last half century, several archeologists and physical anthropologists working in southern Africa have made successive finds of fossil remains, establishing that the so-called "Australopithecines" ("southern apes"), those small, hairy, apelike, erect, bipedal creatures,

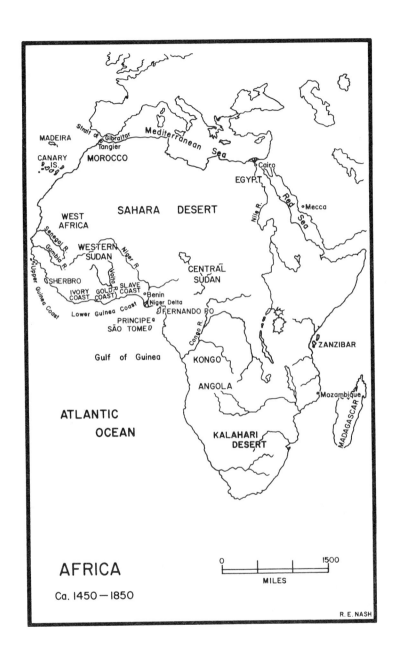

MADEIRA

CANARY
IS.

Strait of Gibraltar
Tangier
MOROCCO

Mediterranean Sea

Cairo

EGYPT

Nile R.

Red Sea

Mecca

SAHARA DESERT

WEST
AFRICA

Senegal R.

Gambia R.

Upper Guinea Coast

WESTERN
SUDAN

Niger R.

SHERBRO

IVORY
COAST

GOLD
COAST

Volta R.

SLAVE
COAST

Benin

Niger Delta

FERNANDO PO

Lower Guinea Coast

PRINCIPE
SÃO TOMÉ

CENTRAL
SUDAN

Congo R.

ZANZIBAR

Gulf of Guinea

KONGO

ANGOLA

Mozambique

MADAGASCAR

ATLANTIC

OCEAN

KALAHARI
DESERT

AFRICA

Ca. 1450 – 1850

0   1500

MILES

R. E. NASH

long the subject of so much controversy, were indeed the immediate evolutionary link with Homo sapiens.[1] Moreover, over a period of some two million years, the Australopithecines, or at least their evolutionary progeny, became tool users, then tool makers; in effect, they created culture, or, in other words, they became humans. Thus, as historian Basil Davidson has observed, "Africa was the mother of mankind."

Details of the movements of early man from Africa to Asia and Europe are still very much a matter of conjecture. It is clear that in terms of evolutionary time, the spread of man was remarkably rapid. But time is a relative matter. It is likely that for some thousands of centuries, Africa remained in the vanguard of human progress. Bohannan contends that "It is not until the Neolithic period [about 8000 B.C.] and the agricultural revolution that we must look outside of Africa for major contributions—and, indeed, only then if we follow the traditional but geologically debatable practice of throwing Asia Minor in with Asia instead of with Africa." Thus, despite controversy and disagreement among scholars, Africa must be considered the cradle of culture.

This chapter is not concerned however, with the course of human development outside of Africa, but with human activity within the continent. And before continuing our consideration of early man in Africa, it is essential that we take note of a tremendously important geological development, one that largely determined the nature of his many migrations and his continuing evolution.

It was a development that produced dramatic ecological change involving the stages of relative wetness and dryness of the Saharan region. The Sahara, like most contemporary deserts, was not always a desert. Prior to its last dessication ("drying up") the area passed through two distinct stages, dating *very* approximately from about 10,000 B.C. to 3000 B.C. The first of these stages was a dry one, but not desert-dry. It was habitable. The second was a wet stage—the so-called "Makalian" wet phase—which lasted from about 5500 to 3000 B.C. During this lush period the area was well able to sustain human life and even to permit a considerable increase in population. It also afforded easy movement of people and hence substantial contact among them. This, of course, permitted diffusion of certain culture elements. Among these elements were the cultivation of cereal and grain and the production of superior weapons—bows, arrows, harpoons, and spears—the use of which spread rapidly. Clearly then, by about 3000 B.C., Neolithic [New Stone Age] culture had diffused over an immense area occupying much of the northern and northeastern two-thirds of the African continent.

But the wet phase did not last; the process of dessication was well under way by about 3000 B.C. As time passed, ever more of the area turned to arid desert waste, incapable of sustaining human life. It became necessary for the inhabitants to move out, and over a long period of time they did so. They moved in all directions, north, northeast, south, and southwest, following the most convenient paths to water supplies. In this way the African people came to be more or less separated by the growing desert. This separation was to have multifold effects. In the first place, the possibility of significant contact among a variety of peoples and cultures was greatly diminished. "Culture-flow" was thus reduced and insularity increased, especially in the more remote areas of the Sudanese grasslands south of the desert and in the forests further southwest along the Atlantic coast and in the western river valleys. There, in relative isolation, the migrants developed their own characteristic cultures.[2]

Not only did culture-flow decrease, so did "gene-flow." The genetic traits associated with the people of sub-Saharan Africa, especially dark pigmentation, were doubtless intensified within the tightly inbreeding populations of the Sudan and beyond. On the other hand, those who migrated north and northeast were to remain comparatively in contact, genetically and culturally, with developments in western Asia and later on, in Europe. This brings us to one of the perennial problems of African history: the historical relationship between Africa and Egypt.

Once again, it would seem that the problem is rooted in racism and ethnocentrism, but this time not solely on the part of the Europeans. The problem centers around the question of the "race" of the Egyptians. Were they near-eastern Asiatics or Africans? The "pro-Asian" school claims that the Egyptians were primarily Asiatics, culturally and genetically, and that the black African influence was minimal. The "pro-African" school contends that Egypt is part of Africa, and that the evidence indicates that the Egyptians were primarily Africans, culturally and genetically. Actually, the traditional historical sources tell us very little about the "race" of the Egyptians in the age of the Pharoahs. It is clear that the lower Nile, seat of the Egyptian civilization, lay precisely in the middle of two burgeoning cultures, one Saharan-Sudanese, the other neareastern. As Bohannan has suggested, "Egypt lay culturally as well as geographically between Africa and Asia." Nor can there be much question that the Saharan dessication lent itself to the peopling of at least part of Egypt by migrants from the west. Egyptian civilization, then, was the product of culture contact and diffusion, plus the enormous natural advantage of great fertility produced by the periodic flooding of the lower Nile valley.

There is, however, at least one period of Egyptian history that is clearly dominated by Sudanic Africans. The ancient land of Kush, located between the third and fourth cataracts of the Nile, was unquestionably inhabited by Africans from the Sudan. By the eighth century B.C. the Kushite rulers had extended their power and authority as far to the north as Upper Egypt. And they continued to press further north, harassing the Egyptians in a long series of border raids. Under Piankhy, who ruled from 751 to 716 B.C., the Kushites completed their conquest of Egypt. The twenty-fifth dynasty of the Pharoahs came to be composed of the next five kings of Kush. For about a hundred years the capital of Kush, located in Napata, was the reigning metropolis of one of the world's great empires. The shift of the capital to Meroë (about 593 to 568 B.C.) gave rise to a complex Sudanic-Egyptiac culture that has come to be called "Meroitic." The rise of the Meroitic phase of East African development following the Assyrian defeat of Egypt provides a point of division between African history and that of the ancient Near East. But their separation was never really complete, because trade contacts and the exchange of ideas and culture materials never completely ceased.

Egyptian-Assyrian contact, however unfriendly, produced technological innovation that quickly reached Meroë. Iron fabrication (and knowledge of the effectiveness of iron) diffused to an area rich in iron ore. The iron spear and the iron hoe were the immediate result, and they may be said to have introduced the early iron age of African history. For when Meroë eventually fell to the Axumites (later to be known as Ethiopians), just after the beginning of the Christian era, the Meroitic armies were dispersed and their leaders retreated into the Sudan. There, once again, diffusion of ideas and technology occurred.[3] But by then the great Sahara had become a desert, a vast internal sea of sand, and Africa had come to be largely separated into isolated population elements divided by vast distances as well as forbidding geographic barriers.

We must now narrow the subject area of our concern; to focus on a smaller area and to telescope our chronology. By now it should be obvious that African history is as vast as the continent itself. The "considerations" that have been the subject matter of this chapter have been treated only to point out this fact, and to attempt to dispel some of the mythology. But keeping in mind that African history *does* have certain unity (a point that will be emphasized again a bit later), we must now focus our attention on a smaller part of the continent, the part that produced the ancestors of *most* of the Afro-Americans: sub-Saharan West Africa. And we must limit the time period of our inquiry to the period before the coming of the Europeans, or at least to the period before the Europeans came to be of much importance in the development of West Africa. Any inclusive, specific dates must, of course, be arbitrary. But there would be some validity in fixing our time-frame *roughly* in the period between 800 and 1600 A.D.

It should not be necessary to state that what follows will not be a complete history of West Africa from 800 to 1600. That would require a large volume, which would only provide an introduction to the subject. Once again we are only going to isolate certain "considerations" that are necessary or at least convenient to the understanding of the African background of Afro-American history. Before undertaking an overview of the prominent historical and cultural considerations of the territory southwest of the Sahara, however, the geographic regions and the "culture areas" of special interest to the student of Afro-America should be more specifically determined. Geographically, the area of greatest concern is the coastal region beginning in the western Sudan just north of the Senegal River, then continuing down the coast to the northern fringe of the Kalahari Desert. Looking inland, our area of concern stretches to the eastern reaches of the major river systems, especially the valleys of the Niger and Congo Rivers.

Generally speaking, this area may be divided into three fairly distinctive regions: the western Sudan, the Guinea Coast, and the Congo. Conveniently, anthropologist Melville Herskovits (a specialist on West Africa) has designated the same three regions as major *culture* areas of the continent, basing his judgment on certain culturogeographic similarities, including "ecological and institutional factors."[4] Despite sufficient differences among the three to warrant dividing them on cultural grounds, in one important respect they were fundamentally similar: the people of all three areas were basically agricultural. They depended chiefly on farming for subsistence. This is an important fact, because, along with the related matter of social organization, it would ultimately provide the basis for elaborate empires, kingdoms, states, and city-states.

The earliest African social organization was very likely no more than the "band," a small group inhabiting a certain "neighborhood," probably also linked by certain kin-

ship ties. But out of necessity, it would seem, the social
unit tended to grow larger, yet continue to exhibit some
elements of a kinship system. This broader kinship system
was the "extended family," a group of people who were all
related in some way to each other and dependent on each
other for survival. As time passed and the social organisms
grew in size, the nature of the kinship system on which
they were based tended in many cases to become even
more complex, although the kinship basis prevailed. The
difference was only in the greater complexity of the relationships, and in the acceptance of "descent" as the ordering principle of the organization; the "lineage" came to
form the basis of the social system, along with the continuing notion of "community." Such descent groups were
ordinarily "unilineal" in nature. The line of descent was
determined through the family of the father ("patrilineal"
descent), or, less frequently, the mother ("matrilineal"
descent). Unilineal descent groups, then, came eventually
to form the basis for most of the social organization among
West Africans.[5] They also formed the basis of the political
and economic structuring of the group, and frequently
even its religious organization. The culture system of West
Africa, and indeed, most of Africa, was and is based on
kinship factors. This is a point of extreme significance,
and one to which we will return later.

It was, to reiterate, out of these kinship-dominated agricultural societies that the medieval African states developed.
The earliest of these were the Sudanic states. The best
known were those that developed into the Sudanic empires: Ghana, Mali, and Songhay. Historians Roland Oliver
and J. D. Fage have noted that the Sudanic states were essentially "parasitic" growths that fastened themselves "upon
the economic base of pre-existing agricultural societies."
On this basis, states were created when one lineage proved
powerful enough to impose its political authority on neighboring villages. But ordinarily, along with political authority, the state-making process brought with it the extension
of new subsistence techniques, most notably in mining,
metallurgy, and trade. On the basis of the diffusion of

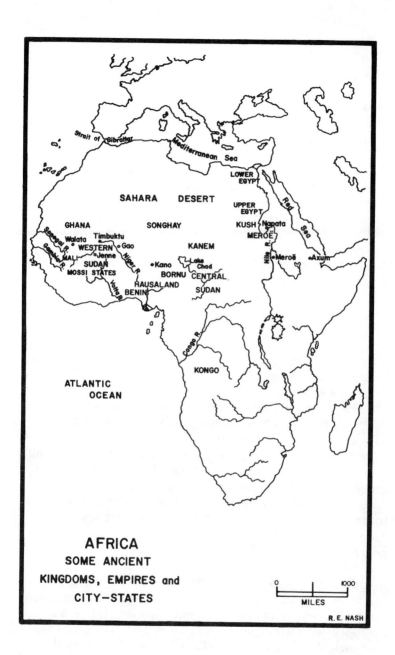

Strait of Gibraltar

Mediterranean Sea

LOWER
EGYPT

SAHARA   DESERT

UPPER
EGYPT

GHANA   SONGHAY   KUSH Napata
                                  MEROË
Senegal R. Walata Timbuktu Gao
         WESTERN   KANEM
Gambia R. MALI Jenne Niger R.   Nile R. Meroë Axum
         SUDAN   Lake
    MOSSI STATES   Kano   Chad
                 BORNU CENTRAL
                 HAUSALAND SUDAN
    Volta R. BENIN

Red Sea

Congo R.

ATLANTIC
OCEAN

KONGO

AFRICA
SOME ANCIENT
KINGDOMS, EMPIRES and
CITY—STATES

0   1000
MILES

R.E. NASH

37

these subsistence techniques the states were able to grow larger and widen their sway. For it was largely the world demand for gold and ivory and slaves that brought West Africa into direct contact with the Islamic world of North Africa and beyond.

The expansion of trade contacts across the great inland sea of the Sahara marked the emergence of the first Sudanic states, early in the ninth century. Muslim demand for Sudanic trade items gave rise to the trans-Saharan trading caravan, which in turn led to the founding of Sudanic trading settlements, which came soon to thrive, prosper, and grow into cities. The leaders who came to control these cities, and thus to control the trade routes, were able to assume great power and influence over the surrounding peoples. And this, greatly simplified, was how the trading empires of the Sudan, nourished by the wealth of West Africa south of the Sudan, were born and nurtured. This is how the Sudanic cities—Timbuktu, Gao, Jenne, Walata, Kano, and others—came to serve as the nerve centers of these dynamic kingdoms. The growth of trade was to continue as was the influence of successive empires, rising, expanding, then falling to a rival. This was the pattern. And as the Sudanese trading centers established connections with other export centers to the south—for example, Begho, in what is now the independent nation of Ghana, or Benin, in modern Nigeria—a complex network of trade routes resulted. By 1400 or earlier, as Basil Davidson has observed, "one should think of the whole of West Africa as being intricately traced with trading trails and market centers, an economic fact of basic importance for understanding the political history of this region. . . ."

Ghana was the first of the great African empires about which much is known. Tradition varies as to the founding of the empire, but it is clear that a small but aggressive group of Soninke people (of the Mande language group), equipped with iron spears, began to attack and conquer their neighbors. By about 800 A.D. they had created a central organization under a divine-right ruler, the *ghana* or "war chief" (thus giving the empire its name.) The *ghana* then gained control over the import of an important commodity: salt from the desert fringes. He also controlled the export of gold to the north, and throughout the reigns of successive kings the area of his hegemony continually increased. By the early eleventh century, when the documentary records left by Arab travelers begin to produce valuable information about the empire, a considerable portion of the western Sudan seems to have been organized under an imperial arrangement that provided centralized administration of the vast territory, including the collection of taxes and tribute throughout the land.[6]

But the Arab explorers found much more than this. They also found practitioners of a variety of crafts in the West African interior. They found great cities with streets and bazaars where the artisans produced their cloth and ornaments of wrought gold and bronze, and where grain was sold, along with kola nuts, ostrich feathers, slaves, and ivory. Incoming caravans brought trade items of equal value and variety. Salt was first in importance, but the desert traders (predominantly the mounted and mobile Tuareg) also brought in horses, swords, mirrors, silks, beads, and other decorative items, and of course, exotic foods and spices from the Mediterranean coast.

By the eleventh century imperial Ghana had reached its zenith, and trouble from the north would soon interrupt the placid flow of commerce across the desert. The trouble came at the hands of warlike Islamic religious fanatics called the Almoravids. Driven by the compulsion to spread the word of Mohammad, these North African Berbers began their invasion of Ghana in 1062. By 1076, after posing considerable resistance, Ghana fell to the invaders and became at least technically a Muslim territory.[7] But the heritage of this first Sudanic state by no means ended with its defeat. Local Sudanic leadership lay quiescent for a time, then reemerged when a powerful leader of another Mande lineage assumed power in the upper Nile valley. His name was Sundiata, and under his rule (ca. 1230 to 1255) an even greater empite, Mali, came into existence.

The sources of power of the rulers of Mali (called

mansas) and the nature of the empire itself were in most
important respects similar to those of Ghana. Power and influence lay in the control of the trading routes across the
desert (to the northeast) and in the forestlands of the
Guinea coast. Under the greatest of the *mansas*, the fabled
Mansa Musa (who reigned from 1312 to 1337), the Mali
empire reached its zenith, stretching along the Atlantic
coast from the fringes of the Sahara to the edge of the
tropical forest, and reaching inland to the great bend of the
Niger. In bringing the middle Niger area under his control,
Musa brought the primary trading centers of Timbuktu and
Gao into the empire. He even came to control such cities
as Walata, the commercial center of the southern Sahara,
rendering his domain in all respects great among the empires of Islam and the world. One important difference between Mali and Ghana is noteworthy; all of the *mansas*
were Muslims, and their concerns with formal learning as
well as their practice of one of the great world religions
lent an added dimension to this kingdom of the Sudan.
Musa's interest in scholarship and religion, as well as his
wealth, have provided him with not the least part of his
historical reputation. According to tradition (one much
repeated by scholars both ancient and modern) his lavish
spending while on his pilgrimage to Mecca wrecked the
local currency by undermining the value of gold. This de-
vout ruler also attracted numbers of scholars to the cities
of his empire, scholars who taught the *Koran* and *Shari'a*,
the sacred law of Islam. Timbuktu and Jenne achieved de-
served reputations as centers of such studies, as well as for
their contributions to architecture. Moreover, as noted by
the medieval traveler Ibn Battuta (who toured the empire
from 1352 to 1353), the land was well governed. He
found a prevailing justice, safe roads, and good lodging. He
also found peace, prosperity, and order.

By the early sixteenth century, however, Mali, too, had
fallen into a decline, mostly because of harassment by
Songhay warriors, who persisted in pillaging the northern
provinces. The third of the great Sudanic states was in
the ascendant under the leadership of yet another great

leader, Sunni Ali, founder of the state of Gao, which was to become the Songhay empire. The Songhay people, long restive under Mande hegemony, had developed an army, won their freedom, and now contested ever broader areas of the old Mali domain. Under Sunni Ali (1464 to 1492) the boundaries of Gao were expanded to the extent that the Songhay ruler controlled an area as large and important as that of Mali, and this was only the beginning. One year after the founder's death another leader, Askia Muhammad (later known as "Askia the Great"), assumed the throne; he reigned for 36 years, bringing Songhay to heights of power and wealth exceeding that of both of her illustrious predecessors. By establishing control of the very heart of the old empire—the trade centers Timbuktu, Jenne, and the captial, Gao—Askia was able to build on the old structure while expanding his boundaries eastward almost to central Africa (near Lake Chad) and north to the very gates of Morocco.

The threat to Moroccan boundaries, however, brought resistance that ultimately spelled the end of this last of the medieval Sudanic empires. In 1591 Morocco mounted a large-scale attack on Songhay. Three thousand troops crossed the desert and grouped on the Niger above Gao. This force was actually smaller than the Songhay army that opposed it, but the Moroccan forces included European mercenary soldiers equipped with muskets, and the superior fire power proved decisive against the troops of Songhay. The defeat marked the beginning of the end, for political collapse of the empire followed in short order. With the fall of the cities, which were the centers of imperial authority and power, envious neighbors and former subjects of the king proceeded to raid at will, taking advantage of the chaos and disorder to achieve greater autonomy or retribution or booty. Trade, always the lifeblood of the empires, suffered immeasurably. The Sudan then entered into another phase of its long history, a phase marked by the absence of central authority and a decline of Islamic civilization. The peoples of the countryside once again assumed the power to rule themselves through the older, smaller social and political units out of which the empires had grown. This dramatic change may be dated with some degree of accuracy in 1600.[8]

Although Ghana, Mali, and Songhay are by far the best known of the Sudanic states, they were by no means the only ones. The fifteenth and sixteenth centuries saw other, relatively smaller and less significant kingdoms run their courses of rise and decline. The Mossi states south of Songhay, for example, lying between the savanna and the rain forest, achieved considerable power and influence over local communities before they fell to the Songhay forces of Askia Muhammad. Similarly, and on an even larger scale, the empire of Kanem-Bornu in the central Sudan, under King Idris Alooma (1580 to 1617), spread both east and west of Lake Chad and began to encroach on the Hausaland. This remarkable administrator established an effective central organization over his widespread domain, maintained diplomatic relations with countries north of the desert, and even established diplomatic ties with the sultan of Turkey through his Mediterranean embassies. By the early seventeenth century, however, Kanem-Bornu had begun to decline; disruptive influences similar to those in the other Sudanic states had taken their toll, and once again, a substantial kingdom receded into history.

What of the "jungle" lying south of the savanna? Surely its inhabitants demonstrated nothing in the way of political organization and statecraft; surely one could not expect great cities or an elaborate trade complex in the forests of the Guinea coast. Here, if nowhere else, the myth of the dark continent must bear some semblance of reality, for the Europeans who created the myths used their early contacts with the Guinea coast to determine that this was truly a land without civilization, a land of savages. As a matter of fact, the Europeans rarely penetrated the coast to reach the Guinean towns of the interior until the nineteenth century, and on the rare occasions when outsiders *did* get to the towns, their impressions were hardly negative. The city of Benin, center of the forest state of the same name, elicited the following observation from a Dutch traveler in 1602:

The town seemeth to be very great; when you enter it, you go into a great broad street, not paved, which seems to be seven or eight times broader than the Warmoes street in Amsterdam.... When you are in the great street, ... you see many great streets on the sides thereof.... The houses in this town stand in good order, one close and even with the other, as the houses of Holland stand....

In some respects—as in the great tradition of bronze sculpture created by its court artists—Benin was exceptional. In other respects it was typical of the forest kingdoms of the coast, kingdoms like Oyo and Dahomey. The rulers of such states, deriving their authority from descent contact with the founders of the states, were the focal points and unifying elements of their fundamentally agricultural peoples. The states themselves varied in size, complexity, and the degree to which they were centrally organized. Oyo, foremost city of the land of the Yoruba, served as an important trade connection between the lower Guinea coast and the western Sudan. By 1600, Oyo had assumed a position of leadership and authority throughout most of Yorubaland, partly because its middle-man position in the trade complex permitted the acquisition of Sudanese horses for her mounted cavalry, which in turn gave Oyo clear military superiority in the area. Others of the forest states were simpler in structure and organization.[9] But even the smallest and least complex states of the central Guinea coast, as Basil Davidson has written, "had chiefs and counsellors, orderly government, firm rules of public behavior, trade with their neighbors and trade with the interior." They were somewhat more isolated, somewhat less complex in political organization, and somewhat less rich in culture content. However, in the sixteenth and seventeenth centuries they were not inhabited by "savages" in a state of culture arrest, as the myths would have us believe.

Far to the south of the Niger basin, southward even from the mouth of the great Congo River, another West African kingdom flourished that must be noted at this point; the

famous kingdom of the Kongo. By the middle of the
fifteenth century this kingdom, actually more a confedera-
tion of several smaller states linked under the king, the
manikongo, was a fully sovereign African state; it was, in
fact, the leader of all the states of the central coast. But
the Kongo state was to be one of the first of the African
areas to come under the influence of the Europeans; indeed, the most famous of the Kongo kings, Nzinga Mbemba
(better known by his Christian name, Affonso), was apparently already Roman Catholic in religion and predisposed
toward strong ties with Europe when he assumed the
throne in 1506. He had great hopes for Kongo-Portuguese
relations, including converting his country to Catholicism
and expanding trade and culture contacts with western
Europe. One of his earliest acts was to call on King Manu-
el I of Portugal for priests and technicians to assist him in
his great plan; until 1512, the plan seemed to be working.
However, the Portuguese ultimately failed Affonso; with
calculation and cynical indifference to the requests of the
king, the Portuguese turned away from all forms of trade
except trade in black slaves. That story, however, belongs
more properly in another place, for the story of Afro-
European contacts and the Atlantic slave trade is an episode in Afro-American history that demands detailed consideration.

We can now leave our discussion of some of the more
important states, kingdoms, confederations, and empires
of West Africa up to 1600 with one final, very general,
consideration. They were all, by 1600, well into their
periods of decline. However, before beginning some other
considerations of precolonial African culture, one further
observation should be made with reference to political
organization. West African political systems did not *always*
take on forms of centralization and bureaucratic organization. Many peoples, usually those furthest removed from
the urban centers, managed very well without central organization of any sort and without any recognizable government at all. We have already noted that the states
grew out of less complex forms of social organization,

usually based on kinship and descent grouping. Many
people remained quite contentedly "stateless" throughout
the period.[10]

An African people who managed very well under a loose-
ly-knit form of organization were the Ibo people, living
generally south of the Benue River in what is now eastern
Nigeria. The political organization of the Ibo was not based
on the idea of the state, but instead on what has been
termed "village clusters," groups of small villages in which
the residents were united by ties of kinship and descent.
Each cluster claimed a common ground on which the leaders could meet to settle disputes and disagreements, usually
under the leadership of the ranking village chief (i.e., the
oldest chief of the oldest village). These common meeting
places were also local trade centers for the village members and meeting places for religious practice for the cults
represented in the cluster. This system was typical of
many similar (although sometimes variant) village systems
quite common throughout the "noncentralized" portions
of precolonial West Africa.

Basil Davidson has argued convincingly that the "middle
ages" in African history ended about 1600. A new period
then commenced, exhibiting some fundamental differences
from what had gone before. The year 1600 was a "turning point" that marked "the outset of a major epoch of
transition that was to steer West Africa out of Iron Age
civilization into the very different civilization of our times."
As noted above, the fall of Songhay indicated the demise
of the authority and significance of the old empires. By
then the trans-Saharan trade had shifted from the western
routes to the eastern routes, which were being largely
supplanted by the Atlantic coastal routes. The great market cities of the Sudan had, consequently, waned in significance and were in the process of decay that would leave
most of them only ruins by the nineteenth century. Finally, the Atlantic slave trade had begun to unravel the fabric
of West African culture. The devastating combination of
such factors (and others) pointed the way to the period of
European domination that would be complete only with

the partition and colonization of the entire continent by the late nineteenth century. After 1600, the impact of Europe was to be indelible and probably permanent. But what was African life like before the Europeans arrived? What were some noteworthy culture considerations that are indicative of the individual's life-style? Until now, we have been concerned primarily with certain dominant *historical* considerations. We must now turn briefly to some *culture* considerations and attempt, however imperfectly, to suggest their contours.

Generalization about the history and culture of sub-Saharan West Africa is difficult. The sources are not always available, and the rich diversity makes meaningful generalization risky, at best. But even so, *some* broad generalization is possible, particularly since, as we have already observed, precolonial West Africa did fall roughly into two "culture areas" manifesting considerable culture unity. There is sufficient unity that we are able to isolate certain patterns or tendencies common to the life-styles of large groups of Africans. Remember that we are speaking here of pre-European, precolonial, "traditional" culture considerations, and that we are speaking in generalities of the "typical" or "normal". There would necessarily be exceptions to practically every statement, exceptions that space limitations preclude our noting. With these things in mind, we will examine some of the dominant aspects of traditional West African culture, especially those related particularly (although often indirectly) to the Afro-American experience.

The first "consideration" is one that we have already noted, and one that is the dominant thesis of this chapter. It relates to the matter of the great diversity and complexity of the cultural experiences of the so-called "primitive" people of the Dark Continent. In the eyes of the anthropologist or culture historian, there are no "primitive" peoples; all cultures are complex, claiming intricate and often highly formalized social, political, and economic institutions, not to mention subtle forms of artistic expression and intricate theologies and religious rituals.[11] As anthropologist William Bascom observed with reference to

West Africa, "the term 'primitive' is valid. . . only if it is used technically to distinguish literate societies from those whose history and culture are transmitted orally." In this sense only the people of precolonial West Africa may be thought of as "primitive," since they were all preliterate except for the Arabic-speaking (and Arabic-writing) sections of the Sudan. In the absence of writing, however, oral traditions were assiduously maintained and, in fact, form one of the major sources of our information about the history and culture of the region.

The second major culture consideration is also one that we have mentioned earlier: "kinship domination," the kinship basis of most social organization. To understand most aspects of African culture—for example, economics, politics, or religion—one must be familiar with the kinship system. Kinship dominated all else. We have already noted the role of kinship in social and political organization. But in kinship-dominated cultures, the very status and role of the individual is determined by his position in his kinship group, not only in such matters as social class and means of subsistence, but also *vis-a-vis* his relationship to the earth, the world at large, and even the hereafter. Who one was, what one did, and his chances for success in the after-life depended on the maintenance of his "place" with reference to his family, nuclear or extended. In the words of one specialist in the subject, "A man's health and securi-ty, his very life and even his chance of immortality, were in the hands of his kin. A 'kinless' man was at best a man without social position: at worst, he was a dead man." Clearly, this was a powerful force operating on each mem-ber of a society. Outside the kinship group, the individual had no status, little security, and nothing to guide him in his role expectations. In short, he was an outsider, whose lot, at best, was that of a tolerated stranger. Inside his group, however, a sometimes complex web of kinship ties linked him with the others in his community and deter-mined his place and role in work, religious observation, government, and recreation. It can almost be said that one's very being, his "personness," depended on the maintenance of his kinship role, because all reference points of existence, all guidelines to behavior, were based on that role.

Kinship also provided cohesiveness to the society, partly through a powerful sense of collective responsibility and shared benefits of kinship relationships. The individual not only had his role fixed by the system; he was also a single but integral part of a complex whole. One member of an Ashanti clan phrased this interrelationship in these words: "I am because we are; and since we are, therefore I am." This dozen words sum up the nature and significance of kinship with astonishing clarity.

Kinship considerations provided much of the structure of African life, but religion infused every aspect of existence. Moreover, despite the stereotypes, religions in Africa were extraordinarily complex systems of belief that sought to provide an explanation of life, death, and the relationship between the individual, his God, his kin (living and dead), and the many intermediaries between man and God. Although they displayed the same incredible diversity we have by now come to expect of the "Dark Continent," and although they lacked any doctrinaire orthodoxy, African religious beliefs did manifest certain common tendencies. All African religions, for example, were monotheistic in that they posited the existence of a supreme being—a "High God," who created himself, other gods, and the world—whether he be called *Nyame, Olorun, Chukwu,* or something else. He was not only the creator of the world, but also the source and author of whatever meaning and order governed the affairs of man. But these religions may also be said to have been polytheistic in that numbers of spirits or lesser divinities were believed to stand between the individual and the High God. These intermediary spirits were frequently invoked in rituals to determine the wishes of God, or of some powerful spirit. Once the wishes of the spirit were determined, ritual propitiation was required, propitiation that frequently came through the intermediary assistance of a priest or an elder, someone believed to be close to the "vital force" central to the African conception of life itself.

This vital force governed the African world view, since it suggested the life-affirming quality so marked in African religion. Life itself, and the power necessary to life and procreation, lay at the summit of the value scale, and the religious practices and symbols suggesting this life-affirming quality often shocked the uninitiated western observer. The importance of sex, for example, was quite openly accepted and formed the basis of symbolic ritual dances. Religious art frequently employed the use of phallic symbols and representations of sexual intercourse. It was all part of the belief in vitalism or dynamism which was central to traditional African religion. In many respects such attitudes are reminiscent of Greek, Hebrew, and Indian recognition of sex, procreation, and the human body as being literally of fundamental good.

But there is also evil to be accounted for in the African world view and, indeed, there were many sources of evil. It was necessary to guard against them constantly; because they varied so in source, the believer had to take appropriate precautions against a variety of possible authors of evil. Ritual, then, was elaborate and demanding, centering around prayer, offerings, and especially sacrifice. One's difficulties might have been the result of having paid insufficient attention to a spirit. Ancestors might have been punishing a descendant for offenses against kinsmen or other shortcomings. Or the trouble might have had a "witch," a human capable of causing great problems through his ability to cast spells, as its source. In any case, it was necessary to get to the source of the problem and then take the necessary action to end it by appeasing the source or countering the spell. This required a diviner to establish the source of trouble; then the person seeking relief could determine the correct ritual or rituals to counter its effects. Rituals varied, but usually they involved sacrifice of one kind or another, either symbolic or actual. In extreme cases, if the trouble was of great magnitude, it might call for the most treasured of all sacrifices, that of human life. How-

ever, human sacrifice was, even in the period of our concern, relatively uncommon. Only rarely did the offended
spirit demand such an extreme sacrifice. Although blood
sacrifice was customary, the blood of a chicken or goat
used symbolically generally satisfied the author of the
trouble.

Religion in Africa provided much more to its faithful
than mere defense against trouble, however. It also taught
moral precepts; it inculcated the individual with a sense of
his responsibility to society. In order to do so, the traditional religion had to offer a body of wisdom and example
and provide a set of guidelines to the good and moral life.
It did this through age-old proverbial guidance, maintained
and preserved by the people even today. This proverbial
wisdom was transmitted in oral tradition and constitutes
a tremendous body of religious literature, comparable in
volume to the New Testament or the Koran. Collectively
the proverbs all serve somewhat the same function; they are
all sources of spiritual guidance. They point the way to
the moral, the right, and the good. They show how to
avoid error and evil. The collected proverbs are at the
very center of traditional religion in that they provide its
"holy writ," and by no means the less so because they
were never written. They were simply known.[12]

It should go without saying that kinship, religion, and
law were integrally related in African culture. Traditional
law (or "customary" law, as it is sometimes termed) is an
enormously complex subject, but one that must be considered, if only briefly, because of the common western
association of "primitive savagery" and "lawlessness."
There is considerable evidence that a sense of justice and
respect for law were vital features of West African culture.
Where kinship and religion failed to provide sufficient
sanctions for correct behavior, the system of law did so.
It was, of course, not written law, nor was it technically
"codified," but the system of precedents based on tradition and maintained by duly constituted judges was as clear
and forthright in its operation as written law. Such tradi-
tion-based "codes" varied in complexity, but Africa could

claim courts (and even hierarchies of courts), the distinction between civil and criminal proceedings, jury trial, witnesses, and counsel: in short, the full panoply of court law manifest in "civilized" states.

Traditional African legal systems did not, of course, always accord with the modern western sense of justice and equity. Trial by ordeal and other arbitrary techniques for determining guilt were employed on some occasions, especially in the absence of witnesses. Punishments were sometimes harsh, including maiming and death by torture, especially for such offenses as witch-craft, sorcery, murder, and treason. But the system was not as a rule capricious or unduly harsh in its operation. Precolonial African law did what legal systems anywhere are supposed to do. It provided a means of recourse to aggrieved individuals; it formed a source of authority that could enforce and maintain order; it protected the group from the sociopathic individual. There is little or no evidence that in its operations the African systems were in the least bit more harsh, cruel, or unjust than those of the "civilized" states of Europe during the same years.

Customary law was not the only law to operate in precolonial West Africa. The Muslim influence was strong throughout the Sudan, and by the mid-thirteenth century, Islamic law, as we have noted, was powerfully entrenched in most of the centralized states south of the Sahara. Based on the *Shari'a*—the sacred law of the Muslims—the Islamic legal system prevailed wherever the influence of Islam was strongly felt, particularly in the urban centers of the western Sudan. There the power of a converted king, a *Mansa* Musa, for example, was sufficient to impose the sacred law on the people under his aegis. Outside the urban areas, however, customary law prevailed or a form of syncretism occurred, producing a cross between the two systems of law. In either case, precolonial West Africans cannot be considered a "lawless" people. That myth, like the rest, simply does not stand the test of historical inquiry.

It would be impossible to conclude our consideration of

West African culture without mentioning art, because it is in that field that even the Europeans, otherwise so unwilling to admit African achievement, are ready to make certain concessions. "Primitive" art, we are told, did have its influence on such modern abstract artists as Picasso and Modigliani, and for that reason may be worthy of recognition, however grudging. In reality, traditional African art proceeded from rather different assumptions than the work of the moderns. It should be judged on its own merit, not on the basis of its "influence" on later artists. So judged, it can stand up well on its merit. In view of the limitations of space, it would be fruitless to attempt a consideration of the aesthetic foundations of African carvings or bronze castings, and even more so to attempt a discussion of individual works. We can only suggest in passing that every African culture manifested an aesthetic dimension, that the greatest percentage of African art was functional, usually religious in nature, and that the aesthetic from which it proceeded reflected the world view and value system, which we have already discussed.[13] The bronzes and ivory and gold carvings of Ife and Benin and the myriad wood carvings in which West Africa is so rich rank with the world's great art of whatever people and of whatever time. The mystery, power, subtlety, and craftsmanship are incontestable and vividly relate the sense of beauty based in functionalism with which their creators were imbued. That they provided inspiration for modern western artists is a secondary consideration at best except, of course, to the painters and sculptors who found their creative impulses in the work of unknown black masters.

So much, then, for our "considerations" of the African heritage of Afro-America. The coming of the Europeans in substantial numbers was to add in a deterministic way to the forces of change that profoundly influenced West Africa in the fifteenth and sixteenth centuries. These forces were largely disintegrative in nature; by 1600 the old empires and city-states were mere vestiges of what they had once been. When more and more slavers began arriving, the pace of disintegration quickened. Africa would never really be the same. In a sense, the beginning of Afro-American history marks the end of a major epoch in the history of mother Africa. Old World Africa would be as deeply affected as Old World Europe by the discovery and development of the New World, and just as Old World Europeans found their way into the New World, so did Old World Africans. African history is tied to American history in the same way that European history is tied to American history, with one notable exception. The end results of the contact were different. New World discovery and development tended to revivify Old World Europe. The effects on Africa were quite the opposite. Yet it was out of the awkward and painful joining of old and new worlds that Afro-America was born.

NOTES

[1] The oldest of the Australopithicine fossils discovered to this time has been determined to be over 2½ million years old, and the Australopithicine stage of human evolution is believed to have lasted from that time until about ¾ of a million years ago. In the specialized language of the prehistorian, this would mean that the little creatures roamed over large areas of Africa from the lower part to the early middle part of the Pleistocene epoch. No hominid fossils even remotely near that age have been discovered on any other continent.

[2] To suggest that the people of the western Sudan moved into relative insularity is not, of course, to suggest that they became culturally sterile and uninnovative. The Africanist Robert July has suggested recently that some tremendously significant innovations in subsistence technique were made by such resourceful peoples as the Hausa, Bambara, and Mandinka. Among the noteworthy innovations were deepplowing techniques for grain and systems of irrigation for cotton cultivation.

[3] The extent to which this diffusion influenced developments in the western Sudan and less directly in sub-Saharan West Africa is another subject of scholarly controversy. Some specialists contend that diffusion did indeed occur, especially in such key matters as iron technology and the principle of divine kingship. Other scholars play down Egyptaic and Meroitic influence, arguing for the indigenous growth of most West African culture elements. Linguistic patterns, the basis of many historical judgments by Africanists, seem to support the latter view.

[4] Herskovits isolated 10 such culture areas in all. In addition to the

three contiguous areas of the west coast, he designated North Africa, the desert, Khoisan (a linguistic family of Southwest Africa that includes the Bushmen and Hottentots), East African cattle area, East Sudan, East Horn, and Egypt.

[5] These groups are frequently called "lineages" or sometimes "clans," which is really a rather broad term designating any kinship group beyond the nuclear family. The concept of "tribe," so often used with reference to African social and political organization, is hard to define. (One authority has noted it is easier for a member than an outsider.) Generally, "tribe" designates a larger group than clan; one distinguished by a special name and occupying and exploiting a more or less well-defined territory, and one in which the members recognize certain cultural (including linguistic) similarities that distinguish them from other similar groups.

[6] A compilation of the Arabic travel accounts of Ghana made in 1067 by the scholar al-Bakri reveals much detail about the wealth and power of the Ghanian kings. Publication of this compilation—the *Kitab al-Masalik wa'l Mamalik*—came only months after the Norman invasion of a little-known northern European island called England.

[7] Such ostensibly wholesale conversions from the traditional African religions to Islam were seldom if ever complete. Usually the rulers would accept the Koran (or at least agree to do so) while the people outside the capital continued to follow their customary religious practices.

[8] It would be well over 100 years before larger, more complex, political units would reemerge in the western Sudan under the auspices of different peoples altogether, most notably the Fulani and Bambara. That story, however, is beyond the scope of this chapter.

[9] The Hausa states of northern Nigeria is yet another group of West African city-states that must be mentioned as an intermediate-level state complex flourishing in the period. The walled cities of the Hausa people (and there were numerous such cities) all maintained relative independence; since no single city ever gained sufficient power to control the others, there was never a real Hausa "empire." Nevertheless, the Hausaland by the sixteenth century had become another part of the system of long-distance trade that linked the Sudan to Guinea.

[10] One technical term often applied to such social structuring is the "segmentary society," or "acephalous society," meaning a grouping of several descent lines under leadership of the elders of each individual line or internal "segment." Such segmentary societies were ordinarily keynoted by a pervasive equalitarianism among its people.

[11] It has long been the tendency of the western world to judge the

relative complexity or "state of advance" of a culture largely in terms of its technology. The more technologically advanced a culture, the more "civilized" it is thought to be. In view of the world's current ecological crisis, the product of human technology, many are coming to question this assumption.

[12] As noted above, religion in West Africa was not limited to traditional religion. Both Islam and Christianity made rather tentative incursions, into the Sudan in the former case and in the Congo in the latter, prior to the full-fledged European invasion. But there was no great popular response to either until the nineteenth century. The traditional religions were simply too strong. Islamic strength in the Sudan was limited to the cities and rarely spread to the countryside and villages outside the urban centers.

[13] The thorough integration of African art into African culture as a whole has led critic Roy Sieber to suggest that "the arts [of Africa] more closely approached those of Egypt, Greece and the Middle Ages in Europe than [the] more recent arts of the Western World."

SUGGESTIONS FOR FURTHER READING

Three brief general introductions to African history and culture provide good points of departure: Paul Bohannan and Philip Curtin, *Africa and Africans* (Garden City, N. Y.: Natural History Press, 1971) reflects the anthropological perspective as well as the historical in a lively and readable prose style. Roland Oliver and J. D. Fage, *A Short History of Africa* (Baltimore: Penguin Books, 1962) is a surprisingly comprehensive and well-written general history. More recent and equally readable is Joseph E. Harris, *Africans and Their History* (New York: New American Library, 1972). Robert W. July, *A History of the African People* (New York: Scribner, 1970) is a balanced and fair-minded textbook, as is the somewhat more detailed but highly competent Harry A. Gailey, *History of Africa from Earliest Times to 1800* (New York: Holt, Rinehart and Winston, 1970).

One could make a fairly extensive and thoroughly enjoyable study of Africa in the books of Basil Davidson, the British free-lance writer and lifelong student of African history. For example, Davidson's *Africa in History: Themes and Outlines* (New York: Macmillan, 1968) affords a fine introduction, while his *The African Past. Chronicles from Antiquity to Modern Times* (New York: Grosset and Dunlap, 1964) provides an excellent collection of primary source documents. His *A History of West Africa to the Nineteenth Century* (Garden City, N. Y.: Anchor Books-Doubleday and Company, 1966), written with the assistance of F. K. Buah and J. F. Ade Ajayi, is a most successful attempt to flesh out the sinews of early West African history and to create some order from near-chaotic complexity.

Davidson is a scholar of strong opinions, however, and should be balanced with J. D. Fage, *A History of West Africa. An Introductory Survey* (Cambridge: Cambridge University Press, 1969), and especially J. F. A. Ajayi and Ian Espie, eds., *A Thousand Years of West African History. A Handbook for Teachers and Students* (Ibadan, Nigeria: Ibadan University Press, 1965), a collection of essays by African scholars that is almost essential for the more serious student. Anyone should enjoy and profit from Alvin M. Josephy, Jr., ed., *The Horizon History of Africa* (New York: American Heritage, 1971), a big, beautiful, well-integrated text-with-illustrations, each section of which is written by a ranking authority in the field. The authorities include Philip D. Curtin, J. Desmond Clark, A. Adn Boahen, and Basil Davidson.

The fascinating subject of the evolutionary process by which near-man became man is treated more dramatically in Robert Ardrey, *African Genesis. A Personal Investigation into the Animal Origins and Nature of Man* (New York: Dell, 1967). More scholarly and no less compelling is the work of a foremost human biologist, Wilfred E. LeGros Clark, entitled *Man-Apes or Ape-Men? The Story of Discoveries in Africa* (New York: Holt, Rinehart and Winston, 1967), a clear and comprehensive summary of the Australopithecine controversy. Equally fascinating is the subject treated in J. Desmond Clark's seminal "The Prehistoric Origins of African Culture," *The Journal of African History*, 5:161-183 (1964).

The monographic literature on West Africa is large and growing larger by the month. Selecting a handful of titles to recommend is most difficult and highly subjective. But the student would probably profit from and enjoy E. W. Bovill, *The Golden Trade of the Moors* (London: Oxford University Press, 1958), a fine study of the trans-Saharan trade routes. Robin Fox, *Kinship and Marriage. An Anthropological Perspective* (Middlesex: Penguin Books, 1967) is a good, clear introduction to an incredibly complex subject, one that is vital to any understanding of African culture. Richard W. Hull, "Law, Crime and Punishment in Pre-Colonial Africa," *Colloquium*, 1:27-33 (1970), also provides a fine brief consideration of its subject, as does Geoffrey Parrinder, *Religion in Africa* (Baltimore: Penguin Books, 1969), an excellent analysis by a specialist in comparative religions. The best introduction to African religion and thought, however, is John S. Mbiti, *African Religions and Philosophy* (Garden City, N. Y.: Anchor Books, 1970), an enormously insightful study by an African theologian-teacher.

To begin the study of African art, Frank Willett, *African Art: An Introduction* (New York: Praeger, 1971) would be excellent. Elsy Leuzinger, *Africa: The Art of the Negro Peoples* (London: Mathuen,

1960), although marred by some peculiar racial assumptions, is a beautiful book featuring scores of superb reproductions. William Fagg and Margaret Plass, *African Sculpture. An Anthology* (New York: E. P. Dutton, 1964) is a profusely illustrated paperback with an excellent text.

Some of the great scholarly controversies concerning Africa are treated in Robert O. Collins, ed., *Problems in African History* (New Jersey: Prentice-Hall, 1968). Collins' "problems" are well chosen and each is given a fine introduction. Finally, the student who wishes to delve more deeply could not do better than to turn to Robert A. Lystad, ed., *The African World. A Survey of Social Research* (New York: Praeger, 1965), a bibliographical survey ranging over 18 different academic disciplines, each treated by a leading specialist in his field.

Chapter 3

THE ATLANTIC SLAVE TRADE AND
THE DYNAMICS OF CULTURE CONTACT

The great Atlantic slave trade from Africa to the New World lasted nearly 400 years and produced one of the truly remarkable instances of population migration in world history. It also evidenced a kind of callous inhumanity and brutality that has been condemned with understandable and justifiable outrage by modern historians, amateur and professional. No sane person could view the trade in its operational aspect with anything but horror and contempt. However, those who would really understand this important historical episode should be prepared to make certain compromises with emotion and view the trade from the perspective of the world and time that produced it.

It is sometimes difficult for people living in the western world today to realize that the concept of individual freedom is a relatively recent notion. For the greater portion of recorded history the majority of the world's population was not free, nor would most people have understood the term in its modern sense. Slavery was an ancient institution by the sixteenth century, when the Atlantic trade first reached sizable proportions. Although most of the people were not actually slaves in 1500 A.D., neither were they fully "free." There were various degrees of "unfreedom" in which a person might—indeed statistically speaking *would*—find himself fixed for life.

Note. Footnotes for this chapter are located on pages 93-96.

An individual might, of course, be a chattel slave, considered a piece of property by his owner, subject to absolute control, whose person as well as his labor belonged to his master. Or he might be a serf, little better off, really, than a chattel, locked in service to the land and the landlord and fixed in his situation for life. Or he might be of a special class of serf termed "villein," possessing the legal status of a free man in all his personal doings except those directly involving his lord. Slavery and various other forms of feudal vassalage were an accepted part of the way things were. Widespread "unfreedom" was a normal condition in most of the world when the Atlantic trade was born.

It should be obvious, however, that in 1500 slavery and the various forms of unfreedom had little or nothing to do with "race." Slaves and other vassals might come from any genogroup or from any ethnic group. During the long period of conflict between Christianity and Islam, during the great crusades and holy wars, *religion* was often significant in bringing about one's loss of freedom, because "infidels" or "nonbelievers" were deemed fair game for enslavement by all sides. Generally, so were prisoners of war. Genes had nothing to do with it, and slaves came in all colors and shapes and from all corners of the earth. Some came from Africa. Others came from what is now Turkey, or the Balkan states, or the Soviet Union. Anyone who was vulnerable to capture was subject to sale, and hence much of the world's labor was performed by land-bound serfs or captive slaves, owned outright by those who were wealthy and powerful enough to purchase or inherit them. This consideration is the first essential to an understanding of the origins of the Atlantic slave trade and the creation of what African historian Philip Curtin has termed the "South Atlantic System."

It is also important to realize that several forms of slavery existed in sub-Saharan West Africa in the same period. There, too, the people were generally divided into the free and the unfree, and free men became slaves in Africa in much the same manner as elsewhere in the world. An individual could be captured in war and be enslaved by his captor, and many were. He could also be "pawned" for debt by his kinsmen and subjected to servitude until the debt was paid off. If it was not paid off, the individual might become a "pawn for life," a lifetime slave.[1] But if there were similarities in the kinds of slavery practiced in Africa and elsewhere in the Old World (and later, in the New World), there were also some pronounced differences.

African slavery as it existed prior to the coming of the Europeans has been termed variously "domestic," "benign," or "household" slavery. The primary difference between this kind of slavery and the kind prevailing in most of the rest of the Old World (and all of the New World, once the system was established there) lay in the great flexibility of the slave's status. In West Africa slaves were not considered "chattels," that is, a slave was not merely an article of personal property belonging to his master. The slave was deemed a person, albeit a person deprived of kin and therefore without place. But his status was by no means irrevocably fixed for the duration of his life. He could and frequently did become free, by hard work or loyal service or by a fortuitous marriage, for nothing in the system of domestic slavery denied the slave the right and the opportunity to marry a free citizen. He might also accumulate wealth of his own if he were a good businessman or a military leader or a skilled craftsman. Sudanic kings, for example, occasionally used reliable slaves as province chiefs in the kingdom. Slaves could even become kings themselves.

The use of the terms "household" and "domestic" suggest that the African slave was in a sense a part of the owner's family, living with the family as a part of the extended household although attached to the household by nonkinship links. At times even kinship links were established, for marriage of a slave into the master's family was not uncommon. An old Ashanti proverb well sums up the potential aspirations of a slave in such a system. "A slave who knows how to serve," it teaches, "succeeds to his master's property." Although a slave assuredly was not a person of exalted status in the society, neither was he held

in contempt as an innately servile and inferior person. He
was simply unfortunate. In a system that viewed slavery
as a fate that could fall to anyone, things could hardly
have been otherwise. Without a doubt, African slaves worked hard and suffered the cruelties and indignities attendant
to any form of unfreedom. Slaves were also the most vulnerable element in the population, and, when the ruler
deemed it necessary, were used for ritual sacrifice. But as
Basil Davidson has noted, the condition of the average
West African *slave* was in many ways comparable to the
condition of most of the *people* of medieval Europe.

The European discovery and colonization of the New
World[2] produced a system of slavery that was in most respects original and in all respects more exploitive than anything preceding it. Slavery took on an essentially new dimension in its New World setting, and the process and dynamics of the New World slave system form a central episode in the Afro-American experience, because it was in
that process that Afro-America came to be.

Europe was to provide the means of transportation for
Old World Africans to their New World homes; she would
be the agent of the trans-Atlantic nexus of West Africa and
the Americas. What has been termed the "Age of Reconnaissance"—the period during which Europe began tenta-
tively to explore southward in the Atlantic—is usually said
to have begun in the early fifteenth century. The Portuguese were in the vanguard. Motivated by the desire to
reach the rich markets of the Far East, and by the desire
to find the kingdom of fabled Prester John (believed to be
a wealthy Christian king somewhere in central Africa), and
by a kind of simple curiosity to discover just what might
be "out there," the able Portuguese seamen began to push
further and further south down the West African coast. By
1445 they had reached Cape Verde and the mouth of the
Senegal River, and had established the beginnings of a
colony in the Cape Verde Islands. In 1472 they made their
first landfall on the "Bight of Benin," the northernmost
projection of the Gulf of Guinea and the area they would
soon come to know as the "Slave Coast." The most fa-

mous of all the Portuguese voyages of exploration along the African coast, those of Bartholomew Diaz to the Cape of Good Hope (1488) and Vasco da Gama around the Cape to India (1497 to 1499), completed the pattern of the African phase of Portuguese "reconnaissance."

While the Portuguese explored to the south, other Europeans pushed out in other directions. In 1492 Italian navigator Christopher Columbus, sailing in the employ of Spain, discovered the West Indies thus initiating the beginnings of exploration and conquest of the Caribbean and the Americas. Other European nations were quick to follow the Spanish lead. Within a year after Columbus landed in the islands, Portugal laid claim to New World territory; the resulting papal arbitration gave the Portuguese control of Brazil.[3] Several other European powers, however, were ultimately to repudiate this agreement between the Pope and the Iberian states. By the middle of the seventeenth century, England, France, Sweden, and the Netherlands would all have claims to New World territory; in fact, they would have claimed virtually *all* of the New World, and to a greater or lesser degree made good those claims by occupying and then colonizing their respective possessions.

In terms of commercial importance, however, the center of the New World remained in the Caribbean and Brazil, for it was there that the Europeans first established the South Atlantic System in its full-blown form. Both Brazil and the islands afforded the temperate climate and rich soil necessary to the production of certain staple crops for which, the Europeans realized, there was worldwide demand. Only a source of labor was necessary to develop the plantation system and the international commercial network made possible by plantation production. Hence, following an initial, largely unsuccessful experiment with the forced labor of the Amerindians, the Europeans were to look to Africa for the labor supply essential to the system.

The economic institution essential to the development of the South Atlantic System was the plantation. Owned by Europeans, producing tropical staples for European consumption, the plantations of the New World provided the basis for the expansion and development of the Americas. But the success of the plantation system rested fundamentally on the continuing supply of efficient, reliable labor, and this obvious fact produced what one historian has termed the "most massive intercontinental migration before the industrial era." An anthropologist concerned with the cultural processes involved in such a vast new contact of cultures has termed the results of the slave trade "the most massive acculturational event in human history." Over a period of about 400 years European traders were to transport several million Africans[4] to work on New World plantations (and in some cases, mines) in order to provide such luxuries as sugar, coffee, chocolate, and dye-woods for the Old World market. Two by-products of the South Atlantic System were to be of staggering consequence to the history of western civilization. The first was the capital accumulation made possible by plantation-mine production. To a significant degree, that investment capital formed the basis for the Industrial Revolution in Europe. The second by-product was the Afro-American population itself. It might reasonably be argued, then, that Afro-Americans produced through their labors the wherewithal for the development of the modern industrial system.

But why Africans? When the Europeans first began to search for potential labor, why was it that they chose the West Coast of Africa as their source of supply? As we have already noted, they turned to Africa only after their initial attempts to enslave the local population had proved largely unsuccessful. But why *did* the early experiments with Amerindian slavery fail? There were several reasons. First, it should be remembered, the Europeans initially did not undertake to establish plantations. They wanted the gold, silver, and precious jewels they believed to exist for the taking in the "Indies." The Spanish conquest of the Aztecs in Mexico (1521) and the Incas of Peru (1532) only added to the urgency of their greed for easy riches. As a result, the native population was initially exploited and then virtually extinguished by the cruelty associated with the frenzied treasure hunt. Within 50 years of the discovery of Hispaniola, for example, the local population was for all practical purposes annihilated. The same could be said for the populations of Cuba, Jamaica, and Puerto Rico. These people obviously could not be enslaved; they were simply killed off by the ferocity of the European aggression and by their inability to resist European diseases.

This second factor was important enough to bear further examination. Isolated from Old World contact, the Amerindian population could not develop resistance to the Old World disease environment. As a result they died off in droves when the inevitable epidemics struck, especially measles, smallpox, influenza, and tuberculosis. Much has been made of the old notion that Africans made good slaves in the New World tropics because they could perform heavy labor in the tropical climate whereas Amerindians (and, of course, Europeans) could not. But the fact is that people do not sicken and die of climate, they sicken and die of diseases to which they have not developed immunities. Africans were better able to counter the European disease environment than the Amerindians were. Consequently the Africans would be thought to be more suitable slaves than the Amerindians. There was never any question of the Europeans themselves performing the labor of plantation and mine.[5]

A third major consideration in assessing the causes of the relative failure of Amerindian slavery as compared to African slavery has received inadequate emphasis in the past: the endemic New World population was, for the most part at least, not culturally conditioned to agricultural labor. In the Brazilian lowlands and the Caribbean, the population simply had not advanced to a level of efficient agricultural production. However, as we have seen, most West Africans were advanced agriculturalists. Thus they were better able to make the adjustment to the plantation system. The Europeans believed (to a degree correctly) that the Indians would sooner resort to suicide than to submit to agricultural slavery. Finally, there was the obvious consideration that the Indian had a fair chance of escape into the hinterlands where he might reasonably expect aid and comfort from his people. The African, of course, had no such advantage. He was alien to the land and to the people, and could thus be subjected to greater restriction and control. For all of these reasons, European planters came quickly to regard one black as the equal of four or five Amerindians in labor potential.

But although Amerindian slavery for the most part failed, the local population was forced to submit to other forms of forced labor throughout the colonial period and into the national period of Latin American history. In some areas—notably the Brazilian upcountry, Mexico, and Peru—the native population was somewhat more advanced in agricultural techniques and social organization than elsewhere in the New World. In these areas the Spanish (and to a certain extent the Portuguese) came to employ a system known as the *"encomienda."* It was a system of labor recruitment and employment in which the people inhabiting a specified group of villages were turned over to a sort of feudal baron, known as the *encomendero*, who could claim their labor and other forms of tribute to put to whatever purpose he liked. In reality, then, the relatively more advanced Amerindian populations *were* employed in a system of "slave" labor, while the relatively backward peoples of the plantation low-lands were tried as slaves and found wanting. It was then that the Europeans turned their attention to Africa as a source of labor for the New World plantations.

European slave raids on the West African coast began on a very small scale. A convenient beginning date is 1441, when the Portuguese Captain Antam Gonçalves made a landfall on the coast of Rio d'Oro north of Senegal and took captive what he later called "two Moors," in reality Sanhaja Berbers. He then took them, along with seven other captives, back to Lisbon where they could be held for sale or ransom (or to be examined by the studious Prince Henry). Similar piratical forays followed over the next several years, perpetrated against essentially defenseless fishermen or cattle nomads of the region north of Senegambia. But these raids were only the early precursors of the great Atlantic trade. Actually, as the Portuguese moved further and further down the West Coast in that succession of voyages of exploration we have already observed, they discovered two significant realities. First, they encountered coastal peoples who were better able to defend themselves from the European raids. Second, they found that Africa offered trade commodities of very considerable value other than slaves, namely pepper, ivory, and gold. They also came to realize that they could trade for such commodities to the mutual advantage of both African and European.

As early as 1445 the Portuguese had begun colonization of the Cape Verde Islands as a potential trade base with West Africa. In 1471 they reached the northern shores of the Gulf of Guinea to discover the mineral wealth that led them to refer to the area as the "Gold Coast." In order to protect this great source of trade from foreign interlopers, the Portuguese built a castle-fortress just off shore at the location they called *"Elmina"* ("The Mine"). This was the first of a series of coastal forts built by the Portuguese to discourage foreign poaching on a trade domain they were beginning to see as their own. By 1500, following the voyages of Diaz and da Gama, the Portuguese seemed well in control of the West African trade. In this stage of trade contact, of course, slaves were only one of several valuable commodities in which the Portuguese were interested. But over the years, as the South Atlantic System developed, the European demand for black slaves increased dramatically. As a consequence, the most valuable trade item came to be African slaves.

From the middle of the fifteenth century the Iberians had been using African slave labor in their colonial plantations located on the string of islands lying just off the West African coast. It was, in fact, from these islands that the plantation system was transferred to the New World. The Spanish took the system from the Canary Islands to the West Indies; the Portuguese made the move from the Cape Verde Islands and the islands of the Gulf of Guinea to Brazil.

Although slaves had been sent to Hispaniola as early as 1502, a more accurate date for the origin of the great At-

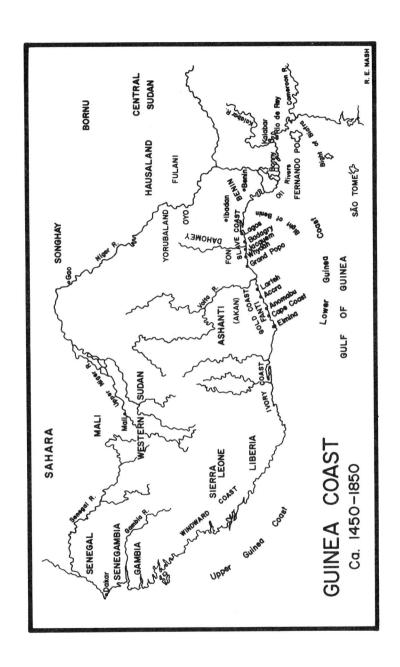

GUINEA COAST
Ca. 1450–1850

R. E. NASH

lantic slave trade would be 1518, the year in which the first "black cargo" shipped directly from the Guinea Coast was landed in the New World, carried there by Portuguese traders dealing specifically and predominantly in slaves. In that same year King Charles V of Spain granted the first license to deal in the slave trade to Spanish America—the so-called *asiento*—which purported to give the grantee the exclusive right to trade in slaves in the Spanish empire. This monopoly soon came to be held in great esteem by those who were actually involved in the trade. Although the development of the trade was initially slow, geared as it was to the development of the plantation system, by the late sixteenth century it had picked up considerably. By that time the great "triangular trade" from Europe to Africa to the New World colonies had begun to develop its familiar shape. By then the enormous profit potential for those involved in the system was apparent.

The profit potential served to increase the dimensions of the New World plantation system both in area and numbers of people involved. Although the Portuguese and the Spanish initially dominated the direct trade from Africa, other European states soon began to make incursions into the Iberian monopoly. By the middle of the seventeenth century the French, English, Dutch, Danes, Swedes, and even the Brandenbergers (Prussians) were all involved in the process of buying or stealing slaves in West Africa and trading them in America. In addition they were attempting to stake their claims (or jump the claims of others) in the area on the West African coast over which they hoped to exercise local control of the trade. All began building their coastal "forts" or "castles" in imitation of the Portuguese original at *Elmina*. The Dutch, in fact, had taken that strategic fortress from the Portuguese in 1637 and had come to play the dominant role among the European powers who had established their beachheads on the coast. By then the Atlantic slave trade had grown to enormous proportions and had achieved the status of a vast international commercial enterprise. At this point, as Basil Davidson has observed, "the slaving tide became a flood."

It is important to note, however, that the South Atlantic System did not come to full fruition until the first quarter of the seventeenth century. By that time the people of the West African slave trading states had come to depend on the Europeans for desirable, even essential, commodities, especially manufactured goods and weapons. Trade interdependence, then, along with the rise of the New World plantation economy and an age-old tradition of slavery in both Europe and in Africa, provided the necessary ingredients for the great Atlantic slave trade of the seventeenth, eighteenth, and nineteenth centuries.

As we have already noted, chattel slavery of the European type, whereby a man was valued only as a piece of property and subject to the absolute control of his "owner," was not a natural feature of African culture. But over the years of the late fifteenth and sixteenth centuries, some African rulers (and some of the people in general, it would seem) underwent a subtle change in attitude toward their "unfree" classes. Demand for European trade commodities gave rise to this change. In the words of historian J. D. Fage, the need for European goods produced "the vital change by which some West Africans began to view some others not as kin or non-kin but as a means by which to obtain wealth and power." Hence, as the trade grew to significant proportions in the late sixteenth and early seventeenth centuries, the European traders seldom had to capture and enslave people themselves; they could depend on African traders to supply slaves in ever greater numbers, in exchange for the European goods that had become, to certain individuals, essential. Chief among these essential goods were firearms.

With the introduction of firearms into a central position in the trade there came a terrible necessity to maintain arms parity with one's neighbors. What followed in certain key areas of the West African coast was a kind of chronic warfare based on slaving raids. To maintain his power and authority, a local ruler found it absolutely essential to trade for European arms. The Europeans seemed to want only slaves in exchange for guns, and there were simply not enough slaves available for trade from normal sources, that is, debtors, criminals, and prisoners of war. It became necessary for the ruler to acquire additional slaves for trading purposes. To do that ordinarily required taking more captives, so he had to raid neighboring peoples. To defend themselves the neighbors also needed European arms, which meant that they, too, had to raid to obtain captives to sell. In short, the Europeans introduced a vicious and malignant cycle involving the capture and sale of hundreds of thousands, and over the years, even millions of Africans by Africans.

In assessing the burden of "guilt" for the origin and development of the Atlantic slave trade, the Europeans traditionally bear the onus for originating the system. But the Africans are commonly blamed for participating in the capture and sale of "their own people." Such a view is overly simplistic and distorts several important considerations. The Europeans were able to justify their participation in the trade on the grounds of historic precedent, economic necessity, and religious sanction; the Africans were "infidels" and thus subject to capture and/or conversion to the "true church." Such rationalizations do not satisfy the moral sensibilities of the twentieth-century western world, but they did satisfy the vast majority of Europeans of the sixteenth, seventeenth, and eighteenth centuries. Similarly, modern man tends to view the selling of blacks by blacks as utterly reprehensible, an outrage on the sensibilities of those who prize "racial" solidarity and pan-African nationalism. But the Africans of the time of the trade viewed the whole thing from a very different perspective. They did not believe themselves to be selling "their own." In fact, they had no sense of continental unity at all, and their religion tended to view the concept of "one's own people" in a purely local dimension. One did not, at least according to moral law and custom, capture and sell one's own people, but *outsiders*, "unbelievers." This was *their* rationalization. Again, although we might view such a justification as cynical and self-serving in the extreme, *they* ordinarily accepted it as part of the way things were.

In reality, neither side of this partnership in the sale of human beings can claim the admiration or respect of the modern world, but neither can either side be accused of being more vicious or inhumane than the other. It is an ugly fact that the world of that period was in many ways a cruel world that had little regard for the niceties and conventions of liberty and justice for all. It was a world that permitted and even encouraged enormous extremes of wealth and poverty, power and vulnerability, licentious freedom and abject slavery. It condoned the use of torture, hideously cruel corporal punishment, prison confinement, and even death for minor offenses against the state, the church, or one's feudal lord. It condoned indiscriminate slaughter in defense of the faith. It also condoned slavery and the horrors of the Atlantic trade, all in the course of what was considered normal and accepted as such. And it should be noted that the "world" to which we refer included both Europe *and* Africa.

The institutional and intellectual background and rationale of the slave trade, then, is relatively clear and understandable. Somewhat more problematic are the actual operational details of the system: where the captives came from, how they were captured, transported, and sold, where they were taken, and over the duration of the system—almost four centuries—the number of people taken out of Africa and transported to the Americas; these questions must be considered in order to gain any real understanding of the slave trade. Unfortunately, the very scope and duration of the trade gave rise to many variables that have rendered the historian's job difficult. There is still much to be learned about all aspects of the system. However, certain generalizations are possible with regard to all of these factors, and from these general considerations a broad picture of the whole emerges.

It is clear, for example, that the vast majority of the slaves came from four general areas on the West African coast. The northernmost of these trade centers might be generally designated "Senegambia": the coastal area of the region drained by the Senegal and Gambia Rivers plus part

of modern Sierra Leone. To the immediate southeast lay
the Guinea Coast, stretching from the eastern boundary of
modern Liberia to the western boundary of Nigeria. The
third center of the trade was the Niger Delta region. This
was the most important of the four centers. Here several
of the most famous slave depot-fortresses were operated,
including Cape Coast Castle, Whydah, Bonny, and Old Cala-
bar, all of which lay in the coastal zones of the two
"Bights" of the Gulf of Guinea: the Bight of Benin and
the Bight of Biafra. Finally, far to the south was a broad
region that the Europeans of the period termed "Angola";
it included the coastal strip adjoining the lower Congo and
reaching south into modern Angola. A few slaves came
from elsewhere on the continent, from the Rio de Oro region north of Senegambia, for example, or even from the
east coast, especially Mozambique. But these areas produced only a relative handful of New World slaves, at least
before the midnineteenth century. The majority of slaves
taken into the Atlantic trade came from the great west
coast centers, and most especially from the Guinea Coast.

A cursory glance at a map of West Africa reveals two
things about the trade centers. First, they were all located
on the coast. Second, they seem to be associated with
river systems reaching into the interior. Both factors were
significant in the trade's development. The Europeans
found it most expedient to center their trading activities
on the coast because they believed that few whites could
survive the disease environment of the interior, and because
the African rulers of the coastal kingdoms were quite able
to resist any European thrust into the interior. The rivers
provided a network of transportation for the captives from
the point of capture to the coast. The vast majority of
the slaves were taken within 200 miles of the coast, and
many were then shipped to the coast on the most convenient river in large river craft similar to canoes. Where river
transportation was not available it was necessary to march
overland with "coffles" of recent captives; this overland
march was considered more dangerous than the journey by
riverboat. In either case, very few slaves were taken from

deep in the African interior. Transportation was too difficult and too dangerous to permit a very long march to the sea.

Considering the fact that the vast majority of the New World slaves came from a relatively limited area, it should be easy to pinpoint the specific ethnic groups (loosely, "tribes") represented in the trade. Unfortunately, this is not the case, except in very general terms. The Europeans involved in the trade were not particularly careful in distinguishing the ethnic origins of the slaves they bought and sold. For example, the slave traders commonly referred to the trade center from which slaves were shipped to designate the nationality or ethnic origin of the people themselves; thus a slave shipped out of Senegambia was likely to be termed "Senegalese" no matter what his actual ethnic origin. Similarly, the Europeans frequently chose one term, ethnic or linguistic, to identify a large group of people coming from a wide geographical area. "Bambara" was such a term, applied generally to all slaves brought in from the interior and sold to slave dealers in the post at Saint-Louis near the mouth of the Senegal River. "Mandingue" ("Mandingo" in English) shifted in meaning over the years. Initially it referred to the Malinke-speaking people of the Gambia Valley; later it came to mean anyone who spoke a Mande language, no matter what his actual tribal affiliation. These are some of the problems involved in pinpointing the precise tribal origins of the Afro-Americans.

Difficulties notwithstanding, however, it is possible to identify several of the ethnic groups that figured prominently in the trade. In Senegambia, for example, the Wolof, the Malinke, the Mende, and the Susu bear special mention. The Akan were associated with the Gold Coast, while the Bight of Benin produced Afro-Americans of Fon, Yoruba, Nupe, and Beni origins. The traders off the Bight of Biafra dealt predominantly with Ibo, Efik, and Ibibio peoples. In statistical terms it is likely that a substantial percentage of all New World slaves were originally the Twi-speaking, Yoruba-speaking, or Ewe-speaking peoples of the Guinea coast, from the areas forming the modern nations of Ghana, Dahomey, and Nigeria.

Earlier in this chapter we noted the variety of ways a man might become a slave in Africa, and, increasingly as time passed, become subject to sale to the Atlantic traders. To reiterate briefly, one could be sold by the king as punishment for a crime, or sold by himself or his kinsmen for debt. He might be kidnapped by a "press-gang" (either European or African or both) specifically for sale to the coastal traders. Or he might be (as most were) a prisoner of war.[6] Once taken into slavery in Africa, the system whereby the individual or group was sold to the European traders remained fundamentally the same throughout the period of the trade. In large and small groups the slaves were sold to the European traders for a price established between the African seller and the European purchasing agent or "factor" in residence at one of the myriad coastal slave collection points. The price was flexible and was usually calculated in terms of a preestablished exchange value agreed on by buyer and seller. The state of the market influenced the price, so in areas where the supply of slaves was generally adequate to fill the needs of the traders, the price per slave was relatively low. If the supply was limited, however, the price went up accordingly. Frequently the African traders were shrewd businessmen, and bargained ably for the best possible deal. Rarely, it seems, were the Europeans able to cheat their African counterparts, nor would they have been likely to try to do so. The factors were extremely vulnerable during the period in which they were collecting slaves while awaiting the arrival of a slave ship. Indeed, they operated only by permission of the local African ruler and dared not risk alienating the host on whose good will their very lives depended.

Having arrived at a price satisfactory to both parties, the dealers effected the actual exchange of goods for slaves. Then the factor, usually with the assistance of black mercenary retainers, proceeded to brand each of the new slaves so that he (or she) might be easily identified as the property of the new owner.[7] Finally, the new slaves were

locked in a corral or pen known as a *barracoon.* The men
were chained in place. In this way began the wait for the
arrival of a ship outfitted to transport a human cargo to
the New World. This wait in the *barracoon* varied in length
from several days to many months as the process of collection continued.

The process of initial capture, transportation to the coast,
sale to the European agent, branding, and imprisonment in
the slave pens was a cruel, traumatic sequence of events for
any human being to endure. Many did not endure. The
mortality rate in the ordeal was high, especially among the
old, the sick, and the very young. In terms of the individual suffering involved, it is doubtful that humankind has ever
witnessed a more spectacular example of man's protracted
inhumanity to man. And yet the next phase of the pro-
cedure—the infamous "middle passage"—was unquestionably
worse than everything that had occurred to that point.

The "middle passage," of course, referred to the leg of
the triangular trade lying between the West African coast
and the New World destination. Slave ships out of Bristol,
Liverpool, and London, Nantes and La Rochelle, Boston
and Salem, manned by hardened captains and crews, made
this heinous voyage thousands of times throughout the history of the trade, and each voyage was substantially the
same as the one before. Despite considerable disagreement
among the nations involved in the trade as to whose slavers
were the worst managed—all agreed that their own were
the best—the real differences were only in degree. All
shared certain features in common simply because necessity, in the minds of the traders themselves, determined
that it must be so.

First among these necessities was the matter of the size
of the cargo. Purely economic considerations determined
that the more slaves one ship could transport and deliver
for sale, the more profitable the venture. Consequently
the slave ships were usually designed to accommodate as
many bodies as possible.[8] Slaves were stored below the
main deck in the cargo area, which was especially designed
to give each slave a minimum of 18 inches of headroom.

Rarely, however, did the black cargo enjoy that much lateral movement because necessity also dictated that the slaves be chained together, either by their legs, their wrists, or their necks. If such a system seems overly restrictive, even to the point of prohibiting the use of sanitary facilities, this factor was of minimal importance; there were rarely any sanitary facilities. On the better-operated ships, however, the crew did wash down the slave decks occasionally with a mixture of vinegar and water.

Necessity also dictated the use of certain other precautions on the part of the captain. Although no slave ship ever landed a cargo without losses in transit, it was necessary to keep the mortality rate as low as possible while maintaining the standards of safety for the crew. It was obvious, for example, that in a crossing of from four weeks to three months the slaves must be fed, cared for medically, and given the opportunity to exercise. Consequently they were fed at least once a day, usually boiled beans, yams, or manioc, a starchy root plant similar to potatoes. If they refused to eat (as many did) they were fed anyway, with the aid of a specially designed instrument called a *speculum oris*, a screw-device that could be forced between (or through) tightly clenched teeth, then manipulated to pry the mouth open so that food could be poured down the resisting gullet. The slave cargo also received the ministrations of the ship's surgeon, who tried to cure whatever illnesses the slaves contracted. If he could not do so, or if the disease were contagious, the afflicted slave was jettisoned. Such losses were insured.

Exercise was required of the slaves, and once each day they were brought out of their hold beneath the main deck for this purpose. They could dance, or just jump about if they preferred. If they did not choose to do either they were beaten until they ceased to resist, either by partaking in the exercise or by losing consciousness from the physical abuse. Refusing to obey any order from the captain inevitably met with quick and often diabolical punishment to the slave. No form of recalcitrance could go unpunished. Any slave showing any sign of resistance was used as an example for the others. They were beaten to death, mutilated, or subjected to any one of many inventive torture-deaths for which the period's sailors were so justly renowned. And yet, it would seem that resistance of one form or another was a constant reality aboard the Guineaman.

The most fearful form of resistance was the slave mutiny, which usually occurred within sight of the African coast. The odds against success were enormous. The Europeans had guns, and the slaves lacked not only weapons but also any familiarity with ships and the sea. Moreover, the slaves were seldom able to communicate with each other effectively; the traders made a calculated effort to keep people able to speak the same language segregated. But despite their minimal chance of success, the slaves did attempt mutiny with relative frequency. The historical record fully documents 55 mutinies aboard slave ships from 1699 to 1845, and includes brief mention of over 100 others. The slave captains remained in constant fear of revolt and mutiny, at least until their ships put to sea and got clear of the African coast; then the chances of mutiny at sea were not as great.

Other forms of resistance also prevailed at times on the crossing. Individual slaves could attack the captain or members of the crew, and did so on occasion, although the attempt meant certain death. More common was a kind of passive resistance whereby the captives would simply refuse food or water, even when threatened with force, including torture. Unless the captain was able to force sustenance on the slave, the slave simply died. More direct forms of slave suicide were also fairly common. Some ethnic groups were more prone to suicide than others—the Ibos were believed to be especially self-destructive—but crews on the slavers had to be constantly alert to the suicide potential of all Africans. Suicide as a means of resistance to slavery was far more common than is generally believed. Actually, the old idea of African passivity and unresisting acquiescence to the slave trade is just another of the great myths that surround the whole story of New World slavery.

Let us assume, however, that the slave ship from the Guinea coast arrived at its New World destination with only the normal losses attendant to the crossing (an average of perhaps 18 to 20% of the cargo). What came next in the system of the Atlantic trade? Chances are the slave ship would put ashore at one of the islands in the West Indies, Cartagena, or Brazil. Immediately upon anchoring, the sale of the black cargo began. First, the captain weeded out those who were sick or badly injured. The incidence of disease, especially dysentery and scurvy, was very high under the circumstances of the crossing. Those who were obviously near death were simply left on the wharves to die. Those who were in doubtful condition were sold off quickly at auction for whatever they might bring from speculators who gambled that one or two of their purchases might survive and become valuable.

After the disposal sale of the disabled came the main work of the whole venture: the sale of the healthy portion of the cargo. Depending on market conditions, any one of several different methods was employed in this merchandising operation. Sometimes a single wealthy planter bought the entire lot directly from the ship captain. More often the sale was handled by a commission merchant or dealer in the islands who tried to get the best possible price for the lot from the would-be buyers. Most common was the method known as the "scramble." In this system the captain or merchant fixed the prices for all slaves in advance of the sale, with one set price for adult males, one price for females, and a third for children under a given age. Then a shot was fired from the ship as a signal to the waiting buyers who quickly rushed onto the ship where the slaves were waiting on the main deck. Each buyer then attempted to round up as many of the best-looking slaves as he could and lay claim to their purchase by marking them with his ensign, frequently a kerchief of a given color. He was permitted to purchase as many people as he could round up and claim at the preestablished price. "For the slaves," one historian has written, the scramble "was the terrifying climax of a terrifying voyage."[9]   The bondsmen were ordinarily then branded again, this time with the marks of their new owners, and were prepared for transportation to their new homes.

Following the sale came the final stage in the process whereby Africans became Afro-Americans. Clearly, a newly imported slave was not conditioned to the kind of life and labor to which he would now be subjected. He was, in the term used by the whites, "unseasoned"; he was still a "Bozal Negro." Before he could be expected to function as part of a large labor force in the plantation system he required a "seasoning" period, which usually lasted from three to four years. The seasoning process involved more than just learning to do a job. It involved adjustment to the rigors of plantation discipline, acclimation to the new disease environment, and a sort of cultural reorientation that was inevitable in the forced adoption of a new way of life. The seasoning process, which many slaves did not survive,[10] provided a period of enculturation during which the slave came to experience and sometimes to accept the realities of his new condition. He came to know new work techniques, repressive discipline, new values, new life priorities, new imperatives for subsistence and survival, a new religion, a new language, a new kinship system, and new modes and styles of day-to-day living. The new slaves were taught these things in the huts and provisioning areas of the older, more established bondsmen in whose midst they were placed precisely for this purpose. Their psychic survival (as opposed to their physical survival) depended on their ability to make the necessary cultural adjustments.

Before continuing with the matter of culture dynamics, however, it is important to examine other aspects of resistance to the slaving process. Once again, contrary to common belief, resistance was a continuing fact of life in the South Atlantic System, and awareness of this is vital to an understanding of that system. As early as 1503 the Spanish commandant at Hispaniola complained to his superiors in Seville that the African slaves recently imported from Spain were causing him great grief. They were, he explained, escaping and frightening the other colonists as well as "teaching disobedience to the Indians." He recommended that no more Africans be sent to the New World. Seville, of course, did not take this advice, although later developments in the islands suggested to many Europeans that it had been good advice. In 1522, for example, the slaves in Hispaniola, by then greatly expanded in number, perpetrated the first substantial New World slave revolt. It was put down with all the hideous cruelty the Spanish could devise. Bloody examples were considered necessary by the whites to deter further insurrections. They knew their lives were at stake.

No matter with what horror the revolts were suppressed, they continued. In 1527 an insurrection broke out in Puerto Rico. Another one followed within two years in Santa Marta, a coastal settlement in what is now northern Columbia. Still another revolt racked Panama in 1531, and in 1532 the Spanish found it necessary to create a special police force to capture fugitive slaves who had escaped to freedom during the periods of turbulence. In 1537 there was a large-scale uprising in Mexico, the first of many such that were to follow the increased use of black slave labor in the Mexican mines between 1560 and 1580.

Each of these revolts was followed by increased restrictions on the personal lives of the slaves and by efforts to limit the relative number of blacks to whites in the colonies. But these restrictions were of little avail. The eighteenth century saw over a dozen documented revolts in Jamaica alone. Moreover, fugitive blacks, termed *maroons* (from the French word *"marron"* or "runaway"), were sometimes able to consolidate their forces and sustain an effective form of guerilla warfare against the white master class.[11] Maroons were known to be operating in Haiti as early as 1620, and their numbers were augmented by successive revolts there in 1679, 1691, and 1704. Considering the incidence of insurrection in Hispaniola from the very beginning, it was quite fitting that the most successful of

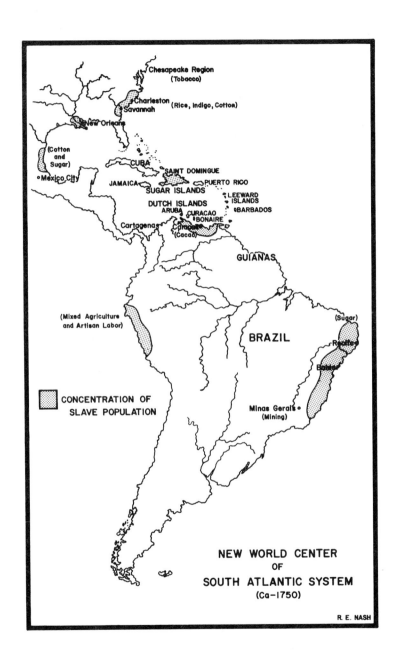

Chesapeake Region
(Tobacco)

Charleston
Savannah
(Rice, Indigo, Cotton)

New Orleans

(Cotton
and
Sugar)

CUBA

Mexico City

JAMAICA

SAINT DOMINGUE

PUERTO RICO

SUGAR ISLANDS

LEEWARD
ISLANDS

DUTCH ISLANDS
ARUBA

BARBADOS

CURACAO
BONAIRE

Cartagena

Caracas
(Cacao)

GUIANAS

(Mixed Agriculture
and Artisan Labor)

(Sugar)

BRAZIL

Recife

Bahia

CONCENTRATION OF
SLAVE POPULATION

Minas Gerais
(Mining)

NEW WORLD CENTER
OF
SOUTH ATLANTIC SYSTEM
(Ca-1750)

R. E. NASH

84

all the New World slave revolts—that of Toussaint L'Ouverture in 1791—should have occurred in Haiti.

The British North American colonies were not spared the terror of slave insurrection. Although revolts were relatively rare in North America, they did occur often enough to keep the white Americans in a state of more or less constant and chronic fear, which on occasion reached hysteria. This was the case, for example, in New York in 1721, when an insurrection brought on open warfare between rebel slaves and the white authorities before the revolt could be put down. Throughout the 1730s and 1740s the colonies in British North America experienced successive waves of panic and hysteria. As early as 1736 Colonel William Byrd of Virginia voiced the fear that slave insurrection was a constant threat in his area. Virginia maroons, he stated, could "flee to the mountains, and turn the Old Dominion into another Jamaica." Despite the contrary claims of later proslave apologists, the fear of slave rebellion was never far removed from the consciousness of the white masters, and this fear lay at the foundation of much of the suspicion and tension and resulting repression and cruelty that so characterized the New World slave system, no matter where it operated.

Still, the South Atlantic System prevailed and the slave trade continued year after year, decade after decade, century after century. Still the various imperatives of the system continued to operate on the people involved to produce the Afro-American population of the New World. We have already noted that the system produced a series of physical and psychic shocks as well as an enculturation process that every slave who survived had to experience. It remains only to suggest some specifics of those culture dynamics and to assess their effects on the Afro-American experience.

It should be obvious that the slave trade brought about a variety of culture contacts, European and African, African and Amerindian, Amerindian and European. For our purposes, however, only the first of these contacts is pertinent. At the outset there are two basic questions we must ponder.

First, what were the culture dynamics involved in the contact of Europeans and Africans in the New World setting? Second, how did those culture dynamics operate to change the basic cultural orientation of the individual's African experience to produce a new product, the Afro-American? In other words, what was the degree of acculturation that occurred between the Europeans and the Africans in the South Atlantic System?

Let us begin from a wholly negative point of view. In some respects the slave system itself precluded the possibility of cultural borrowing from the Europeans, while at the same time it deprived the slave of his African heritage. It was patently impossible for the slave, for example, to retain his old economic and political institutions. Yet neither would the system permit the possibility of his borrowing from ("acculturating to") the European master's equivalent institutions. The abolition of slavery and the freedman's rise to political and economic equality would have to precede the Afro-American's full participation in the European political system and market economy. The slave might *learn* of these matters, but he could hardly "borrow" them to make them his own. In these areas, then, the Europeans actually practiced what sociologist E. Franklin Frazier has called an "anti-acculturation" policy.

But what of the acculturation process that did occur? What were some of its dimensions and dictates? First, one distinction must be made. There were obvious differences between the experience of an African newly imported to the Americas and an Afro-American born and raised in the New World. The former individual not only had to adjust to his new circumstances but also had to shed a considerable portion of the cultural baggage he took with him out of Africa. On the other hand, the person born into the system had only to adjust to the circumstances of his birth and to learn his culture without having to cast off practically everything that had given his life pattern and meaning before. But what was the nature of the culture that the infant born into the plantation system had to learn? This question brings us back to the whole matter of the acculturation process, since in order to identify some aspects of the emerging Afro-American culture we must examine that process at work in the Americas.

The acculturation process, as we have seen in Chapter 1, requires direct, sustained contact of the two cultures involved, that is, the dominant society, whose culture elements are being "borrowed" and the "acculturating" society, the group doing *most* of the borrowing. The acculturating group must have sufficient knowledge of and experience with the way of life of the dominant group to permit the effective transfer of culture elements from one group to the other. Without sufficient direct contact only a kind of partial and incomplete acculturation can occur, and that, it would seem, is precisely what happened in the contact of European and African in the New World environment. The dominant Europeans permitted contact only to the degree that served to enhance the operation of the slave system, and no more. Efficient control of the black population, the whites believed, demanded that blacks be kept in a servile and inferior caste, distinctly apart and separate from the master class. Contact that occurred could by the very nature of the system be only brief, selective, and transitory. Most generally the contact ocurred only in areas directly relating to the slave's labor on the plantation.

Moreover, it is clear that very early in the history of black-white contact the whites developed a set of distinctly negative attitudes toward Africans as a "race."[12] Europeans came quickly to see Africans not only as socially inferior, but also as "racially" inferior. This antiblack racism tended to inhibit direct social contact between the races even more. In short, the Europeans refused to permit complete acculturation, and the result was of great significance in the creation of an essentially unique and new Afro-American culture.

Take, for example, the matter of language, always a key element in the development of ethnic identity and solidarity. Of necessity the African had to give up his original language, or at least its vocabulary, almost completely. He was instructed in his duties by his fellow slaves or by the overseer on the plantation in a language taking its vocabulary from the European language of the master, be it Spanish, Portuguese, French, or English. Only rarely were groups of West Africans speaking the same language kept together in the Americas. But there is more to language than mere vocabulary, and there is some solid evidence that certain common African language patterns and structures did continue to prevail in the plantation setting, as did certain *attitudes* toward the uses of language.[13] The majority of the slaves came from a *relatively* small area geographically, small enough that structural similarities could aid in the communication among the slaves even though it was necessary to assume European vocabularies. In linguistic terms, African grammatical systems partially survived and were overlaid by European vocabulary or lexical items. The result was a new "Creole" tongue, a kind of Afro-Caribbean language born and developed in the islands and on the mainland plantations. Neither African nor European, this language, or more correctly, these languages, served their speakers quite well, and were passed on from generation to generation. Individually, each of these Creole languages served as a complete, functioning system of oral communication and expression for its Afro-American users. These Afro-American Creole languages were not "bad" languages or "bastard" languages; linguists all agree that there are no "inferior" languages.[14] They were simply different languages, the products of a quasi-acculturation process, and an important part of the cultural tradition born of New World plantation circumstances out of the internal dictates of a slave subculture.

A somewhat similar development occurred in the area of religion. The Catholic powers of Europe demanded that slaves taken into their colonies be converted to Christianity. To a lesser degree so did the Protestant powers, especially following the initiation of the counter-reformation. In both cases, there is ample evidence to suggest that real efforts to convert the slaves were rare. Nominal "baptisms" of large groups of blacks were more common, but slaves rarely became fully "Christianized." Instead, a process of religious syncretism occurred whereby certain aspects of traditional African religions were incorporated into a Christian framework. Once again, the result was not a "bastard" religion, but a complete, functioning, relatively well-integrated religion capable of sustaining the spiritual needs of its believers. We have already observed that *vodun* (or voodoo) is a classic example of New World religious syncretism, but other cults also emerged out of the melding of European and African religions. The Shango cult of Trinidad, for example, is apparently composed largely of Yoruba elements combined with both Catholic and Baptist traditions. Shango himself is identified with John the Baptist. Similar combinations are also present in the Candoble and Macumba cults of Brazil and the Obeah cult found throughout the Caribbean. Because African religion permitted a certain flexibility in the pantheon, its practitioners could accept and adopt European objects of worship while retaining the essentials of the old religion. Even in the cases where Afro-Americans seemed to reject African religious practices completely and to accept Christianity without reinterpretation, there is evidence that Christian theology and practice did not always mean exactly the same thing to the new converts as it did to the European believer, born and raised in Christian traditions. As historian George Rawick has cogently observed, although many slaves did adopt the "outward forms of Christianity," syncretism permitted the blacks "to develop Christianity's interior meanings and practices in their own way." Considering the incredible pervasiveness of culture, it could hardly have been otherwise. This suggests that at the outset, European Christianity and Afro-American Christianity were not exactly the same thing. As we will see a bit later, in many ways the differences persisted for a very long time.

A third area of possible acculturation in which the Europeans took a positive interest was the area of subsistence technique. Here again only partial borrowing was permitted by the whites. The Afro-American was given the opportunity to learn new agricultural techniques and the use of new tools, but only so that he might better serve the plantation system. Indeed, there is some considerable doubt that plantation agricultural techniques employed by the Europeans marked a real improvement over the techniques existing in many parts of West Africa at the same time. Many improvements in agricultural mechanics were introduced by the slaves themselves; when sugar cultivation was first introduced in Louisiana it was necessary to import two West Indian blacks skilled in cane cultivation before the experiment was successful. Still, it was to the advantage of the whites to keep the blacks tied to the soil or to the mines, so no real development in subsistence techniques was afforded the Afro-American by virtue of his contact with Europeans in the New World. The potential for acculturation toward a more "advanced," more productive means of subsistence was suppressed by the dominant whites.

There were, however, elements of the blacks' day-to-day life style over which the Europeans exercised little control simply because they did not care whether the blacks retained certain African traits or characteristics; that is, the European masters permitted the retention of African culture traits not deemed injurious to the plantation system. Chief among these continuing African traits were folklore, music, and the dance.

The Europeans believed, quite correctly, that Africans placed great value on music and dance. Consequently, seeing no threat in either, both were permitted and even encouraged. Although the Afro-Americans borrowed some European elements over the years, notably in instrumentation and musical notation, they apparently retained such African qualities as rhythmic patterns, tonal system, phrasing, and voicing. They also retained certain forms of African instrumentation, chiefly in the area of rhythm and percussion instrumentation. One leading contemporary specialist in Afro-American music, the folklorist-musicologist Alan Lomax, has gone so far as to conclude that Afro-American music has been and is "a sub-system of a continental Black African style tradition. . . ." In this area, too, Afro-America has clearly maintained continuity with the African past. A similar development seems to have occurred with the dance technique, although perhaps with less pervasive results. Scholars have long been impressed with the evidence of substantial retention of African tales, maxims, parables, and folk beliefs. There can be no doubt that New World folklore has been greatly enriched by these African retentions handed down from generation to generation by Afro-Americans who placed value on them.

It should be emphasized, however, that although the African influence was strong in all of these areas, including religion, only rarely did anything resembling a *pure* African trait persist beyond the first or second generation. Afro-American cultural development, even though based in the African background, was tempered and shaped by experience in the crucible of the New World's plantation system. The cultural patterns that emerged from this experience grew out of special historical and cultural circumstances peculiar to the system.[15] The Afro-American culture that developed over long years of black subjection to the cultural imperatives of the plantation system was unique. It was a thing unto itself, new to the world and destined to play a role all its own in the world historical setting.

To some extent *all* Afro-Americans who participated in the South Atlantic System shared the same experiences and were shaped culturally by the dictates of the system. But as we have already noted, there were certain variables, depending on where and when the individual lived and to which European power he found himself subjected. The experience of New World slavery did have its comparative dimension, which admitted some degree of diversity in the system. However, at this point we must again restrict ourselves in the area of our coverage. Although the comparative aspect of the Afro-American experience will continue to be of concern, our *primary* focus from this point must be British Colonial North America and the United States. Such a shift in focus is necessary if we are to examine in greater detail the particulars of the Afro-American experience in the formative years of its *North* American manifestation. In many respects, those formative years determined the general course and direction of that experience even to today.

NOTES

[1] The Ashanti, for example, had four categories or degrees of unfreedom: (1) *Akyere* was one under death sentence for crime, a slave pending execution; (2) *Odonko* was a foreign-born slave, usually a captive; (3) *Awowa* was a pawn to a creditor; (4) *Akoa pa* was a "pawn-become-slave." Bornu, similarly, had three classes of "slaves" with differing degrees of freedom: *Kamba, Kalia,* and *Zusanna.*

[2] Use of the term "New World" clearly demonstrates the abiding ethnocentrism of those who initially coined the phrase and of those who have persisted in its use. The New World was hardly "new" to those who had lived there for centuries prior to the coming of the "Old World" Europeans.

[3] The division of the New World was accomplished by means of a "demarkation line" established by the Pope in 1493 and adjusted to the advantage of Portugal in 1494 by terms of the famous Treaty of Tordesillas. In 1500 Pedro Alvares Cabral landed in Brazil, thereby formally initiating Portuguese sovereignty.

[4] The African historian Philip Curtin has made a close study of what he terms "the numbers game" in an effort to determine at least approximately the number of Africans actually transported to the New World in the Atlantic trade. Prior to recent investigation estimates ranged from a low of some 8 million to a high of over 50 million. Curtin concluded that no precise estimate is possible with available data, but suggested that the number was probably between 8 and 10.5 million, and that 9.5 million would be a reasonable figure if he were pushed for a specific estimate. This figure would work out to an annual average of 22,800 between 1451 and 1870. Curtin's figures pertain to slaves who actually made it to the New World.

Many did *not* make it, and the total number of victims of the slave trade would likely be several times Curtin's 9.5 million estimate.
[5] The African ability to resist the European diseases, although only *relatively* greater than the Amerindian, came quickly to be accepted by Europeans as absolute. An early Spanish historian of the Indies, Antonio de Herrera, observed in 1601 that the Africans so "prospered" in the islands "that unless a negro should happen to be hung he would never die, for as yet none have been known to perish from infirmity." The idea of Afro-Americans invulnerability to disease appeared early as one of the myths justifying black slavery.
[6] There were some noteworthy variations on these techniques of taking slaves. The "Aro system" of the Niger Delta involved the use of a powerful religious oracle to provide a steady supply of slaves by accusing people of a variety of transgressions, then finding them guilty and fining them beyond their means to pay. Thus they were sold into slavery and transported to the coastal traders by the Aro "priests." The "Egbo" (leopard) Society of the Efik, a secret society of wealthy and powerful men, served in a similar capacity to produce captives for sale, then controlled the terms and nature of the trade with the European dealers.
[7] The "owner" at this point was usually one of the chartered European trading companies licensed to participate in the slave trade. The British Royal African Company, the Dutch West India Co., and the French Company of the Senegal were among the more important such companies. Each company had its own insignia used in branding its slaves for purposes of identification.
[8] The British Guineaman *Brookes* out of Liverpool was a famous slaver, considered fairly typical, about which detailed information has survived in the records. In the cargo hold of the *Brookes*, men, women, and children were maintained in separate storage areas. Each man was allotted a space 6 feet long, 16 inches high, and about 2½ feet wide. Women were given spaces only 5 feet 10 inches long; children 4 to 5 feet long by 12 to 14 inches wide. The *Brookes*, a 320 ton vessel, was permitted by law to carry 454 slaves. It was reliably reported, however, that before passage of this law the ship had carried as many as 609 slaves on one voyage. From time to time considerations of high mortality risk in such "tight-packing" (as it was known) gave rise to experiments in "loose-packing." By the eighteenth century, however, "tight-packing" seems to have won out as being most profitable.
[9] There is evidence that some Africans believed the European traders to be cannibals. From the time of their sale, then, they harbored the fear that they were being taken away to be eaten by whites. The

scramble seems to have been traumatic in the extreme to such slaves, now convinced of their fate by the sheer frenzied eagerness of their newest captors.

[10] It has been reliably estimated that 20 to 30% of the new slaves did not survive the seasoning process.

[11] Some of the *maroon* bands were able to sustain themselves as quasi-independent "republics" for varying periods of time. Termed "Bush Negroes" by the Europeans, they have in some cases produced fascinating historical episodes. Especially noteworthy were the Brazilian fugitives who in 1650 established a forest settlement called Palmares. By successive raids on the area plantations the Palmares maroons were able to build their population and ultimately produce a military force 10,000 strong. They were defeated in 1696, but only after a fierce struggle in which the Portuguese army employed heavy artillery. Elsewhere in the New World, however, maroons often survived to maintain their independence and continue to exist as distinct tribal groups even to today. The best known of these groups are now found along the inland waterways of Surinam and French Guiana and include the Boni or Aluku, the Djuka or Aucaner, the Saramacca, the Mataway, and the Paramaka.

[12] The origins, nature, and causes of white European racism are complex and scholars are not in complete agreement on many details. It is clear that the symbolic function of "blackness" as the representation of evil was deeply rooted in the European mind. It is also clear that as the slave trade developed, the Europeans subconsciously sought justification for enslaving blacks, especially those blacks who converted to Christianity. This "rationalization need" lay at the base of several European attitudes that reached full fruition as the South Atlantic System developed. Among these attitudes were the notions that Africans were not really human, but somewhere between man and ape, and that as such, blacks were clearly underdeveloped in certain "human" capacities, especially intelligence and sensibility. Finally, in casting about for justification of the system, the Europeans were able to cite Biblical sanction for black servility and enslavement by whites in the so-called "Curse of Canaan" (in *Genesis*, IX), which, according to some biblical scholars, condemned all blacks to eternal service of whites. Such attitudes were to serve the whites well in their justification of chattel slavery even after slavery came under severe attack by the humanitarians of the eighteenth century.

[13] Melville Herskovits has suggested that numbers of West Africans, although speaking different languages, shared a "grammatical matrix" and a "deeper-lying structural similarity" of language that facilitated

communication when provided with a rudimentary European vocabulary.

[14] Anthropologist Sidney Mintz writes: "Once a generation of children had been born, for whom one of these languages was a native tongue, the languages themselves had become *creole* languages, and were no longer pidgins." "Haitian Creole," he continues, "is no more 'corrupted' French than French is 'corrupted' Latin. . . ."

[15] A more detailed analysis of the operation of cultural imperatives in the plantation system of the United States appears in Chapter 6.

SUGGESTIONS FOR FURTHER READING

Most of the titles recommended for use with Chapter 2 contain material pertinent to the slave trade and culture contact. On the background to slavery and other forms of involuntary servitude, and particularly on western attitudes *toward* servitude, see David B. Davis, *The Problem of Slavery in Western Culture* (Ithaca: Cornell University Press, 1966), a Pulitzer Prize winner. Two standard works on the slave trade are Basil Davidson, *The African Slave Trade. Precolonial History, 1450-1850* (Boston: Little, Brown, 1961), which stresses the effects of the trade on African history and development, and Daniel P. Mannix and Malcolm Cowley, *Black Cargoes. A History of the Atlantic Slave Trade, 1518-1865* (New York: Viking, 1965), a good synthesis that assumes a New World perspective. Both works are quite readable. Also readable but more flamboyant is James Pope-Hennessy, *Sins of the Fathers: A Study of the Atlantic Slave Traders, 1441-1807* (New York: Knopf, 1968). The title is somewhat misleading, for the book treats the whole of the trade's functioning, not just the traders themselves. No serious student of the subject should fail to consult the four-volume primary source collection compiled by Elizabeth Donnan entitled *Documents Illustrative of the History of the Slave Trade to America* (Washington: Carnegie Institute, 1935, reprinted, New York: Octagon Books, 1965). Philip D. Curtin, *The Atlantic Slave Trade. A Census* (Madison, Wis.: University of Wisconsin Press, 1969) is the most reliable study of the numbers of Africans brought into the South Atlantic System, although the author emphasizes throughout that his figures are at best approximate. Eric Williams, *Capitalism and Slavery* (Chapel Hill: University of North Carolina Press, 1944) is primarily a study of the international economic effects of slavery, with its central focus on Britain.

Anthropologist Melville J. Herskovits has written extensively on the contact of Africa and the New World; even though some of his conclusions have been questioned by later scholars, he is still quite persuasive on important details of the dynamics of culture contact. See especially his *The Myth of The Negro Past* (New York: Harper, 1941, reprinted Boston: Beacon Press, 1958), and *The New World Negro*, edited by Frances S. Herskovits (Bloomington, Ind.: Indiana University Press, 1966), a collection of his many articles published over the years relating to the subject. Also on the contact of cultures see E. Franklin Frazier, *Race and Culture Contacts in the Modern World* (Boston: Beacon Press, 1957), which is partly devoted to the Afro-European contacts of the slave trade period, and Marvin Harris, *Patterns of Race in the Americas* (New York: Walker, 1964), a most provocative study by a modern anthropologist. Two collections of readings are worthy of perusal in connection with this chapter. They are Laura Foner and Eugene D. Genovese, eds., *Slavery in the New World. A Reader in Comparative History* (Englewood Cliffs, N. J.: Prentice-Hall, 1969), and especially Norman E. Whitten, Jr., and John F. Szwed, eds., *Afro-American Anthropology: Contemporary Perspectives* (New York: Free Press, 1970), a most interesting collection of recent scholarly articles.

On the still controversial subject of slavery in Africa, see two journal articles: Walter Rodney, "African Slavery and Other Forms of Social Oppression on the Upper Guinea Coast in the Context of the Atlantic Slave-Trade," *Journal of African History*, 7:431-43 (1966), and J. D. Fage, "Slavery and the Slave Trade in the Context of African History," *Journal of African History*, 10:393-404 (1969). Two other recent articles also pertain broadly to the present chapter. They are Sidney W. Mintz, "Toward an Afro-American History," *Journal of World History*, 13:317-332 (1971), and Richard B. Sheridan, "Africa and the Caribbean in the Atlantic Slave Trade," *American Historical Review*, 77:15-35 (1972).

Chapter 4

THE BLACK EXPERIENCE IN EARLY AMERICA:
Origins of Status Duality

Malcolm X, a most perceptive and sensitive observer of Afro-American matters, told a black audience on one occasion that "no matter how long you and I have been over here, we aren't Americans yet." He went on to explain: "Being here in America doesn't make you an American. Being born here in America doesn't make you an American." Years before Malcolm made this cryptic comment another great black leader, W. E. B. DuBois, had said something rather similar, employing the poetic imagery he used so well. DuBois wrote: "One feels ever his two-ness—an American, a Negro; two souls, two thoughts, two unreconciled strivings; two warring ideals in one dark body, whose dogged strength alone keeps it from being torn asunder." Both men were referring to the fact that "America" has historically been defined by its white Euro-American majority, and that somehow blacks had never been included in the definition of an American.[1] Blacks were not fully "American" because the dominant whites had never permitted them to be so. Thus a black man born and raised in America could never really consider himself a part of America and could never wholly share the ideals and values and aspirations of the nation's dominant ethnic majority. He might know no other homeland; he might feel the same attraction for a place that most men feel for their homes.

Note. Footnotes for this chapter are located on pages 130-133.

But he could never attach the same value to "country" that the dominant element in the population felt. Black Americans were, in one sense, American, but a very special kind of American. Their value attachments were divided between their *Americaness* ("My home is America") and their *Afro*-Americaness ("I am a black American").

This ethnic duality (DuBois's "two-ness") has been part of the Afro-American experience from the very beginning of American history. The dominant cultural patterns of America on the one hand and Afro-America on the other developed simultaneously in the mainland provinces of the British Colonial System, the portion of the empire that ultimately became the United States. As the South Atlantic System spread to the North American mainland, black people spread there, too, as an essential part of the system. Although the mainland colonies were never fully a part of the system, except possibly in South Carolina, the black population itself became a permanent part of colonial America virtually from the onset of the colonial period.

Even though blacks constituted a significant portion of the total population and provided much of the manpower that built America into a productive unit in the empire, blacks were always a racial and cultural minority, differentiated as such, subjected to an inferior class status, and denied the opportunity to move into a higher class and to share in the benefits America afforded to countless hundreds of other poor people. Blacks were excluded from full participation in American life by the dominant culture (Euro-American) into which they were thrown. Not only were they forbidden to share in the value system of the dominant culture, they were denied American advantages by that value system itself. The black American was not only a man-out-of-culture (a "marginal man"), but also a man-condemned-by-culture. The conflict of culture imperatives acted to produce what Melville Herskovits once termed "socialized ambivalence." How was a black American to accept the values of a dominant culture that condemned him as innately inferior and servile? On the other hand, how was he to reject his home? It was a real dilemma.

America was "home" for black people from very nearly the beginning of America. Although it is impossible to determine precisely when the first black man settled in America, we definitely know that about 20 blacks arrived in Jamestown, Virginia, just 12 years after its founding. In August 1619 a Dutch frigate, probably a privateer, exchanged a group of 20 captive blacks for food and provisions. The Dutch captain had probably taken the prisoners during a raid on a slave vessel in Caribbean waters. It is noteworthy that the blacks were sold to the governing officials of the little colony. Their status was nonfree; they were exchanged as commodities for other commodities. Whether they were actually *slaves* is a matter that has plagued historians for years.[2] There is a good chance that they were not chattel slaves, doomed to a lifetime of servile labor for their owners. They may have been considered indentured servants whose "indentures" (terms of obligation to servitude) were limited to a certain number of years. Certainly many of the white Europeans living in the area had come as indentured servants, and it is possible that the blacks were of the same status.

In any case, over a period of years other blacks trickled into the colony, so that by 1650 there were perhaps 400 in all of a total population of some 18,500. Their status seems to have varied; some were free, some were held in indentured servitude, and some were held as lifetime slaves, even though as yet there was no formal legal recognition of chattel slavery in America. A similar process occurred in Maryland, Virginia's sister colony on the Chesapeake, following its founding in 1634. In both colonies the black population remained a small minority until much later. For two generations blacks lived and worked among whites who in many cases had no clear status advantage. From the outset, blacks were distinguished from whites in a small but very real way. They were called "Negroes" (following the Iberian usage). Such labeling is always important. As Winthrop Jordan has observed, "A distinct name is not attached to a group unless it is regarded as distinct." So, from the time of the first arrivals in 1619, blacks were set apart from whites. The degree and dynamic of that distinction would greatly increase with the passage of years.

In the second major group of North American colonies, the Puritan commonwealths of New England, the slave status seems to have been attached to blacks from the outset of their arrival. In 1638 Captain William Pierce of the Salem trading vessel *Desire* arrived with what were probably the first blacks in New England. They were slaves. Pierce had obtained them in exchange for Amerindian captives taken in the Pequot War (1637), very likely from the Providence Island colony in the West Indies. The lively trade that soon developed between New England shippers and the Caribbean gave rise to other such dealings, but the black population of New England was never to be very large; there were only a relative handful of slaves in 1680, and blacks never constituted more than 3% of the total population in the eighteenth century.

The demand for slave labor in New England was not sufficient to warrant extensive slave importation.[3] However, there was never any doubt about the status of blacks brought into New England in the early trade. New Englanders had the example of the West Indies, where, by the seventeenth century, slavery had been accepted as a matter of course. There was no reason why the idea of bond slavery should not be borrowed from the island colonies and planted on the rocky shores of New England. To allay any possible doubt as to the legality of slavery there, Massachusetts specifically legalized the institution in 1641.[4]

In the middle colonies of America the origin of the black population was less distinctly tied to slavery than in New England. There were blacks in the colony of New Netherlands (later New York) as early as 1628, but their status is unclear. Only much later, perhaps not until the 1650s, did a fully developed system of slavery emerge. Under the auspices of the Dutch West India Company, the slave trade was encouraged and many blacks were introduced into the colony from Curaçao, the Company's primary slave *entrepôt* in the New World. Additional slaves were smuggled in or brought in as contraband or prizes.

The majority of this midcentury black importation were employed as slaves in the agriculture of the rich Hudson River Valley or on public projects of the colony. When the English took over in 1664, there was no difficulty involved in transferring the blacks into the emerging system of British-American slavery. Outside the plantation south, New York was to claim the greatest black population in America, about 14% of the total throughout the colonial period.

The institution of slavery never really took firm hold in colonial Pennsylvania, the other major middle colony, and consequently the black population remained small throughout the period. The black population that did exist in Pennsylvania remained tied to the urban areas, especially Philadelphia, where slaves were occasionally employed as domestic servants and mechanics. Generally, in the northern colonies slavery was a relatively common and accepted practice by the early eighteenth century, even though the slave populations were in some areas small.

It was, however, in the colonies of the South that slavery was to have its greatest impact on the total Afro-American experience because of the tremendous number of black people drawn to that area by the colonial plantation system. As the seventeenth century progressed and the nascent plantation economy developed, the black population increased greatly. Tobacco planters in Virginia and Maryland, spurred on by the international demand for their commodity, imported greater numbers of black laborers to work their fields. By the early eighteenth century the black population of the Chesapeake region had reached some 31,000, out of a total population of 121,000. In South Carolina the population increases were even more striking. Following the introduction of rice cultivation in 1694 and the subsequent success of rice in the world market, black people arrived in greater numbers, greater even than the number of white Europeans. One contemporary estimate fixed the black population in 1708 as 4100, while the whites numbered only 3500. By 1720 the figure was even more disproportionate. By then blacks outnumbered whites more than two to one (approximately 12,000 to 5000).[5]

In Carolina the plantation system (including slavery) closely resembled the system in effect in the West Indies. From the outset of Carolina plantation cultivation the institution of slavery was intended to be a replica of that prevailing in Barbados; indeed, many Barbadian planters moved to Carolina in the 1660s, taking their slaves along with them. As a result there was never any doubt as to the status of blacks coming into Carolina. They were chattel slaves. There was no need to develop an endemic system of slavery, since the white Carolina settlers brought a ready-made system with them. It was a harsh and repressive system. Because the primary concern of slaveowners, who were outnumbered by their chattels, was slave control, the system they developed in the islands and in Carolina was concerned primarily with the policing of blacks and with creating a deterrent to any form of slave recalcitrance or rebelliousness. Consequently the first law concerned exclusively with slavery in Carolina, passed by the colonial assembly in 1690, provided horrendous penalties for slave offenses, including whipping, branding, mutilation, and castration. In 1696 Carolina enacted a complete slave code virtually copied from the Barbadian code and again including many of the barbarities typical of Caribbean slave law.

It was in the Chesapeake area, especially in Virginia, that the slave system developed that would ultimately provide British Colonial North America with its own peculiar version of chattel slavery, a system that would be accepted by all the slave states following independence. In Virginia the slave system developed not according to the dictates of some foreign slave system, but according to its own strange logic and unique local conditions. And, it should be emphasized, it developed along with and coordinated to a system of race relations in colonial America. The effects were to be profoundly important to the Afro-American experience. For this reason, we must give detailed consideration to the simultaneous development of slavery and race relations in Virginia.

At the outset it should be carefully noted that in Virginia as elsewhere in the seventeenth century the laboring classes were commonly held in a variety of nonfree statuses. Indians were enslaved in Virginia as well as in Latin America, the Caribbean, and New England. Indentured servants, whose terms of service were fixed in their contracts, were not free men until their indentures expired. It is true that when the original blacks arrived in 1619 they were not considered actual chattels, but it is equally certain that they were not considered fully free. In short, the question of how black chattel slavery developed in Virginia does not involve the question of whether black labor might have been free labor, but only what sort of unfree labor it was to be. The evolution of racial slavery began with the fact of an unfree status for blacks and proceeded to the ultimate definition of black chattel slavery as provided in the black codes of the early eighteenth century and subsequently. Surveying the evidence closely, one is struck by the fact that for all the early status confusion, the road from the undetermined involuntary servitude of 1619 to the systematized slave codes of the eighteenth century was as straight as it was short.

For years now, historians have puzzled over a thorny problem. Why was it that while other laboring people in colonial America gained ever greater freedom to determine their own fortunes, black Americans and only black Americans were reduced to hereditary chattel slavery? In other words, why did *racial* slavery evolve in America? The definitive answer has not yet been found, but certain considerations loom large in any discussion of the matter. The immediate, but too infrequently noted answer, we have already considered. Racial slavery did not *originate* in colonial America. It already existed in Latin America and the Caribbean before it appeared in North America, and, in fact, had existed in Europe since the early fourteenth century. Black slaves were a familiar sight to Europeans long before the plantations of the Chesapeake region began to flourish. Africans, as noted earlier, were *available* for enslavement and use in the plantations. There was, then, a tradition of black slavery on which the colonial planters could draw for guidelines as they cast about for the most efficient kind of labor available to them. The use of black slaves seemed a natural choice, perhaps the only choice.

But if racial slavery did not originate in Virginia, it did develop certain unique forms and tendencies there, and these forms and tendencies would later earmark the peculiarly American version of the system. By the middle of the seventeenth century, black slavery existed in several areas of the world, but the institution had not been defined and institutionalized in English or English-colonial law. The growing number of black "slaves" was significant in itself in producing the necessary motivation for the colonial institutionalization of racial slavery. To Europeans, large numbers of blacks required regulation and control. From the outset, Euro-American racism/ethnocentrism was at the base of the white determination to effect a totally subservient, totally inferior status for the black population.

The earliest evidence of the relationship between antiblack racism and the evolving slave status for blacks is slim but nevertheless convincing. Virtually from the beginning of the colonial period certain distinctions were made between blacks and whites in the mainland colonies, distinctions that reflect European prejudices against Africans. Blacks were distinguished from whites in the tax rolls. As indentured servants, black women worked in the fields; white women did not. Blacks were forbidden sexual contact with and/or marriage to whites, largely, it would seem, to avoid the production of "spurious issue"—genetically mixed offspring—considered "unnatural" by the Euro-American establishment. "From the surviving evidence," writes Winthrop Jordan, "it appears that outright enslavement and . . . other forms of debasement appeared at about the same time" in the Chesapeake region. Antiblack prejudice clearly accompanied and reinforced the emerging slave status.

Antiblack prejudice, however, was not enough in itself to condemn Afro-Americans to hereditary chattel slavery.

Blacks had other distinct disadvantages. First, as previously noted, they were vulnerable. Blacks were not protected by legal contracts limiting their service to a given number of years. Instead, a custom developed whereby blacks were normally considered "servants for life," in other words, slaves. As time passed white indentured servitude diminished in significance, while black servitude grew more important. Availability, vulnerability, and antiblack prejudice, then, combined to point the way toward racial slavery.

The combination began to crystalize in the final third of the seventeenth century. A series of laws passed by the colonial assemblies of Virginia and Maryland began to mold the institution of slavery into its familiar ante-bellum form. The first of these enormously important laws was passed in Virginia in 1662. Oddly, it pertained only indirectly to slavery as such, yet it established one of the essentials of any system of chattel slavery. The exact wording is noteworthy. "Whereas," it stated, "some doubts have arisen whether children got by any Englishman upon a negro woman shall be slave or free, . . . all children born in this colony shall be bond or free only according to the condition of the mother." The slave status, then, was to descend through the mother. Children of slave mothers were to be considered slaves, presumably for life.

Two years later, in 1664, the Maryland assembly passed a law declaring categorically that blacks were to be held to service *Durante Vita*, for the duration of their lives. The exact wording of the act is again of considerable consequence: ". . . all Negroes and other slaves already within the Province and all Negroes and other slaves to be hereafter imported into the Province shall serve *Durante Vita*. And all Children born of any Negro or other slave shall be Slaves . . . for the terms of their lives." Both of these key acts apparently use the words "Negro" and "slave" interchangeably. It is apparent that by the mid-1660s "Negro" and "slave" meant the same thing. There was never a need for laws specifically enslaving all blacks, because by that time custom had provided all the sanctions that were necessary. By then, the presumption of whites in Virginia and Maryland was that blacks were slaves. Black color was tantamount to slave status. In both of the above cases, legislation served only to clarify certain ambiguous points involved in an established institution.

The same was true of two other laws of the same period that are also worthy of special notice. In 1669 a Virginia statute exempted a slaveowner from prosecution for felony if a slave died as a result of punishment. The reasoning was that no felony could be perpetrated unless there was malicious intent, and it was inconceivable that any person would destroy his valuable property with malice aforethought. The reasoning, of course, is inherently faulty; it assumes an unswerving rationality in man that, in fact, does not exist. But the implications of the statute are clear. Slaves were property under the law, no more, no less. If there was still room for doubt, that doubt was totally dispelled in 1705 when the Virginia Assembly passed a law stating flatly that "all Negro, mulatto, and Indian slaves, in all courts of judicature, and in other places, within this dominion, shall be held, taken, and adjudged to be real estate. . . ." The knot was tied. Slaves were slaves for life, they inherited their status through their mothers, they were property, not persons under the law, and their owners had virtual life and death power over them.

These factors were to be the essentials of the fully developed American slave system, a system that would ultimately operate to deprive the great majority of Afro-Americans of any claim to personal liberty. By about 1700, when great numbers of blacks had begun to make their involuntary appearance on American shores, racial slavery along with the police powers deemed necessary for control of the black population had been enshrined in law. In 1705 Virginia compiled the random statutes pertaining to slavery into a "slave code," and the system of chattel slavery was complete.

The cluster of laws beginning with the act of 1662 and culminating with the Virginia Black Code of 1705 was passed, it was believed, out of necessity. Large aggregations of black slaves represented potential danger to the whites of the colonies. This danger had to be minimized. Consequently, slaves had to be controlled, policed, and contained. Moreover, white landowners had come to depend on black labor, and laws were necessary to perpetuate the labor supply by making slavery hereditary. Finally, antiblack prejudice, European blood pride, and malignant racism all dictated that blacks must be kept apart from (and beneath) the dominant whites. Thus, a combination of interrelated forces operated to condemn black Americans to abject chattel slavery.[6]

Perfecting the system of racial slavery did, of course, require the resolution of some thorny problems. Most urgent among these problems was the status of mulattoes. In spite of all efforts of the authorities to prevent miscegenation, the practice that began with the first contact of black and white continued to be common. Basic human sexual desire plus the vulnerability and availability of black women to whites pointed inevitably to racial mixture. Equally inevitable was the tension associated with racial mixture in a culture committed to the idea of maintaining racial "purity" and to the related notion that racial mixture was somehow a violation of natural law and proper order. The very logic of racial slavery demanded that there be a clear demarcation between white and black, and racial mixture prevented clear demarcation. Moreover, every mulatto child was living evidence that some white had sinned with some black, since each colony had laws forbidding intermarriage. Finally, the presence of mulattoes was a constant and unwelcome reminder that things were not all black and white in the world. Racial lines were *not* clean-cut and clear even though racial considerations loomed large in the determination of status and rank in colonial America.

The white response to these problems was to pretend that mulattoes did not exist. This was a simple way to solve a difficult problem; if it was grossly irrational, it was nonetheless effective. So in British Colonial America, and *only* in British Colonial America, mulattoes simply were not recognized or distinguished by custom or in law. Mulattoes were blacks, subject to all the forms of degradation blacks were subject to, including racial slavery. As we have already noted, in 1662 the Virginia Assembly established in law that the slave status was to be inherited through the mother, even though the child was fathered by a white. In this way the lawmakers of colonial Virginia resolved the problem of genetic mixture as it related to racial slavery, thereby snipping off one of the raveled edges of the system. At the same time, white America established a precedent that would persist even to modern times. In the United States, mulattoes were to be considered blacks both in law and, for the most part, in practice. The resulting clarity of genotypic distinction would make it even easier to hold the "blacks" as a class in a subordinate and inferior status.[7]

A second problem to be resolved before racial slavery could be perfected was posed by religious conversion of the slaves. If one of the historical justifications for enslaving an individual was his adherence to the wrong religion—if a "pagan" might legitimately be enslaved—what effect would his conversion to the *right* religion have on his slave status? This was a big problem, particularly in seventeenth-century America, where religion was taken quite seriously by the great majority of the people. The first blacks in America were probably Christianized and permitted to be baptized like other servants. But as the status of "servant for life" (or slave) evolved in Virginia and Maryland the fear arose that under Christian precept baptism might mean freedom from life bondage. This was a troublesome prospect to the white owners of such chattels, and the slaveowners' first reaction was simply to forbid baptism to all blacks. This proved unacceptable to the religious authorities, who continually sought new converts. To resolve the dilemma the Virginia Assembly in 1667 passed a law designed to permit (and even to encourage) conversion without endangering slavery. The law stated that conversion was to have no effect on a person's status, bond or free. It was that simple. But for those seriously disturbed by the dilemma of conversion, it was *too* simple. There was some doubt whether a group of provincial lawmakers could settle an essentially theological question so expediently.

In 1727 the Bishop of London spoke on the matter, re-solving the remaining doubt. "The Freedom which Christi-anity gives," the Bishop declared, "is a Freedom from the Bondage of Sin and Satan, and from the Dominion of Mens Lusts and Passions and inordinate Desires; but as to their *outward* Condition, whatever that was before, whether bond or free, their being baptiz'd, and becoming Christians, makes no manner of Change in it. . . ." So good Anglicans could now rest easy. Conversion freed no one. Indeed, as the Bishop himself had observed, conversion to Christianity carried an obligation to all slaves to perform their duties and obey their masters with unquestioning obedience. Con-version, said the Bishop, places slaves "under stronger Ob-ligations to perform. . . [their] duties with the greatest Dili-gence and Fidelity." The Reverend Hugh Jones of Virginia echoed this notion when he wrote "Christianity encourages and orders them [slaves] to become more humble and bet-ter servants, and not worse, than when they were heathens." And the Reverend Thomas Bacon, addressing the slaves themselves, added "your Masters and Mistresses are God's Overseers." So conversion to Christianity, instead of weak-ening the restraints of chattel slavery, could actually be used to strengthen them.

With the most difficult problems resolved, complete and systematic black codes could be developed. By the early eighteenth century such codes were in effect from New England to Georgia, and indeed, in all the English and French colonies of the Caribbean and Latin America. More-over, despite a great diversity of conditions in the colonies, the codes were remarkably similar in their fundamentals. Two factors account for this similarity. First, although slavery could (and did) exist without statutory sanction, laws clarifying certain ambiguities and establishing the le-gal details of the system were deemed practical and even essential. Consequently, the laws and judicial precedents of all the colonies established, as we have already noted, that the slave was conveyable property (i.e., a chattel) and that his status was inherited from his mother. In addition, it was perfectly clear that some system of *control* was necessary to the existence of slavery, and so all the black codes incorporated stringent provisions for policing the blacks and punishing those who failed to submit to the system.

Control was absolutely essential to slavery, and most whites agreed that *fear* must necessarily lie at the base of the system of control. Bryan Edwards, a West Indian planter and slave owner, tacitly acknowledged this reality in his famous *History of the British Colonies in the West Indies* (London, 1801). "In countries where slavery is established," he wrote, "the principles on which the government is supported is fear: or a sense of that absolute coercive necessity which, leaving no choice of action, supercedes all questions of right. It is vain to deny that such actually is, and necessarily must be, the case in all countries where slavery is allowed." Accordingly, police and control provisions of the black codes provided certain essentials of the system.

In general, the control provisions of the eighteenth century black codes were quite similar. Slaves were forbidden to congregate in large groups without white supervision. They were ordinarily forbidden to carry weapons. They could not, under any circumstances, strike a white person or otherwise show disrespect. They were clearly subject to the authority of their owners, and as we have already seen, the slaveowners had acquired virtual life-and-death power over their slaves. When the laws called for specific punishments for certain crimes they were invariably applied more severely to slaves, and in fact to all blacks, than to whites. The latter point bears emphasis, for in most cases of special legislation, *blacks*, not just slaves, were set apart for special treatment. New York and New Jersey actually barred all blacks from property ownership. Several colonies created special criminal courts for blacks, thereby depriving them of participation in "white" justice. Several other colonies, including Pennsylvania in 1700 and New Jersey in 1704, passed laws calling for the castration of blacks convicted of attempted rape of a white woman,[8] emphasizing yet another distinction made in law between black and white. Under the law of colonial America, white and black were not considered equal. Blacks were different, subordinate, subject to discrimination in law as in practice. The laws of slavery and the laws excluding free blacks from the course of normal affairs developed simultaneously in colonial America. Together they established a tradition that was to prevail for a long time.

No tension associated with the institution of racial slavery was more pervasive than that produced by white fear of slave insurrection. Despite all the efforts at control, the possibility of revolt was an ever-present reality to whites, particularly in areas of high black concentration. The slightest rumor of slave unrest was sufficient to throw whites into near panic and to produce quick and often brutal reprisal. And although actual slave insurrections were not common in colonial America, *rumors* of slave unrest were quite common. Consequently, the white population was never able to relax completely. Fear was chronic and was expressed in terms of the harsher and more repressive legislation that invariably resulted from the rumors. Sometimes there was more involved than mere rumor.

The largest slave insurrection of the colonial period in British North America occurred, not surprisingly, in South Carolina. The decade of the 1730s was a period of great prosperity for the Carolina planters, and throughout the period slave importations increased dramatically, at an average rate of 2500 a year. By 1740 blacks outnumbered whites two to one (approximately 30,000 to 15,000), with most of the slaves concentrated in the coastal rice districts. Moreover, South Carolina had relatively more recent arrivals among the slave population than did the colonies to the north, and "unseasoned" slaves tended to be less docile than those born into the system. The situation consequently was ripe for revolt. On September 9, 1739, a group of about 20 slaves broke into a plantation warehouse near the Stono River and obtained guns, ammunition, and supplies. The initial group of insurrectionists then attacked and killed about 10 whites and burned their homes, thereby initiating the so-called "Stono Revolt."

It appears that the slaves who planned the strike for freedom had received word that the Spanish authorities at St. Augustine, Florida, were offering liberty to any Carolina slaves who escaped south to Spanish territory. With this offer in mind, the rebels, who increased in number to about 60 as the group proceeded, began the march toward Florida. The South Carolina militia, desperately summoned to service, set out in pursuit. When they overtook the insurrectionists a pitched battle ensued in which the slaves, outnumbered and untrained, were defeated. About 40 blacks and 20 whites were killed; the white Carolinians had now experienced what they had so long feared.

The Stono Revolt initiated a shock wave of panic and hysteria that was felt in every American colony and did not subside for some time thereafter. Indeed, the memory of Stono gave rise to the insurrection panic in New York that has come to be known as the New York slave "conspiracy" of 1741. Although the circumstances are not entirely clear, whites evidently attributed certain occurrences—a series of fires, for example—to a group of black conspirators in New York City. Scholars now believe that there was probably no real conspiracy, although there might have been instances of incendiarism. The white fear of the black population was so great, however, that the whites of the city were stampeded into a witch hunt of considerable proportions. The chief informant, an attention-seeking white indentured servant by the name of Mary Burton, claimed to have accidently overheard much of the plotting, and as she named more and more participants in the "conspiracy," the number of black executions mounted ever higher. By the time the episode had come to an end, the total stood at 14 slaves burned at the stake, 18 other blacks hanged, and 72 deported. Such was the extent of white fear, and of the determination of the whites to instill an equally compelling fear of horrible reprisal in the hearts of blacks. Mutual fear was, then, inherent in the system of slavery and was a constant reality of race relations in the colonial period. Whites feared blacks, and blacks feared whites. This fact was primary in the functional relationships between whites and blacks. The residual effects of longstanding mutual fear would profoundly influence race relations in America even until today.

Despite the occasional rebellion or conspiracy, however, the system of control was generally effective in colonial America. Most slaves, even though they may have dreamed of freedom, dared not revolt. Most slaves simply did as they were commanded and took what pleasure they could in their woefully restricted lives. The typical slave worked on a southern plantation, was involved in some aspect of agricultural production, and worked long hours in the fields as part of a labor gang. His life was limited to the plantation on which he had been born and on which he would, barring sale or escape, die. But even within the confines of the plantation, there were further limitations on the slave's personal contacts. For the most part, his interpersonal relations were confined to his contact with other slaves or, in some cases, free blacks. His contacts with whites were limited in the extreme, limited as to both *frequency* and *nature*. When the contacts with whites did occur, it was under strained and unnatural circumstances, marked by mutual distrust, fear, and a general difficulty of communication. The *mutuality* of this fear and distrust bears special emphasis. For all that has been written about the benevolent "paternalism" that supposedly characterized American slavery, it is clear that the son did not know or trust the father; the father did not know or trust the son. Their relationship ordinarily was one of exploiter and exploited rather than one of patriarch and people.

Generalization is quite difficult regarding the degree of brutality and physical cruelty associated with the system of plantation slavery in the eighteenth century.[9] A great deal depended on individual masters, and they varied in their attitudes on the treatment of slaves. In a period not noted for its high regard for human sensibilities, some degree of physical cruelty is to be expected. It assuredly existed. Slaves were forced laborers who gained little but the barest subsistance for their efforts. Forced labor demands the use of physical coercion and on the plantation this usually meant the whip, shackles, and the threat of much worse. And as we have already noted, the slightest show of resistance to the system met with quick and sometimes brutal punishment.

However, for all the inevitable cruelty associated with black slavery in colonial America, a curious fact remains. Of all the slave systems in the New World colonies, only in British North America did the black population increase in size by natural reproduction over the years. Despite high mortality rates, the black population grew continually as a result of the excess of live births over deaths. The necessity for importing vast numbers of Africans was thus diminished. Philip Curtin, the leading authority on the statistics of African importations, contends that British North America received no more than 5% of all Africans brought to the New World. The creole black population (i.e., blacks born in America) thus developed according to the dictates of largely internal considerations without very much in the way of continuing African influence. As the years passed, more and more blacks were born and raised as slaves in America, knowing no other way of life. This fact was to be of profound significance in the development of an endemic and near-autonomous Afro-American culture system based on the imperatives of plantation slavery.

Not all the slaves of colonial America lived and worked on plantations, of course. Slaves were to be found in the towns of all the colonies, living under conditions quite different from those on the plantation. Generally speaking, the lot of the town dweller was somewhat easier, even more pleasant than that of a plantation slave. Most of the urban slaves were household, domestic servants, but many others were artisans or craftsmen with valuable skills. They were most frequently carpenters, but in addition, many plantations and towns claimed slave shoemakers, blacksmiths, butchers, coopers, and even barbers and tailors. (We should note that throughout the colonial period white workingmen were consistently antagonistic toward the use of

slaves in any trade.) In New England, slaves were commonly used as assistants in whatever businesses their owners practiced. Such slaves came to be so valuable to their masters
that they often managed to gain some freedom of movement. Opportunities to congregate with other blacks were
generally greater in the towns, and the urban slaves were
unquestionably able to enjoy far more flexibility in their
social lives than plantation slaves did. In New England, too,
there were never very *many* blacks about, so the fear factor
among whites was significantly weaker than in areas of high
black concentration. This situation operated to give slaves,
and free blacks as well, the opportunity to live relatively
unrestricted lives. Indeed, slaves in New England often
occupied a place, albeit a subordinate one, in the family
circle, attending the same church, living on the same premises, and sometimes sharing the same table. But, it should
be emphasized, slaves enjoying such a life style were only
a tiny minority of the total slave population.

To this point we have been dealing for the most part
with slavery and slaves in early America. Needless to say,
there were also free blacks in the colonies, black men and
women who had been born into free families, who had run
away from slavery and made good their escapes, or, less
frequently, who had been "manumitted" (i.e., freed) by
their owners. Because early census figures are notoriously
unreliable, the precise number of free blacks is impossible
to determine, but it is certain that each of the American
colonies sustained a free black population, varying in size
in proportion to its total black population. It is equally
clear that in the southern and middle colonies, the only
colonies claiming substantial slave population, free blacks
were considered undesirable and potentially dangerous by
the majority of whites. Consequently, by law and by custom the whites cast the blacks into a markedly inferior
status. As David B. Davis has pointed out, "The grim and
overriding fact is that in every colony free Negroes . . . suffered from legal and social discrimination, and were at
once condemned for idleness and prevented from enjoying
economic opportunity, accused of being disorderly and de-

prived of equal justice." Moreover, as racial slavery evolved
in the late seventeenth century, the free black status became ever more an anomaly in the minds of the white authorities. When slavery and blackness came to closely associated, the minority of blacks who were not slaves stood
out as abnormal or unnatural. Moreover, slavery functioned
in part as a system of race control for the great majority
of blacks, but the control mechanism of slavery did not
apply directly to free blacks. Their status was insufficient-
ly clearcut and distinct for the increasingly race conscious
whites. The result was twofold. First, special laws (and
customs with the force of law) were used to hold the free
blacks in a distinctly inferior status. Second, every effort
was made to hold the free black population to an absolute
numeric minimum.

The initial legal efforts to set free blacks apart from
whites took the form of distinctions made in the laws as,
for example, in the 1640s when the statutes began making
specific reference to blacks as distinct from whites. Then,
in 1668, the Virginia Assembly became even more specific,
declaring that free blacks "ought not in all respects to be
admitted to a full fruition of the exemptions and impuni-
ties of the English . . . ." The intent of this declaration was
to place the free black population in a category separate
and distinct from the whites and, of course, inferior to
them. This same general principle was readily accepted by
the other colonies, although again more particularly in the
South. For example, in no southern colony could free
blacks testify against whites in courts of law. In no southern colony except North Carolina could free blacks vote,
even if they were property owners. Virginia in 1705 passed
a law forbidding any black (or Indian), free or slave, to
"lift his hand" against a Christian white, a principle soon
adopted by the other colonies. Free blacks were generally
forbidden sexual encounters with whites. Many colonies
also forbade blacks to own arms or to participate in militia exercises, but these laws frequently went unenforced,
and blacks participated in most of the colonial wars. Still,
the very existence of such legislation demonstrates all too

vividly the feeling of whites about free blacks, and the determination of whites to keep free blacks separate from and inferior in status to the increasingly mobile white population.

The desire to keep the free black population at a minimum is also clearly indicated by the laws of the seventeenth and eighteenth centuries limiting the right of slaveowners to free their slaves. As early as 1691, Virginia passed a law restricting private manumission, stating that no slave might be freed unless his owner agreed to transport him out of the colony, and pay for the transportation. But even this restriction proved insufficient to satisfy the white population. In 1723, as part of an elaborate package of antiblack legislation, the assembly passed an act forbidding manumission altogether without the approval of both the governor and the council. By terms of this statute, manumission as a path to freedom was virtually closed. And again, the other southern colonies ultimately adopted a similar policy. Not until the era of the American Revolution and the coming of a more libertarian-humanitarian spirit did any colony decide to ease these rigid restrictions on manumission.

The free black population, then, could be augmented only by births into free families, by slaves escaping to freedom, by self-purchase, or by free black immigration. In none of these categories was the increase substantial. Although the birth rate was apparently high, mortality was fierce, and self-purchase and immigration were rare. The incidence of successful runaways who managed to establish themselves as free men was relatively small. This is not to say that runaway slaves were rare. Quite the contrary. As one historian has said with reference to colonial Virginia, the number of runaways was "large, large enough to sap a part of the economic advantage of a slave labor force." But many runaways were recaptured; others were killed in their escape attempts. Those who made it to a distant town or even another colony were by no means safe. White authorities were simply too suspicious of a new black face in the community to fail to ask questions and to take action that all too often resulted in the return of the slave to his owner.

But though the free black population remained relatively small, it was none-the-less important. In every colony there were free black people who lived and worked in their own fields or at their own trades. Although their lot was frequently made difficult by discriminatory laws and practices, they considered themselves better off by far than their slave brothers. For all their difficulties, very few chose to give up freedom and submit voluntarily to slavery. Many were able to transcend all their disadvantages and to succeed remarkably well in a world in which they were held as pariahs by the majority population.

Free blacks also played an important symbolic role in early America. They stood as a constant reminder to everyone, white and black, free and slave, that *all* blacks were not slaves, that the coincidence of blackness and slavery was not perfect, and that blacks could aspire to freedom even in white America. Thus they remained a constant thorn in the side of the whites and a constant source of tension in a racial climate marked by many tensions. But it was as a source of inspiration to black slaves that free blacks threatened the slave system. Whites realized this, and most of them despised and feared free blacks all the more for it.

In the course of historical dynamics, certain periods produce notable breaks in the general continuity; these breaks clearly mark one "age" off and distinguish it from what had preceded it and what would follow it. Such a period was the Age of the American Revolution. Inspired by such lofty visions as the eighteenth century enlightenment produced—natural law, the rights of man, human liberty and equality, a general humanitarianism—the American patriots determined to strike off the metaphorical shackles binding their country to Britain. It was inevitable that with such thoughts sustaining the spirit of the age, some men would begin to question the justice of the more tangible shackles binding human beings in chattel slavery. If slaves were men, and they surely were, why should they, too, not share in the benefits of liberty? As James Otis concluded in 1764 in his famous *Rights of the British Colonies Asserted and Proved*, "the Colonists are by the law of nature free born, as indeed all men are, white or black." The "founding fathers" who spoke out against slavery in the period included John Adams, Franklin, Gallatin, Hamilton, Henry, Jay, and even Washington. The Declaration of Independence included in its list of "self-evident truths" the assertion "that all men are created equal" and that they all had the God-given rights ("unalienable Rights") to "Life, Liberty, and the Pursuit of Happiness."[10] To most Americans, slavery was clearly inconsistent with the fundamental principles on which the Revolution was based. The ideas of the enlightenment, and the Revolution based on those ideas, produced a growing abolitionist movement in America (and, in fact, in western Europe, too).

Abolitionist sentiment in America actually predated the Age of the Revolution. The Quakers, practically from the outset of their religious and social experiment in the wilds of Pennsylvania, had opposed slavery and forbidden slave-holding among their coreligionists. But they had been able to accomplish little until libertarianism and humanitarianism became popular notions. Then they found people more willing to listen and even to act. Of all the early abolitionists, none were more eloquent in their pleas than the Quakers Benjamin Lay, John Woolman, and Anthony Benezet, who devoted their lives and careers to the cause. Under their leadership, abolitionist societies multiplied.

Blacks also participated actively in the early abolitionist campaigns. Some petitioned for individual freedom from slavery; others memorialized state legislatures demanding abolition. Moreover, they provided numerous instances of impressive accomplishments by blacks who had to achieve under the most difficult of circumstances. The late eighteenth century produced some remarkable black men and women to whom the abolitionists could point in support of their argument that blacks, if permitted to exist under more favorable circumstances, would be the equal of whites in all respects.

Among the prime exemplars of the innate ability of blacks, none achieved greater fame than Benjamin Banneker, the freeborn, self-educated mathematician, surveyor, astronomer, almanac maker. Banneker attracted the attention of Thomas Jefferson, who, as Secretary of State in 1791, appointed Banneker to survey the national district that later became Washington, D.C. Equally noteworthy was the black New Orleans physician James Derham, who was acclaimed as a brother scientist by Benjamin Rush, unofficial head of America's medical profession. Thomas Fuller, a Maryland slave of African birth, was another favorite of the abolitionists. He was a self-taught mathematician of considerable ability whose talents received international attention. However, black talent in the period was not limited to the scientific fields. Richard Allen and Absalom Jones, both of Philadelphia, were renowned for their ability as preachers and their power as writers. Prince Hall, the leader of the black community in Boston, founded the black Masonic order. All of these men, and many others, achieved fame, and engendered admiration and, perhaps indirectly, support for the abolitionist cause. But a young woman, an untutored slave, born in Africa and raised in Boston, received more attention than any of them. She was Phillis Wheatly, the first Afro-American poet to be published and widely read. The first edition of her collected poems was printed in London in 1773; it was so popular that five editions appeared before 1800. Although her work seems dated to modern readers, heavily rhymed and metered and overly effusive, it was considered excellent by the critical canons of the times, and Miss Wheatly was compared to the great Alexander Pope. Although she argued against slavery only indirectly, she served the abolitionist cause very well.

In yet another way blacks aided themselves in the cause. They actively participated in the Revolutionary War. In spite of traditional fears of armed blacks and foot-dragging on the part of the slaveowning Commander-in-Chief, George Washington, the chronically low white enlistments and the necessities of a long war led the Continental authorities to authorize the recruiting of blacks. The desire to win the war overcame a reluctance to admit the possibility of an advance in black status, and ultimately all but two states accepted black enlistment. In Georgia and South Carolina the slave population was considered too large and the necessities of race control too pressing to overcome white fears of defeat by the British and the loss of independence.

Black military participation in the war actually began with the minuteman companies of Massachusetts as early as 1775. Then, in 1777, Massachusetts officially declared slaves to be eligible for service, and Rhode Island followed in 1778, with the legislature voting to raise two slave battalions. The other northern colonies followed suit. Virginia and Maryland turned to blacks when white manpower proved insufficient, and more particularly when the center of military activity shifted toward the South. Many states used black troops to make up a part of their quotas called into continental service, so blacks served not only in state militia forces but also in the continental line. They also served frequently in the American navy and aboard privateers, acting as pilots in coastal waters they knew well. As one Hessian officer serving under Burgoyne observed, speaking of the American forces in general, ". . . no regiment is to be seen in which there are not Negroes in abundance: And among them are able-bodied, strong, and brave fellows." The consensus among the contemporary observers was that the approximately 5000 blacks who served the patriot cause served it well.

It is of extreme importance to note, on the other hand, that blacks also participated on the side of the British throughout the war, enticed by the offers of freedom to all who would escape behind British lines. When Lord Dunmore, deposed governor of Virginia, made his famous offer in 1775 to free all who would join him, some 800 slaves did so, despite the great risks involved. Thousands more responded similarly when the offer was expanded by Commander-in-Chief Sir Henry Clinton in 1779 to include all blacks in America. Clinton made good on his offer. When the war ended, many hundreds of former slaves were evacuated with the British troops.

Clearly, the great majority of blacks who participated in the war on either side did so primarily out of personal motivation, not out of devotion to country or cause. As the *New York Weekly Mercury* noted on November 27, 1780, "A desire of obtaining freedom. . . reigns throughout the generality of slaves at present." Benjamin Quarles, the leading authority on black participation in American wars, has admirably summed up black motivation in the Revolution:

> The Negro's role in the Revolution can best be understood by realizing that his major loyalty was not to a place nor to a people, but to a principle. Insofar as he had freedom of choice, he was likely to join the side that made him the quickest and best offer in terms of those 'unalienable rights' of which Mr. Jefferson had spoken. Whoever invoked the image of liberty, be he American or British, could count on a ready response from the blacks.

The liberty for which the blacks fought was more personal and immediate than that for which the white patriots did battle. Once again, the factor of status duality is apparent. The blacks who fought for American independence fought both as *blacks* (slaves seeking freedom) and as *Americans* (people for whom America was home). Ironically, the same may be said of those who followed the British.

Nevertheless, the fact of black participation in the cause strengthened the hand of the abolitionists. North of the Potomac, antislavery sentiment grew more pronounced, and by 1777 began to be reflected in constitutional provisions of the newly written state constitutions, in state laws, and in judicial decisions. Vermonters, for example, banned slavery in their state constitution of 1777. The Pennsylvania legislature passed the first gradual emancipation law in 1780, and Rhode Island and Connecticut followed suit in 1784. In Massachusetts, a famous court decision *(Quock Walker* v. *Nathaniel Jennison, 1781)* eventuated in the abolition of slavery by judicial interpretation. New Hampshire ended slavery by court interpretation of the state bill of rights. Public opinion in New England and Pennsylvania simply would not tolerate the continued existence of chattel slavery during this period of rampant libertarianism, and the slaveowners, despite considerable complaining and some overt resistance, were not numerous enough to prevent abolition. Moreover, the black population was not large enough to represent a vital economic interest.

Abolition in New York and New Jersey met with considerably greater opposition. There were relatively more blacks in these states,[11] and the proslave minority was able to hold off the abolitionists for several years. In New York, the state Manumission Society, founded in 1785, was the prime agent of abolition, and its distinguished leadership—John Jay was its first president and Alexander Hamilton the second—exerted continual pressure for a gradual emancipation bill. They were finally successful in 1799. New Jersey passed a badly emasculated and ineffective bill in 1804. In reality, slavery was not completely ended in New York until July 4, 1827, while New Jersey did not pass effective legislation until 1846, and the New Jersey census continued to list slaves among the population until 1860. The last slaves there were not emancipated until the ratification of the Thirteenth Amendment.

Contrary to a very persistent myth, slavery was not abolished in the North because it was unprofitable. Slave prices remained high throughout the revolutionary period and afterward because slaves were serving productive functions for their owners as skilled field hands, artisans, factory workers, and domestic servants. Slaveowners fully appreciated their value and the general benefits of slavery in making their lives more pleasant. Consequently they resisted abolition efforts to the best of their ability. It was only because they were in a minority that they lost out to abolitionist fervor. And as the gradual emancipation laws were effected, the free black population of the North increased steadily, from about 27,000 in 1790 to 122,000 in 1830.

In the South there was a similar reaction against slavery, led by the libertarians of the revolutionary era. Many white southerners initially felt the dilemma posed to slaveowners by the revolutionary principles they claimed to hold sacred. Their initial effort was directed toward easing the restrictions on individual manumission. Virginia, for example, in 1782 passed "An Act to Authorize the Manumission of Slaves," and some slaveowners took advantage of the law to free their chattels. Only in South Carolina and Georgia did the slaveowners resist all efforts to diminish the size and importance of the institution of slavery. But although the upper southern states did take some action toward deemphasizing slavery, none of them went as far as abolition or even gradual emancipation. The reasons for this failure demand brief exploration.

First, the popular belief that Eli Whitney's cotton gin saved a dying institution is highly questionable. Prior to 1793 and Whitney's invention, slavery had been doing quite well in the lower South. The cotton gin, by providing the potential for enormous expansion, doubtless strengthened the determination of slaveowners to retain the institution. But slavery would not likely have died a natural death even if the gin had never been invented. Slavery was profitable to slaveowners and was retained mostly for this reason.

A second important reason for the retention of slavery in the South lies in the matter of white attitudes toward blacks. Even those whites of a pronounced libertarian bent, Madison and Jefferson, for example, believed that the dominant white Euro-American culture was incapable of assimilating or even of accommodating to any sizable black population. Blacks, they believed, were an unassimilable element. Thus abolition was conceivable only if accompanied by some form of "colonization"; the black population must be removed to some other area, preferably a considerable distance away. Said Jefferson on this subject, "Deep rooted prejudices entertained by the whites; ten thousand recollections, by the blacks, of the injuries they have sustained; new provocations; the real distinctions which nature has made; and many other circumstances, will . . . produce convulsions which will probably never end but in the extermination of the one or the other race." In Jefferson's view, white prejudices were based on "real distinctions which nature has made"; blacks were inherently "different" and the differences were the object of white abhorrence. Moreover, the former slaves might choose to make war on their former masters, just as a group of former slaves were making very effective war on their ex-masters in Haiti under the leadership of Toussaint L'Ouverture. The situation would be intolerable to the whites. It was better to keep the blacks in slavery until some system of colonization might be worked out. Slavery was, to the liberal Virginians, a "necessary evil" that could ultimately be extinguished by eliminating not only slavery but all blacks. This was the argument that carried the day against the white abolitionists of the South. The passage of time and the increasing productivity of racial slavery would make the institution appear ever more necessary and less evil.

When the federal constitutional convention met in the summer of 1787, the issue of slavery occupied a considerable portion of the debate. Ultimately the southern pro-slave delegates triumphed. As one of the numerous compromises necessary to create a document acceptable to a majority of the delegates, slavery was written into the fundamental law of the land. Though the Constitution nowhere specifically mentions slavery, it implicitly recognized the institution in three places: in the famous 3/5 compromise, which provided that five slaves would count as three persons for purposes of direct taxation and representation; in the "Fugitive Slave Clause," which provided for the return of any runaway slave escaping into a different state; and in the stipulation forbidding Congress to close the foreign slave trade for 20 years.[12]

The acceptance of slavery by the constitution-makers marked a portentous compromise with principle. Because of the greed, fear, and prejudice of a minority of southern whites, chattel slavery was written into the fundamental law of the land. The nation born of a determination to acquire "liberty" and based on the principles of human equality

and the right of individual pursuit of happiness had accepted the compromise that would later lead the militant abolitionist William Lloyd Garrison to call the Constitution a
"covenant with death and an agreement with Hell." The
great promise of the revolution was deserted, left to die
unfulfilled. For all the hope raised in the minds and hearts
of the libertarians, the results of the American Revolution
were strictly limited in regard to slavery. In the states
where the institution was weakest it was set on the road
to extinction. But where it was strongest and the black
population most heavily concentrated, slavery persisted as
before, little if any changed by the catharsis of the first
of the great Democratic Revolutions.

And just as slavery survived the American Revolution,
so did slave resistance. As news of the happenings on "the
French island"—Haiti—reached American slaves, rumors of
slave unrest spread over the United States. Then, toward
the end of the summer of 1800, rumor became reality.
The blacks in the Richmond, Virginia area, led by a slave
"general" by the name of Gabriel, rose in revolt. They
had begun to plan their uprising as early as June 1800, and
by the time they made their move in early September they
had gained the support of several hundred (possibly as many
as 1000) men. They developed an elaborate plan involving
a three-columned march on Richmond, the taking of the
Virginia state arsenal, and the promotion of a general slaughter of the whites, to be followed by an effort to spread revolt throughout the state. The plan was well-conceived.
However, one day prior to its execution a slave informer
reported the plot to the white authorities, giving them time
for preparation. Then, as the uprising got underway, tor-
rential rains retarded the progress of the slaves toward their
rendezvous point outside the city. The result was the abor-
tion of the whole plan, the capture of scores of participants,
and the execution of from 30 to 40 of them, including
Gabriel himself. Two slave informants were granted their
liberty for the valuable services rendered their masters and
the state of Virginia.

On December 31, 1800, the Virginia legislature passed a notable resolution. The governor of the state, it held, should be requested "to correspond with the president of the United States on the subject of purchasing lands without the limits of the United States whither persons obnoxious to the laws or dangerous to the peace of society may be removed." The persons to whom the legislators referred were free blacks, whom the whites irrationally associated with slave revolts. Thomas Jefferson's notion that whites and free blacks could not live together had received legislative support. If the president (ironically, it was Jefferson himself) should take action, all free blacks in Virginia (and presumably everywhere else in the United States) would be removed onto "lands without the limits" of the country; they would be "colonized." By this means whites sought to solve the problem of the presense of blacks who were not slaves. Black Americans, some of whom had gained their freedom by fighting to achieve American independence, would be removed from their homes and settled elsewhere.

The black colonization plan was never adopted by the nation at large.[13] However, as the eighteenth century came to a close the movement was initiated. Despite a century and a half of participation in the American experience, free black men were still considered foreign and alien and dangerous by most whites. Blackness was still more significant than birth in establishing a claim on nationality. As the nineteenth century opened, Afro-American status duality was an established fact, and slavery was a fixed and seemingly permanent reality for the vast majority of America's black population.

NOTES

[1] The classic inquiry into "Americanness" in the eighteenth century was posed by the French emigré J. Hector St. John Crevecoeur in 1782. "What then is the American, this new man?" he asked. He then proceeded to answer his own question. "He is either an European, or the descendant of an European . . . ." This was the prime prerequisite.

[2] The precise status of this initial group of blacks became a major issue when the question of the origins of white racism began to receive considerable scholarly attention, that is in the mid-1950s. Some historians argued that the first black Americans were considered servants and in no way distinguished from whites of the same class. They maintained that antiblack prejudice *followed* the development of slavery and was a result of value attachments that began to link blacks with slavery. A contrary argument held that prejudice existed from the beginning and was the *cause* of slavery. Blacks were enslaved because they were considered inferior and naturally servile. Most recently, historians have come to agree that neither side was wholly right or wholly wrong; antiblack prejudice existed from the outset and this factor was significant in the emergence of racial slavery, but after slavery came to be established, prejudice and slavery were interactive and mutually reinforcing realities.

[3] The Puritan ship captains and merchants thus had to satisfy themselves with providing slaves for other colonies where the demand was greater. In the seventeenth century the New England traders were not generally able to compete profitably with the powerful Dutch West India Company slavers or those of the British Royal African Company, but by the early eighteenth century the Americans had

overtaken the European monopolists. By then the Puritan traders would come to rank among the largest slave dealers in the world. Massachusetts and Rhode Island in particular were to establish slave trading as New England's most profitable economic endeavor.

[4] Apparently the New England Puritans used precedent and biblical sanction for slavery to support their legalization of the institution. Enslavement of captives of "just wars" was a long accepted practice by the seventeenth century, and *Leviticus*, 25:45-46 gave the Israelites encouragement to enslave "strangers that do sojourn among you." As seen in Chapter 3, enslavement of the Amerindians was a common practice in all the New World colonies.

[5] In the meantime indigo had been introduced as a supplemental staple crop. The significance of black labor in producing a strong and profitable colony was profound. One British historian, Reginald Coupland, has gone so far as to assert that America "as a productive economic unit . . . was saved by Africa."

[6] This combination of forces was neatly itemized in the preamble to the South Carolina slave code of 1696, which had been borrowed from the Barbadian code. Its assumptions were shared by white Virginians and indeed by all whites of the English planting colonies. The preamble stated:

> Whereas the plantations and estates of this province cannot be well and sufficiently managed . . . without the labor and service of negroes and other slaves; and forasmuch as the said negroes and other slaves brought unto the people of the Province for that purpose, are of barbarous, wild, savage natures and such renders them wholly unqualified to be governed by the laws, customs, and practices of this Province; but that it is absolutely necessary, that such other constitutions, laws and orders, should in this Province be made and enacted, for the good regulating and ordering of them, as may restrain the disorders, rapines and inhumanity, to which they are naturally prone and inclined; and may also tend to the safety and security of the people of this Province and their estates . . . .

[7] Such was not to be the case in the European colonies of Latin America and the Caribbean. Although color was always to be a consideration in determining status, several intermediate shades of color were recognized between black and white. The mulatto had, as Carl Degler has cogently argued with reference to Brazil, an "escape hatch" that in many cases permitted his social and economic advance. Caste color lines were never as clearly drawn anywhere in the

New World as they were in the plantation colonies of British Colonial North America and the United States.

[8] The English Crown ordinarily disallowed such laws as excessively cruel and maintained that convicted black rapists should be legally subject to the same penalty as whites: simple hanging. There are, however, numerous records of extralegal castrations and torture deaths in the colonial period. One scholar has suggested that until 1769 castration was employed in Virginia as punishment for chronic running away as well as for rape of white women.

[9] The question of the comparative aspect of New World slavery has been the subject of a long scholarly controversy. In its basics (and somewhat distorted for that), the argument is between those who contend that slavery was comparatively less severe in the colonial possessions of the European Catholic powers, especially Spain and Portugal, than in the colonies of Protestant European nations. The Catholic Church (and hence the state), one group of scholars contends, recognized the humanity of black slaves and insisted that slaves be afforded the ministrations and protection of the Church, including baptism, marriage, and the inviolable family. Conversely, in the Protestant colonies there was no church strongly committed to the recognition of the slave's humanity and to the protection of his human rights. In those colonies, the relationship between master and slave was purely exploitive, hence cruel and severe. On the other hand, those opposing this viewpoint contend that in actual practice differences between the slave systems of the New World were few and slight no matter the religion of the metropolis. Although *theoretically* the Catholic Church did afford protection, in reality that protection was minimal, and, in fact, slavery was probably more cruel in parts of Portuguese Brazil than anywhere else in the world. The matter is still under scholarly contention, but the weight of evidence seems to favor the latter viewpoint. In the Iberian colonies, for example, there was a chronic shortage of black women, and consequently fewer families than in British North America, where the sexual balance was favorable to family development. Even though slave families were not recognized as binding by church or state in Protestant colonies, they did exist and produce enough children to sustain a continuing population growth. This was not the case in the Iberian possessions. Moreover, there was always an insufficiency of churches and priests in the Catholic colonies to insure the protection of slaves in their humanity. The laws protecting slave rights frequently went unenforced. Finally, plantation slaves were plantation slaves no matter where they lived, and as such ultimately subject to the authority and control of the master. Accordingly, so great was the

diversity of treatment slaves received that meaningful generalization about comparative severity is extremely difficult.

[10] Not all white Americans believed that these principles applied to blacks. Jefferson in writing the Declaration, was probably not thinking of blacks as "men" (i.e., citizens). And the Virginia Convention of 1776 rephrased George Mason's original statement on natural rights to read:

> ... all men are by nature equally free and independent, and have certain inherent rights, of which, *when they enter into a state of society* [italics added], they cannot, by any compact, deprive or divest their posterity; namely, the enjoyment of life and liberty, with the means of acquiring and possessing property, and pursuing and obtaining happiness and safety.

Thus, according to the Virginia lawgivers, slaves (and possibly all blacks) were not members of the body politic and were not really "Americans."

[11] In 1780 there were roughly 21,000 blacks in New York, or about 10% of the total population. The approximate figures for New Jersey were almost 10,500 blacks to 140,000 whites.

[12] In 1807, as soon as it was constitutionally capable of action, Congress passed a law declaring the foreign trade illegal. The law went into effect January 1, 1808, the same day on which an identical British law went into force. Although slave smuggling was to continue until the abolition of slavery in the United States, the legal trade ceased in 1808.

[13] Something very similar to colonization was adopted as *Indian* policy, however. Indian "removal" into supposedly uninhabited areas of the trans-Mississippi West was a plan suggested by Jefferson and later promulgated by Andrew Jackson.

SUGGESTIONS FOR FURTHER READING

Winthrop Jordan's *White Over Black*, despite its primary focus on white attitudes toward blacks, remains the most important single volume treating the black experience in early America. Jordan's treatment of the origins of slavery and prejudice is likely to remain the last word. Other works recommended for previous chapters that contain material pertinent to the chapter at hand include: David B. Davis, *The Problem of Slavery in Western Culture*; Marvin Harris, *Patterns of Race in the Americas*; and the reader edited by Laura Foner and Eugene D. Genovese entitled *Slavery in the New World. A Reader in Comparative History*.

Of the two standard works on slavery in the United States, the earlier one, Ulrich B. Phillips, *American Negro Slavery* (New York: D. Appleton and Co., 1918; reprint edition Louisiana State University Press, 1968) contains far more material on the early phase of the history of slavery. Most of it, however, deals with economic, legal, and constitutional matters and not the slaves themselves. Kenneth M. Stampp, *The Peculiar Institution. Slavery in the Ante-Bellum South* (New York: Knopf, 1956) includes only brief treatment of the first two centuries of the Afro-American experience.

The many monographs treating the early history of the blacks in individual provinces range widely in value. Gerald W. Mullin, *Flight or Rebellion: Slave Resistance in Eighteenth Century Virginia* (New York: Oxford University Press, 1972) is a recent, provocative work by a student of Jordan's. Another fine monograph is Thad W. Tate, *The Negro in Eighteenth Century Williamsburg* (Charlottesville: The University of Virginia Press, 1966), a model of careful scholarship. Lorenzo Johnston Greene, *The Negro in Colonial New England*,

1620-1776 (New York: Columbia University Press, 1942; reprint edition Atheneum Press, 1968) is dated in attitude and perspective but still contains much useful material on a relatively small but important group of people. It should be supplemented by a journal article, Robert C. Twombly and Robert H. Moore, "Black Puritans: The Negro in Seventeenth Century Massachusetts," *William and Mary Quarterly*, 24:224-242 (1967). Somewhat thin in research but still adequate for an introduction to its subject is Edgar J. McManus, *A History of Negro Slavery in New York* (New York: Syracuse University Press, 1966). A much older study of a second of the middle colonies contains valuable information but little in the way of analysis. It is Edward R. Turner, *The Negro in Pennsylvania. Slavery—Servitude—Freedom, 1639-1861* (Washington: The American Historical Association, 1911). Frank J. Klingberg, *An Appraisal of the Negro in Colonial South Carolina: A Study in Americanization* (Washington: The Associated Publishers, 1941) is primarily a study of Christian missionary activity among the blacks of South Carolina, but it includes well-selected excerpts from valuable documents. Two older studies containing material on free blacks in plantation colonies are John H. Russell, *The Free Negro in Virginia, 1619-1865* (Baltimore: The John Hopkins Press, 1913), which is quite useful, and James M. Wright, *The Free Negro in Maryland, 1634-1860* (New York: Longmans, Green, 1921), which is badly flawed by strong racist overtones.

The standard study of black participation in the American Revolution is Benjamin Quarles, *The Negro in the American Revolution* (Chapel Hill: University of North Carolina Press, 1961). It is brief, well-written, thorough, and scholarly to a fault. Robert McColley, *Slavery and Jeffersonian Virginia* (Urbana, Ill.: University of Illinois Press, 1964) is competent but contains little that is fresh or new on the slaves themselves. Abolition of slavery in the northern states is reliably treated in Arthur Zilversmit, *The First Emancipation: The Abolition of Slavery in the North* (Chicago: University of Chicago Press, 1967), which also contains a useful brief survey of slavery in the northern colonies. Staughton Lynd, *Class Conflict, Slavery and the United States Constitution* (Indianapolis: Bobbs-Merrill, 1967) is a series of essays of which the central three treat slavery in the United States Constitution and the "Compromise of 1787."

A most provocative recent study is Carl N. Degler's Pulitzer Prize-winning *Neither Black Nor White. Slavery and Race Relations in Brazil and the United States* (New York: Macmillan, 1971), which conveniently summarizes much valuable Brazilian material in arguing that the chief distinguishing factor in the comparative analysis of race

relations in the two countries has been the mulatto "escape hatch."
Of the many collections of readings in black history with material
pertinent to the period covered by this chapter, Seth M. Scheiner
and Tilden G. Edelstein, *The Black Americans. Interpretative Readings* (New York: Holt, Rinehart and Winston, 1971) is recent and
valuable. It contains two journal articles worthy of special mention:
Paul C. Palmer, "Servant into Slave: The Evolution of the Legal
Status of the Negro Laborer in Colonial Virginia," originally published in the *South Atlantic Quarterly*, *65*:355-371 (1966), and
Leonard Price Stavisky, "Negro Craftsmanship in Early America,"
which originally appeared in the *American Historical Review*, *54*:315-
325 (1941).

Chapter 5

PLANTATION SLAVERY I: The Institutional Dimension

The institution of slavery and the experiences of millions of black slaves under that institution are of obvious significance to the student of Afro-American history and culture. Most blacks in the United States at any time prior to 1863 were slaves, and a high proportion of the remainder of the black population had either been slaves or had had some intimate association with slavery. It was as slaves that nearly all African immigrants made adjustments to the new environment in which they found themselves, and it was as slaves that their descendants worked out the best lives possible for themselves in white America. This chapter and Chapter 6 focus on slavery, the central feature of the Afro-American experience prior to the Civil War. The present chapter deals with institutional development and operation, while Chapter 6 examines the patterns of life created by black slaves and the psychocultural imperatives of the slavery experience.

In a single chapter it is possible to develop only in broad outline the institutional dimensions of a system as varied and intricate as plantation slavery in North America. No simple definition of institutionalized slavery is adequate. Slavery was a complex, pervasive aspect of American culture, with wide-ranging implications for American thought, values, and institutions. Slavery was more than simply a system of forced labor. From the beginning, as we have

Note. Footnotes for this chapter are located on pages 162-164.

seen in the preceding chapter (pp. 105-113), it was a police
system, an instrument to control blacks, who seemed to
whites to threaten the social order and civilization itself.
But slavery was also a means of governing the conduct of
whites. As a system of race relations, it provided a broad
umbrella under which the myriad contacts and relationships
between blacks and whites could be regulated. The institution, of course, assumed a particular importance in the
American South; here, over the course of years, it became,
in the words of historian Stanley Elkins, "interwoven with
the means of production, the basic social arrangements,
and the very tone of Southern culture." In the South
slavery provided the cornerstone for a distinct way of life,
dominated by the white planter class.

The fact that the historical discussion of slavery has
largely focused on the system as it existed in the late antebellum period has oversimplified the institution and thus
distorted our understanding of it. Slavery was not a conscious, rational creation that followed along logical patterns
of development until it reached a logical fruition in the
1840s and 50s. Contrary to the traditional viewpoint,
slavery in 1850 was not identical to the institution that had
existed in 1800. Slavery was never a static institution;
over the course of years it underwent constant change, its
development, like that of other social institutions, influenced by a great number of diverse factors. Even in the
last years of its regime, slavery never became the uniform,
monolithic institution described in so many textbooks.
Hence, although we must concentrate in this chapter on
the most characteristic form of American slavery—southern, agricultural, plantation slavery—we should not forget
the variety that characterized the institution in North
America. Racial slavery existed for over 150 years in
the "free" North and for over 200 years in the South.
Even within the South there was wide variation in the size
of individual slaveholdings and in the geographic distribution of the slave population. Slaves were employed in a
variety of jobs, in rural and urban settings, in the older,
border South, the burgeoning deep South, and on the de-

veloping southwestern frontier. Moreover, approximately 10% of southern slaves lived in towns and cities, and in 1860 a half million slaves (of a total of nearly four million) were employed in nonagricultural jobs.

Undoubtedly the greatest variable in slavery was the human factor involved in the system. In its organic development, slavery was not solely the creation of whites. This is not to say that the various forms that slavery took in North America were equally the products of black and white activity. Whites exercised predominant, coercive power, but blacks countered white power with various strategems of self-defense, particularly the use of their intimate knowledge of whites. Historian U. B. Phillips' contention that mutual concessions and understandings produced "reciprocal codes of conventional morality" may exaggerate the harmony of the slave regime; however, it is nonetheless true that Afro-American slaves exercised considerable influence on the development of slavery. As historian Winthrop Jordan has noted, "slavery was a genuine, if crude and perverse variety of common bond." Slavery was, above all, a human institution and its human quality made it a complex and intricate thing.

Slavery in the United States, as in nearly every New World country, was, in its particular shape and dimensions, unique and peculiar. European colonists who shared the same cultural heritage helped create rather different systems of slavery in different parts of the Americas. English colonists in the West Indies, for example, behaved differently in enslaving blacks than Anglo-American colonists did. The particular national culture of New World slaveholders did not alone determine the paths along which slavery would develop in a particular country; economic, geographic, and demographic circumstances and the patterns of settlement of white colonists were also of major significance. In short, the systems of slavery in the New World were shaped by the historical experiences of the countries involved.

The development of slavery in North America was influenced by certain key factors, introduced in Chapter 4, which bear further elaboration here. First and foremost, the confrontation between blacks and whites was largely shaped by the white American sense of mission. Euro-American colonists emigrated to the mainland colonies in family groups to establish permanent homes in the new land. They came in enough numbers, Professor Jordan writes, "to create a new culture with a self-evident validity of its own, complete with the adjustments necessary to absorb non-English Europeans." The success of their experiment in transplanting and modifying English culture encouraged in the colonists a determination to preserve their integrity and identity as a distinct people, and the large degree of self-government they exercised allowed them to translate their attitudes and prejudices into both law and practice. Euro-Americans were determined that the American people would be white, not black or red, and they firmly resisted any encroachment on their world by a people as unlike themselves as Afro-Americans.

Yet, by the end of the seventeenth century, large numbers of blacks were being brought into the English mainland colonies in response to the need for agricultural labor. From the beginning, however, blacks were distinctly a minority group, in numbers and in political and social influence. Racial slavery provided the mechanism of control and of insuring the integrity of white society. Moreover, slavery provided the only clear-cut definition of the black man's social status. In Euro-America the black man who was not a slave was an anomaly. Free blacks filled no imperative societal need; whites were numerous enough to meet the demand for essentially all nonplantation labor and to defend the country in time of crisis. In short, free blacks in Euro-America were generally unable to perform functions that could modify the narrow view of their capabilities which predominated among whites. Whites tended to lump all blacks together, believing that free blacks, who could never be incorporated fully into white society, naturally identified with black slaves. Hence, race came to be inseparably linked with slavery and blacks were considered natural slaves. Because they operated outside the major mechanism of racial control, free blacks were considered a potential threat to the system of slavery and to the American mission itself.

The institution of slavery in the United States was also shaped by another previously mentioned development, which was, in the words of historian Carl Degler, "unique in the world history of slavery." Early in the colonial period, perhaps by the late seventeenth century, the slave birth rate began to exceed the death rate and the slave population began to increase naturally. North American slavery became the only system of slavery in history to expand significantly by natural reproduction instead of by dependence on an external slave supply. The large-scale importation of slaves into the United States had declined considerably by 1800, and it ceased in 1808 with the official closing of the slave trade. Prior to that date, between 376,000 and 500,000 slaves were imported into this country; the number of slaves illegally imported after 1808 is variously put at between 54,000 and 270,000. In any event, the annual increase in slaves, averaging 20,000 in the 1790s and 70,000 in the 1840s, far exceeded average annual slave immigration. As a result of this demographic phenomenon, a very small percentage of the total emigration from Africa produced by 1860 the North American slave population of nearly four million, the largest slave population in the New World.

Slavery in the United States was a homegrown, peculiarly American institution. The peak of slave importation had come in the middle of the eighteenth century, so that by 1800 a large majority of slaves were American born. Because their numbers were not systematically augmented by large-scale immigration from Africa, North American slaves did not maintain the intimate contact with Africa that was characteristic, for example, of Brazilian slaves. Hence, Afro-Americans in the United States shed their African culture, at least the external aspects, more quickly and thoroughly than their Latin American counterparts, and African survivals were less apparent and numerous in the United States than in other parts of the New World.

Afro-American ties with Africa remained so tenuous that until the 1850s free blacks in the United States expressed little interest in returning to Africa, and repatriation schemes generally met with an unfavorable response from blacks, free or slave.[1]

It is also significant that slavery in the United States developed under relatively stable political, economic, and social circumstances. A large slave population had been present since the middle of the eighteenth century, with a large proportion of the slaves concentrated in the South. The fact that slavery was largely a self-contained system that expanded through natural increase kept slave importation and the introduction of new cultural elements low. Moreover, the nearly equal proportion of men and women in slavery and white dependence on the natural increase of slaves promoted a family and social order that facilitated the passage of cultural heritage from generation to generation. And throughout the period of bondage, a well-defined system of race relations paved the way for intimate but carefully limited black contact with white culture. Finally, nearly all blacks, whether slave or free, and regardless of their diverse African backgrounds and circumstances in life, were lumped together by whites and experienced discrimination and subordination at their hands. The peculiar historical circumstances under which slavery developed encouraged a unique pattern of cultural exchange in the United States. The result was the creation of a new Afro-American way of life that borrowed, but differed, from both African and Euro-American culture. The development of this black slave culture is the topic of Chapter 6. It is sufficient to note here that the institutional development of slavery in the United States actually encouraged the fashioning of a distinct and viable Afro-American subculture with its own life-styles and values.

Chapter 4 explores the obscure origins of racial slavery in the seventeenth century and traces its development down to the key year of 1800. According to Winthrop Jordan, the foremost expert on North American slavery in its early years, the system had shared in the "overt brutality" that was a common feature of American life in the seventeenth and eighteenth centuries. Slaves generally lived and worked under atrocious conditions, and they died at a considerably higher rate than whites, especially in fever-wracked areas such as the rice lowlands of South Carolina. Slaves not uncommonly bore branding marks and whip scars on their bodies, and occasionally they suffered degrading punishment, including castration, disfugurement, or other forms of sadistic atrocity. They received little medical attention, the coarsest food and rudest quarters, and scant opportunity to establish viable relations, familial or fraternal, with other slaves. In short, slavery in the seventeenth and early eighteenth centuries was particularly brutalizing.

The two decades on either side of 1800 were critical ones in the history of North American slavery. They constitute, in effect, a watershed period. As we have seen in the preceding pages (see Chapter 4, pp. 120-128) slavery had come under strong attack in both the North and South in the Revolutionary era. Antislavery writers were sharply critical of the treatment of slaves, and the general humanitarianism of the period operated to improve their condition. Prior to 1795 many states liberalized their slave codes, expanding the recognized rights of slaves and prohibiting the most flagrant maltreatment. The revised codes contained stronger prohibitions against the murder of slaves and outlawed brutal punishments. Northern states prohibited the sale of slaves outside the state or required special licenses for selling slaves to persons in southern states. Many states authorized jury trials for slaves in capital cases, and the states of the North and upper South provided stringent penalties for kidnapping free blacks.

Moreover, many slaveholders, motivated by economic interests as well as the dictates of natural rights philosophy and humanitarianism, began to provide more humane treatment for their slaves in the late eighteenth century. Apparently the punishment of slaves became less severe and the disruption of slave families less arbitrary. There is evidence that in Virginia planters began to provide slaves with better food and housing, to use the whip less often, and to curtail, if possible, the disruption of slave families. Historian Eugene Genovese concludes that the liberalization of slavery carried over into the nineteenth century and argues that the standards and conditions of life improved steadily for the generality of slaves in the years from 1800 to 1860.

The relative amelioration of slavery did not, of course, make the slave's lot an enviable one. The slave codes were enforced with varying degrees of effectiveness, and not all masters were swayed by humanitarian impulses. But slaves did benefit when the standards of slave treatment sanctioned by society underwent important change in the direction of improvement. Significantly, the change was a permanent one; even when the structure of race relations was hardened after 1800, prohibitions against exceptionally cruel punishments remained on the statute books, and the new standards of treatment retained the support of most planters.

In the first decade of the 1800s, however, the mechanisms of racial control were tightened by legislative action throughout the South. As occasion demanded, the structure of slavery was remolded, hardened, and polished in subsequent years until slavery became the familiar "peculiar institution" of the 1840s and 1850s. The hardening of the institution after 1800 did not involve the treatment of slaves as much as it involved their control. Outbreaks of slave violence at the turn of the century alarmed whites and prompted in them the determination to keep the slaves under firmer control. The growing profitability of slavery and slave-raising, increasing distress over antislavery agitation, mounting concern over the growing numbers of free blacks, and especially fear of slave violence prompted whites to relegate blacks, slave and free, into what Professor Jordan calls "an ever-shrinking corner of the American community."

The hardening process took various forms in the different slave states. South Carolina, which was most firmly committed to slavery, responded directly and vigorously to the challenges to the institution. The state assembly passed laws strictly regulating black gatherings, tightening up patrol procedures, narrowing the conditions under which slaves could be manumitted, and restricting entry of blacks into the state. Both South Carolina and Georgia passed acts asserting that a person who aided a slave revolt was guilty of treason. Virginia's response was less direct and more hesitant, and it was directed more at free blacks than at slaves. But Virginia, Maryland, Georgia, and North Carolina also strengthened the system of racial control, curbing nighttime religious meetings, providing severe penalties for arson, and regulating the conditions under which slaves could be hired out to work. More significantly, newly-adopted laws made the manumission of slaves more difficult throughout the slave states. Winthrop Jordan argues that the adoption of such legislation in Virginia in 1806 "was the key step in the key state and more than any other event marked the reversal of the tide which had set in strongly at the Revolution." There was now a sense of permanence about the South's "peculiar institution," particularly in those areas where its economic viability was strongest.

In the early decades of the nineteenth century, as slavery was gradually being hardened into its classic antebellum form, it was also undergoing a major geographical expansion. Cotton was in steadily increasing demand in British textile mills, and Eli Whitney's improved cotton gin provided the impetus for an enormous expansion in the production of cotton. In the early 1790s tobacco, rice, and long-staple cotton had formed the basis for a prospering staple agriculture in the lower South, which had helped to keep the demand for slaves high. Nevertheless, the cotton gin was a major technological advance that revolutionized the southern economy and sped the opening of the virgin land of the southwest, thus giving renewed importance to plantation slavery.

As the demand for cotton increased, slaveholders flocked into the undeveloped regions of the South and their slaves went with them. Slave population increased steadily from

1790 to 1860 as the center of slave population underwent a progressive shift from the Atlantic seaboard states to the lower South and the southwest. In 1790 Virginia had by far the highest proportion of the 700,000 slaves in the United States. By 1830, the slave population had grown to over two million, nearly one third of whom lived in the new states of the lower South. In 1860 slaves numbered nearly four million. Although Virginia's slave population of 548,000 was still the largest of any state, the cotton states of the lower South now had over 50% of the slave population. The geographical center of slave population had shifted to northwestern Georgia, hundreds of miles to the southwest of its 1790 position in Virginia.

By 1845, the dynamics of slavery expansion had produced a flourishing empire of slavery stretching from Delaware southward and westward to Texas. The 15 slave states were bound to the institution by strong economic ties. The states of the lower South demanded slave labor for the development of new cotton lands. The states of the upper South, where the post-Revolutionary economic depression and surplus of slaves had helped spawn a serious questioning of the slave system, could now retain the institution and reap the profits of supplying, on a permanent basis, the slave markets of the lower South. After 1810, each state in the empire of slavery was firmly committed to the perpetuation of the institution.

Although white Southerners in the late antebellum period would defend the concept of slavery as a positive good, their commitment was actually to an institution, a complex institution that regulated economic activities, governed interpersonal relationships, provided essential definitions, and was so thoroughly interwoven into the cultural fabric of the region that they could not conceive of functioning without it. The form and dimensions of this institution had been shaped and defined, of course, not only by law and formal regulation, but also by actual practice and accepted custom. The organic development of slavery since its origins in the seventeenth century had been sporadic and uneven. At times, when the commitment of white

Americans to slavery sagged, the institutional supports of the system were weakened. At other times, such as the period after 1810, conditions favored the strengthening of the institution through the addition, refinement, and systemization of law, judicial decision, practice, and custom.

By the late antebellum period American slavery had become an established, well-systematized institution. A large and growing body of law was being incorporated into the slave codes of states, cities, and local governing bodies, and over the years an increasing number of judicial decisions operated to delineate more precisely the legal dimensions of the institution. At the same time slaveholders consciously sought to bring greater system and order to slave management, primarily through the publication of manuals on the subject and through letters and essays in such journals as *DeBow's Review*, the *Southern Cultivator*, the *Southern Planter*, and the *Farmers' Register*. These publications were widely circulated throughout the South and influenced the thinking of many planters in matters relating to the care and control of slaves. Operating on still another level to systematize slavery was the large accretion of customs, traditions, and folkways involving the peculiar institution. The most prominent students of slavery agree that in the 1830s, 1840s, and 1850s slavery in the United States was becoming a more thoroughly organized and highly formalized system that increasingly regimented the lives of slaves.[2]

As was the case elsewhere in the New World, a special body of law was developed in the United States to apply to the slaves. Most of the laws and regulations were formulated by state, city, or local governments, but there were also legal and constitutional provisions at the federal level dealing with slavery. We have already pointed out (Chapter 4, pp. 127-128) that chattel slavery was written into the fundamental law of the land, the Constitution itself. In the early nineteenth century Congress passed legislation outlawing the foreign slave trade and implicitly sanctioning the domestic trade in slaves. The first fugitive slave law, passed in 1793, implemented the constitutional clause requiring states to aid owners in recovering runaway slaves. More stringent legislation dealing with fugitive slaves was enacted as part of the famous Compromise of 1850. The new law placed the power of the federal government solidly behind slaveholders seeking to recover runaway slaves; the claimant had only to present an affidavit to prove ownership. Alleged fugitives were denied any semblance of due process, and officers or citizens aiding runaways, interfering with their recovery, or failing to carry out specified duties were subject to heavy fines, imprisonment, or civil damages.[3]

Every slave state had a body of laws and regulations devoted to the full definition of the slave's status in society. As was the case with constitutional and legal statutes in general, the newer states of the South tended to borrow heavily from the codes of the older states. For this reason, and because slavery necessitated certain basic regulatory provisions, there was a striking uniformity in the slave codes of the southern states. The fundamental provision of the codes, as we have already noted, defined slaves as conveyable property and gave slaveholders perpetual rights of ownership over the persons and labor of the slaves and their descendants. In most states slaves were defined as chattels personal and were denied the fundamental civil rights. Slaves could not legally own property, make contracts, or hold any sort of public office. Nor did the law recognize slave marriages, as a Virginia court noted when it ruled a slave father "incapable of contracting matrimony . . . ." "A slave has never," a Maryland official observed, "maintained an action against the violator of his bed." Slaves were also unable to testify in court against a white person. "A slave is in absolute bondage," an Alabama jurist argued, "he has no civil right, and can hold no property, except at the will and pleasure of his master."

Another central feature of the slave codes was the set of regulations providing for the routine discipline of slaves. In order that masters could be assured of the maximum use of slave labor and services, the principle that slaves must submit to the authority and control of the owner and his representa-

tives was firmly fixed in law. The slave also owed un-
bounded respect and complete obedience to his master's
family. Numerous provisions gave the master wide-ranging rights of police and discipline. In matters not involving criminal conduct, the slaveholder was generally em-
powered to act as judge, jury, and enforcer. A North Carolina judge wrote, "The power of the master must be absolute to render the submission of the slave perfect . . . .
[This proposition] is inherent in the relation of master
and slave." Thus, the master was legally justified in whipping or otherwise punishing his slaves, although by the
late antebellum period brutal and cruel treatment was
prohibited by statute law. Nevertheless, if a slave died
while receiving "moderate correction" or in resisting punishment, the slaveholder was not legally accountable.

The slave codes also contained elaborate regulations to
protect the white community against whatever dangers the
slave population might present. These provisions were the
direct embodiment of the doctrine of white supremacy.
Slaves were required to be respectful to all whites. In
South Carolina any white could legally seize and adminis-
ter moderate correction to a slave not carrying a pass and
refusing to "submit to examination." Slave patrols operated in all the southern states to forestall slave violence, to
prevent escapes, and to apprehend violators of the slave
codes; in general, the patrols served as enforcement agen-
cies in the system of slave control. There was greater necessity for the patrols in localities with high concentrations
of black population and they were usually more effective
in such areas, but they were organized throughout the
South. The operation of the patrols and the overall commitment of southern whites to total control over the activities of slaves turned the South into what historian Gilbert Osofsky has termed a vast "prison house," where "all
white men, solely because of their skin color, were prison
keepers." Nowhere else in the New World, suggests historian David B. Davis, were slaves so "sharply differentiated
from the remainder of society."

To prevent slaves from organizing, acquiring useful but

dangerous knowledge, or gaining a sense of independence, the slave codes greatly restricted slave movement and contacts. The codes prohibited slaves from leaving the plantation without authorization and from visiting or entertaining whites or free blacks. In most southern states, laws enjoined slaves from hiring themselves out, engaging in their own work, or finding their own living quarters. Slaves could not legally gamble, possess firearms, liquor, or incendiary literature, practice medicine, assemble in the absence of a white person, or preach, except under supervision. In several states, a slave was not allowed to beat a drum or blow a horn. All of the slave states prohibited anyone from teaching slaves to read or write and from giving them books or printed matter. These prohibitions were of major significance in the system of slave control, as Professor Osofsky has so pointedly emphasized: "Through the ages, in the most widely divergent cultures, the right to proscribe letters or command a man's name is understood as the power to subordinate—the 'word' has quasi-magical, mystical connotations. The right to control it is the power to order reality, to subjugate man himself." Slave codes at the town and county levels supplemented the state codes and regulated slave activity in the locality in considerable detail. They set time limits during which slaves could be present in towns or villages, specified the types of persons they were allowed to visit, and spelled out the conditions under which they could carry on various activities.

Slaves and free blacks were subject to a more severe criminal code than whites were. Acts that were felonies when committed by blacks were only misdemeanors if the offenders were white. Moreover, penalties were considerably heavier for blacks than for whites committing the same crime. Blacks could receive capital punishment for rape of a white woman, murder, insurrection, robbery, and arson; attempted rape, murder, or insurrection, or simply striking a white person could also bring the death penalty. The regular courts, special slave tribunals, and juries made up of slaveholders tried blacks accused of offenses. After the 1780s there was a trend to provide slaves with a fairer judicial process. In the nineteenth century slaves were sometimes given the protection of the common law, and most states provided for jury trial in capital cases. There was some reform, but as historian David B. Davis has noted, the southern states "stood firm in refusing to place in the bondsman's hands the full power of the law," and as long as slaveholders composed courts and juries slaves could hardly expect evenhanded justice.

It is highly significant that southern lawmakers and jurists considered the regulation of free blacks essential to slave control and discipline. As indicated above, whites saw free blacks as anomalies, persons who were out of their proper place in the social order. As natural allies of the slaves, they might be expected to assist in, or even to instigate, slave flights to freedom or slave insurrections. Southerners received reinforcement of their fears in 1830 when Bostonian David Walker, a free black formerly from North Carolina, published his *Appeal* to the slaves to use any means necessary to achieve their freedom (see Chapter 7). Subsequently, the lives of free blacks in southern states were more thoroughly regulated. Free blacks were generally denied most civil rights other than those of contract and property, and their freedom to leave and enter states was severely restricted. The ultimate intent of southern lawmakers was to rid their states of free blacks altogether. Arkansas attempted in 1859 to force the state's free blacks to leave, and most southern states adopted legislation in the 1850s providing for the sale or voluntary return of free blacks into slavery.

A concurrent development was the pronounced trend in southern law to discourage the freeing of slaves by any means. Constitutional provisions in most states prohibited general emancipation without the owners' consent, and after 1800 most states from Virginia southward severely restricted private manumission by masters. The movement against manumission was strongest in the Deep South, but even in Virginia and North Carolina laws were passed requiring manumitted slaves to leave the state within specified time limits. By 1831 Tennessee required that eman-

cipated slaves leave the state immediately; Louisiana allowed 30 days. With the exception of Louisiana, all the
states of the Deep South had very early adopted general
prohibitions against private manumission within the state,
and by 1860 five of them had totally outlawed emanicpation
by last will and testament. If a living owner desired to
free his slaves, means were still available to him, but legislation greatly restricted the most common method of manumission, by will or deed. Law and an unfavorable public
opinion made the manumission of slaves much more difficult and much less common in North America than in
the other slave societies in the New World.

On the surface, it would appear that the laws governing
slavery and defining the status of slaves indeed delineated
a rigid, closed system of slavery that absolutely denied the
moral personality of the slave. In actuality the effect of
the laws was modified not only by the degree to which
they were observed by slave and master alike, but also by
the way in which they were interpreted by judges and
courts throughout the South. The institution of slavery
in the antebellum South never functioned perfectly. Instead, it was a system shot through with tensions, conflicts,
and compromises spinning off from the central contradiction of slavery: How can a man be both a person and a
"thing"? The logic of slavery demanded the full development of the conception of the slave as private property
that need not be extended basic human rights or consideration. But this conception flew in the face of the reality
that the slave was a man with a human will and moral
consciousness.

The insistence with which black slaves over a period of
200 years demonstrated their humanness significantly influenced the shape that the institution of slavery took in
North America. The black slave was human, and many
events and activities of daily life shared by blacks and
whites reinforced that fact in the minds of whites. Blacks
walked, talked, ate, propagated, played, sang, laughed, and
cried like other human beings. They sickened and died as
whites did; they loved, sacrificed, and suffered as other

people did; they struggled and fought against the adversi-
ties of life as men always have; they also lied, cheated,
stole, burned, and killed like other men. These things
were not lost on the whites of the South; white Southerners knew that slaves were human. Indeed, it was the humanness of slave activity in all its diversity that led to such
elaborate institutional development in the late antebellum
period, particularly the attempts to regulate more thoroughly the daily lives of the slaves. Elaborate measures of control were necessary, abolitionist Theodore Dwight Weld observed, because the slave was "an intelligent being." "Who-
ever heard," Weld questioned, "of cows or sheep being deliberately tied up and lacerated till they died?" Ultimately,
it was white awareness of the slaves' humanity that frustrated
the logical development of chattel slavery and produced
the ambiguities and compromises that characterized the
institution.

The central contradiction inherent in slavery was reflected not only in the words and actions of the small number
of well-meaning, conscience-ridden slaveholders who sought
to manumit their slaves, but in the operation of the law
itself. The decided tendency of statute law was to protect
the property of slaveholders and the security of white society through emphasis on the property status of slaves.
However, even statute law recognized slaves as rational
human beings in holding them accountable for committing
crimes. Moreover, judicial interpretation often went much
further in recognizing the basic humanity of slaves. The
ruling of a Tennessee court in the late antebellum period
included the following statement by the presiding judge:

A slave is not in the condition of a horse or an ox. His liberty is
restrained, it is true, and his owner controls his actions and claims
his services. But he is made after the image of the Creator. He has
mental capacities, and an immortal principle in his nature that constitutes him equal to his owner but for the accidental position in
which fortune has placed him. The owner has acquired conventional
rights to him, but the laws under which he is held as a slave have
not and cannot extinguish his high-born nature nor deprive him of
many rights which are inherent in man.

Among the rights of slaves recognized in statute law and by the courts were the rights to life itself, and to humane treatment and care by masters.[4] Occasionally courts convicted and punished masters, overseers, or other whites for negligence, cruel treatment, or murder of slaves. The courts in numerous instances recognized that slaves could possess personal property. In 1842 a South Carolina Judge cited legislation, court precedent, and "the usage of our people" to support his conclusion *"that a slave may acquire and hold in possession personal property . . . ."* (Legally, however, such property belonged to the owner of the slave.) Undoubtedly the most important recognition of slave rights by the courts involved the right to freedom acquired through manumission or some other lawful means. American courts frequently upheld the ability of slaves to make contracts for the purchase of freedom, and thousands of slaves purchased their freedom under such contracts. Courts sometimes ruled that a slave had become a free man as a result of some action of the slaveholder, and some jurists went to considerable lengths to protect the validity of testamentary manumissions. Although statutory law placed more and more restrictions on private manumission, Professor Davis maintains that "a judicial bias in favor of freedom" lingered throughout the antebellum period.

Now that we have considered the legal foundations of the institution, we should examine the organization of slavery in its daily setting in the rural areas of the South. The vast majority of slaves lived in rural areas and worked on staple-producing plantations and farms. Of the 2,800,000 rural slaves in 1850, approximately 1,800,000 lived and worked on cotton plantations; most of the remainder labored on tobacco, rice, and sugarcane farms. Although most slaves in the South were farm laborers, some were occupied in a wide range of other tasks. Some were skilled artisans, mechanics, or house servants; some worked in lumbering, mining, or construction; others were employed as industrial workers in the cotton, turpentine, iron, and tobacco factories of the South; still others were dock workers, deck hands on river boats, or cowboys on the Texas frontier.

Almost all the slaves were owned by a relatively small proportion—approximately ¼—of the white families in the South; of these families nearly 50% possessed fewer than five slaves. However, the concentration of large numbers of slaves on large plantations sharply raised the median of the number of slaves per slave-worked farm unit. Over 50% of the slaves worked on plantations with 20 or more slaves; approximately ¼ resided on farm units with 50 or more slaves, while only ¼ worked units with 10 slaves or less.

The range of occupations, the size of the farm units, and the geographical location of plantations made for a significant degree of institutional variation. The organization and operation of slavery differed with time, place, and circumstance. On smaller plantations and farms, slaves often worked in the fields alongside the owner, and the master, his sons, or a slave foreman supervised the work rather than an overseer. Ex-slave Rueben Saunders claimed that in Georgia the treatment of slaves "seemed to depend on the number a man had. If few, they got on well, if many, they fared worse." At present, however, we lack historical studies to evaluate Saunders' individual assessment. Moreover, the common assumption that slave treatment in the Deep South was generally harsher than in the border states has not been supported by the work of the historians of slavery in the latter states.[5]   Hence, despite variations in the organization of slavery, there was apparently great similarity in the crucial aspects of the system. Professor David B. Davis maintains that "within the encircling limits and modifications, which varied from region to region [and under differing circumstances], the hard core of slavery was much the same."

Ultimately, of course, the slaveholder was the key to the effective operation of the slavery system. By law and long-established practice the master had practically absolute power over his slaves, and it was only through the exercise of his authority that slavery could achieve its purpose. Because his chattels were "a troublesome property" who

did not take readily to bondage, the successful master had
to establish order, control, and discipline throughout his
domain. Not every master governed in the same way.
Most worked out their own rules and techniques to manage
the slaves who came under their province. As Kenneth
Stampp implies, the effective master had to be a keen student of human psychology adept at dealing with the individual personalities of his slaves.

On the plantations two basic methods were used in employing the bulk of the slave agricultural work force. In
the common "gang" or "time" system, slaves worked in
groups for a given time, usually daybreak to dusk, with
one half to two hours off for the noon meal. Work in the
gang was steady, routine, repetitious, and hard. Supervision was close and constant, with slaves beginning and ending work and taking any break on command only. On the
rice plantations, where supervisory personnel were reluctant
to work under acutely hazardous conditions, slaves worked
under the "task" or "piece" system, in which each slave
had an assigned amount of work to complete daily. He
could work at his own pace with little supervision and
when his task was complete, his time was his own. Theoretically, this system provided greater incentives for slaves
to work industriously, but in actual practice the tasks were
large, usually requiring the typical sunup-to-sundown routine to complete. The evidence suggests that under both
systems slaves were frequently overworked, even by the
standards of the day.

Each master determined his own method of exercising
discipline and control. Generally, rather elaborate rules
and regulations governed routine labor and all other aspects
of slave life. All slave activity was restricted as the master
saw fit, to the degree that supervision permitted. Regulation extended even into the slave quarters; slaves were told
when to retire at night and when to get up in the morning. The maintenance of discipline and control on the plantation commonly involved the threat of pain or deprivation
of certain privileges. The whip was invariably present, and
slaves lived and worked under its threat. The evidence is

overwhelming that the whip was used with great frequency. Ex-slave Soloman Northup remarked that on one of the plantations on which he labored, the lash was "flying from morning until night." Very few slaves went through life without feeling the sting of the whip at one time or another. A system of rewards was also used at times to motivate the slaves. Free time, extra rations, clothing, liquor, holiday festivities, and special privileges were utilized to encourage hard work and obedience.

The management and supervision of slaves might be accomplished by the owner himself or through a command system, depending primarily on the number of slaves held. Owners of less than 10 slaves usually handled matters with little or no assistance. Masters on farms units of 10 to 30 slaves most often lived on and operated their plantations without hired overseers. These masters were often assisted by their sons or by slave foremen. The large planters who owned 30 slaves or more almost always used white overseers, employed on a year-to-year basis. In fact, in 1860 the number of overseers was nearly equal to the number of plantation units with 30 or more slaves. The overseers generally appointed a number of slave drivers to help maintain discipline and order. Often a head driver was chosen to serve as a suboverseer.

Slaves lived under widely differing circumstances, but it would be accurate to say that the overwhelming majority existed at a basic subsistence level. The slave quarters were generally small, cramped, crude, and dirty cabins, huts, or shacks arranged in rows some distance from the plantation house. The buildings were usually constructed of logs or rough clapboard, although there were more substantial frame, brick, or adobe dwellings. Frequently there were no floors or windows, and the quarters were sometimes drafty and leaky. The size of the cabins varied from one to four rooms, and some had usable lofts. Furnishings were extremely sparse and of the poorest quality, although cast-off furniture from the owner's home occasionally went to the quarters. One fugitive slave claimed that he slept on the "soft side of a board." Kitchens and eating utensils were also in short supply. The quarters were generally quite crowded, with entire families frequently living in a one-room hut or sharing one room of a larger cabin.

Slave clothing, especially that of the field laborers, was barely adequate to cover the slave's nakedness and to protect him in the mildest weather. The typical annual clothing allowance was a woolen jacket, two heavy shirts, and two pairs of woolen pants for the winter, and two cotton shirts and two pairs of trousers for the summer. Each slave received a pair of crude, generally ill-fitting shoes each year. The clothing and shoes were of the poorest quality and often were in tatters before the end of each season. Despite the relative mildness of southern winters, slaves were often unable to keep warm and dry when the weather was inclement or particularly cold.

Slaves normally existed on the proverbial "hog and hominy" diet. The typical weekly allowance was a peck of cornmeal and three to four pounds of pickled pork or fatback. A pint of salt was the usual monthly allowance.[6] In the winter sweet potatoes were sometimes substituted for the meal, and occasionally fresh pork, mutton, or beef was issued in place of the salted or pickled pork. Molasses was commonly issued and fresh vegetables were sometimes added to the diet. Although ex-slaves complained that they frequently did not have enough to eat, the slave diet was generally adequate in quantity to sustain life if not health. However, the food was of the lowest quality. Sometimes it was spoiled or had been partially eaten by mice, rats, or insects. At best the slave diet was monotonous and unappetizing.

Even when the slave got enough to eat, he often did not receive adequate nourishment. The typical slave fare provided a surfeit of starch and fat, but its protein content was sometimes seriously low. Even the occasional consumption of vegetables did not furnish the amino acids necessary to a balanced diet. Hence, some slaves lived in a state of chronic malnutrition, and considerable numbers suffered from zerothalmia, beriberi, pellagra, and scurvy as a result of vitamin deficiency. The slave diet usually produced the appearance of good health, but it often failed to provide stamina for sustained labor in the fields and adequate resistance to infectious disease.

It is extremely difficult to measure the relative severity or moderation of a system of slavery and to judge the general condition of slaves under that system. In the United States, a number of important variables modified the system and influenced the quality of slave life. Most important was the character and disposition of the slaveholder. In the situation in which the master lived on the plantation and played an active role in slave management, humanity and the profit motive were constantly struggling against one another in the mind of the planter, and humanity had its victories on occasion.[7] When the overseer was the key figure in slave management, the situation was different. The overseer, whose annual salary was generally based on productivity, was in a purely economic relationship to slavery. This operated against anything resembling coddling of the slave. Fugitive slave Jacob Stroyer noted that where overseers had "full sway," the slaves were generally treated "more cruelly."

Other variables also influenced the condition of slave existence. The distance of the farm unit from towns, cities, or well-settled areas was significant, because social pressure could and did temper the behavior of slaveholders. The status of the slave himself within the social hierarchy of slaves was of immediate importance, since domestics and artisans, in that order, generally fared better than the mass of field slaves. Another factor was the master's knowledge of such subjects as dietitics, hygiene, and cause and treatment of disease. The quality of slave housing, food, and clothing was influenced by economic considerations, but also by the prevalent belief of the slaveholding class that slaves had greater resistance to temperature variants and disease than whites did. For both economic and humanitarian reasons, owners were greatly concerned with slave health, but their best intentions were often tempered by ignorance. Doctors and masters themselves often treated slaves with calomel, castor oil, emetics, bleedings, sweattings, and opium. But slave mortality remained much higher than that of whites, especially in infancy and old age. The death rate was particularly high in the marshy, fever-ridden swamps and low-lying tidewater rice areas, but slaveholders continued to employ slaves in these regions.

Because of the decline in the external supply of slaves after 1807, slaveholders in the United States were necessarily greatly concerned not only with slave health but slave reproduction. Hence masters encouraged or even demanded the pairing of slave men and women, in the accurate expectation that such a practice would provide a source of new slaves. Although slaves were generally encouraged to live in what might roughly be called single-family units, most masters did little to discourage promiscuity or to preserve the sanctity and unity of the slave family. Slaveholder Edmund Ruffin observed that North American slaves generally had "every inducement and facility to increase their numbers with all possible rapidity without any opposing check, either prudential, moral, or physical." It should be noted, however, that despite the slaveholders' monetary interest in slave offspring and frequent references to "breeding wenches," examples of the deliberate and systematic breeding of slaves in the antebellum South are extremely rare.[8] On the other hand, many masters rewarded fecundity and some used practically every means except those used on stock farms to encourage the production of slave children.

In a purely physical sense, slaves probably received better treatment in the United States than anywhere else in the New World. Slaves in other areas of the Americas felt the pinch of famine and disruption of war more often than their North American brothers, who lived in a land of general peace and plenty. Moreover, David B. Davis argues persuasively that Brazilian and West Indian planters, who routinely acquired fresh slaves from Africa, probably "were less sensitive than North Americans to the value of human life." In measuring the relative treatment of slaves in the United States, a number of scholars point to the success of North American slavery in reproducing itself. "Nothing

[else]," Eugene Genovese contends, "so clearly demonstrates the relatively good treatment (in the strictly material sense of the word) of the slaves and the paternalistic quality of the masters." "At the very best," Carl Degler agrees, "that fact offers testimony to a better standard of physical circumstances and care than a system of slavery that did not reproduce itself."

But however mild North American slavery was comparatively, it always retained that fixed, indivisible feature that could not be altered without demolishing the system itself. The tragedy of slavery, in Professor Davis' words, "lay not in its cruelty or economic exploitation, but in the underlying conception of man as a conveyable possession with no more autonomy of will and consciousness than a domestic animal." As a system based ultimately on force and coercion, slavery was in the profoundest sense a violent institution that operated to severely limit human development and fulfillment. Whites as well as blacks paid the price, for in debasing the black man, whites inevitably debased themselves. Ex-slave Austin Steward eloquently expressed the tragedy of slavery:

Everywhere that Slavery exists, it is nothing but *slavery* .... Whips and chains are everywhere necessary to degrade and brutalize the slave, in order to reduce him to that abject and humble state which Slavery requires. Nor is the effect much less disastrous on the man who holds supreme control over the soul and body of his fellow beings. Such unlimited power, in almost every instance transforms the man into a tyrant; the brother into a demon.

Slavery necessarily had a direct and intimate impact on the millions of slaves that bore its yoke, but the exact nature of that impact is not easy to determine. The response of slaves to life under slavery was extremely complex, as it involved their very personalities, their consciousness of themselves, of whites, and of the world itself, and the manner or style in which they were able to live. In Chapter 6 we will consider some necessary psychocultural adjustments that slaves made to the system of North American slavery, and their shaping effects on the Afro-American experience.

NOTES

[1] It should be pointed out, however, that despite the relative paucity of pure African cultural traits in the United States, the African heritage was of much greater significance in the Afro-American experience than scholars have generally believed. See above, Chapter 3, fns. 13 and 14, and below, pp. 171-178.

[2] However, there is some disagreement over the meaning of such institutional development as it pertained to the essential nature of the institution itself. Stanley Elkins, for example, argues that from the late 1600s the law developed in a way that removed any question of slave status, operating methodically to deprive the slave of "rights of personality" and to grant virtually "absolute power" to the master "over the slave's body." In Elkins' view, the profit motive operated to create "unmitigated slavery," a system "finely circumscribed and . . . cleanly self-contained." Any modifications of the system, whether legal or practical, and any achievement of independence by individual slaves were exceptional and did not challenge the system itself. David B. Davis, on the other hand, contends that ambiguities and contradictions persisted in North American slavery despite the systematization that occurred over the years. Various legalities, practices, and customs tended, he believes, to circumscribe and modify the institution much as they did slave systems elsewhere. Slavery in North America was still slavery, but in Davis' view it was no more rigid or total in nature than other modern systems of slavery. As more emphasis is being placed on the study of slave life and culture and on viewing slavery from the perspective of the slave himself, scholars are supporting the Davis interpretation more and more. As is evident later in this chapter and in Chapter 6, the authors of this vol-

ume emphatically reject Elkins' interpretation that slavery was essentially a "closed" system.

[3] Persons interfering with the enforcement of the act were liable to fines of $1000, prison terms of up to six months, and civil damages of $1000 for each slave whose escape they aided. For comment on the enforcement of the act, see pp. 248-249.

[4] This is not to say, however, that these rights were generally protected. The violators of even the most fundamental right of man, the right of life, often went unpunished when their victims were slaves.

[5] For comment on the state of historical study on the comparative treatment of slaves *within* the antebellum South, see historian Eugene D. Genovese's "Foreward" to the Louisiana State University reprint edition of U. B. Phillips' *American Negro Slavery*. The absence of historical studies supporting the assumption in question does not necessarily mean that there were no substantial differences in the treatment and lives of slaves in the two sections. Ex-slave William A. Hall recalled that a number of slaveholders who had taken their slaves from Tennessee to Mississippi treated them much more severely in the latter state: "No man would have thought there could have been such a difference in treatment, when the masters got where they could make money." Slaves almost universally feared and dreaded being sold "South" or "down the river," and not simply because it meant separation from their loved ones and friends and the only homes they knew. Fugitive slave Jacob Stroyer, for instance, noted that slaves considered Louisiana "a place of slaughter." It is the authors' contention that slaves generally had a realistic, down-to-earth outlook on the world they faced; hence, we would suggest that there is a central core of truth in the assumption that life was harder, rougher, more onerous, and more precarious in the Deep South than in the older states of the Upper South.

[6] The standard food allowances for slaves inspired the words for several stanzas of one of the best-known of black freedom songs:

No more peck of corn for me,
No more, no more;
No more peck of corn for me,
Many thousands gone.

No more pint of salt for me,
No more, no more;
No more pint of salt for me,
Many thousands gone.

[7] Obviously, slave treatment varied greatly according to the individual

differences of slave masters. Numerous fugitive slaves described
their masters as kind, humane, and indulgent; the judgment of former slave David West, however, was quite different: "The slaveholders so far as I know are generally mean people." Another ex-slave,
Austin Steward, denied emphatically that slaveholders were "respected for kindness to their slaves": "The more tyrannical a master is,
the more will he be favorably regarded by his neighboring planters . . . ." The testimony of Moncure D. Conway, the disillusioned
son of a Virginia slave owner, lends weight to Steward's claim:

> My observation leads me to believe that kindness to the slaves is
> rather the exception than the rule. And I . . . trace this fact to the
> necessities of the institution itself . . . . [I]f the slightest defiance or
> disobedience is passed over, there is danger that the general discipline
> of the estate may be impaired. So far from a man's interest in his
> slave as property being a guarantee against the laceration of that
> slave, such laceration may be, and frequently is, the only means of
> retaining him as property.

Former slave James W. C. Pennington agreed with Conway. Noting
that the delicate master-slave relationship might be "entangled at
any moment," like a "skein of silk," he commented bitterly: "Talk
not then about kind and christian masters. They are not masters of
the system. The system is master of them . . . ."
[8] But sexual exploitation of slave women by the master class was so
pervasive—as both slave and white sources clearly demonstrate—that
it is reasonable to speak of "unsystematic" breeding by the slaveholders. Former slave Austin Steward believed "that in three-fourths
of the colored race, there runs the blood of the white master,—the
breeder of his own chattels." The Southern slaveholder was motivated, Steward argued, not only by a desire "to gratify his lust" but
also by an ambition to "swell the enormity of his gains . . . ."

SUGGESTIONS FOR FURTHER READING

Many of the major works on slavery that have been recommended for use with previous chapters are important for the consideration of the institutional aspects of slavery. Winthrop Jordan's *White Over Black* is the most important source on the institutional development of slavery in the seventeenth and eighteenth centuries, and it offers suggestive insights on the maturation of the system in the nineteenth century. Two studies in comparative history, David B. Davis' *The Problem of Slavery in Western Culture* and Carl Degler's *Neither Black Nor White*, are particularly helpful because of the broad perspective from which the authors treat North American slavery. Useful for the same reason are Eugene D. Genovese's extended essay, "The American Slave Systems in World Perspective," in *The World the Slaveholders Made; Two Essays in Interpretation* (New York: Pantheon, 1969), and two essays by C. Vann Woodward, "Protestant Slavery in a Catholic World" and "Southern Slaves in the World of Thomas Malthus," in *American Counterpoint: Slavery and Racism in the North-South Dialogue* (Boston: Little, Brown, 1971). Carl Degler, Eugene Genovese, C. Vann Woodward, and Philip D. Curtin, in *The Atlantic Slave Trade: A Census* and in an article in Nathan I. Huggins, Martin Kilson, and Daniel M. Fox, eds., *Key Issues in the Afro-American Experience*, Vol. 1 (New York: Harcourt Brace Jovanovich, 1971), emphasize the exceptional demographic patterns that characterized and helped to shape North American slavery. In another useful essay in the collection cited immediately above, Herbert S. Klein deals with "Patterns of Settlement of the Afro-American Population in the New World." Stanley M. Elkins' *Slavery: A Problem in American Institutional and Intellectual*

Life (Chicago: University of Chicago Press, 1959) provides full treatment of the institutional development of slavery in the nineteenth century South, but his conclusion that slavery became a system of "total dependence and absolute control" should be weighed against the interpretations of scholars such as Davis, Genovese, and Degler. Henry Allen Bullock, "A Hidden Passage in the Slave Regime," in James C. Curtis and Lewis L. Gould, eds., *The Black Experience in America: Selected Essays* (Austin: University of Texas Press, 1970), also disagrees with Elkins. A capsule version of Elkins' views in an interesting format is contained in John A. Garraty, *Interpreting American History: Conversations with Historians* (New York: MacMillan, 1970), Part I.

Both of the classic works on slavery in the United States, Ulrich B. Phillips, *American Negro Slavery*, and Kenneth M. Stampp, *The Peculiar Institution. Slavery in the Ante-Bellum South*, contain a wealth of information on the slave codes, the legal aspects of slavery, the statistics of slave ownership, population, and distribution, slave management, and slave life and labor, as well as on many other topics relating to the organization of slavery in the antebellum South. Two of the standard texts in Afro-American history, John Hope Franklin, *From Slavery to Freedom: A History of Negro Americans* (New York: Knopf, 1947), and August Meier and Elliott Rudwick, *From Plantation to Ghetto* (New York: Hill and Wang, 1966), include excellent summary chapters on plantation slavery. Eugene D. Genovese, *The Political Economy of Slavery: Studies in the Economy and Society of the Slave South* (New York: Random House, 1967) contains much material on slave diet and slave illnesses, but it should be used with caution because Genovese himself now feels that he exaggerated slave health problems and the inadequacy of slave diet. Gilbert Osofsky's lengthy introduction to *Puttin' on Ole Massa: The Slave Narratives of Henry Bibb, William Wells Brown, and Solomon Northup* (New York: Harper and Row, 1969) is particularly useful for the insights it contains on the system of control in the antebellum South. A collection of readings well worth perusal in connection with this chapter is Allen Weinstein and Frank Otto Gatell, eds., *American Negro Slavery: A Modern Reader* (New York: Oxford University Press, 1973).

Of the contemporary accounts of slavery by white authors, the following contain valuable information and insights: Frederick Law Olmsted, *The Cotton Kingdom: A Traveller's Observations on Cotton and Slavery in the American Slave States* (London: Sampson Low, Son & Company, 1861); Theodore Dwight Weld, *American Slavery As It Is: Testimony of a Thousand Witnesses* (New York:

American Anti-Slavery Society, 1839); and M. D. Conway, *Testimonies Concerning Slavery* (London: Chapman and Hall, 1864). From the black perspective, the narratives of former slaves such as Solomon Northup, Austin Steward, and Jacob Stroyer contain material particularly pertinent to this chapter. Their accounts may be found in four excellent and recently published collections of slave narratives, including the Osofsky edition cited above. The others are *Five Slave Narratives; A Compendium* (New York: Arno Press, 1968); *Four Fugitive Slave Narratives* (Reading, Massachusetts: Addison-Wesley, 1969); and Arna Bontemps, ed., *Great Slave Narratives* (Boston: Beacon Press, 1969). An indispensable primary source is the five volume collection compiled by Helen H. Catterall entitled *Judicial Cases Concerning American Slavery and the Negro* (1926 edition reprinted New York: Octagon Books, 1968).

Chapter 6

PLANTATION SLAVERY II: Psychocultural Dynamics

Scholars can discuss the institutional aspects of slavery with considerable confidence. We know a great deal about the laws and regulations that governed the system and about the practices of slave management that prevailed in the cities and on the plantations, and we are learning more about the customs and traditions that influenced slave treatment and control. But the most informed treatments of institutional slavery tell little about the lives of slaves, in particular about such important matters as slave consciousness and self-expression, slave behavior, and slave personality. What was the impact of slavery on its subjects? How did slavery influence the character and personality development, mating and childbearing patterns, family structure, and overall cultural condition of slaves? This chapter seeks to investigate these questions, to explore, in other words, the psychocultural dynamics of slavery.

Scholars have universally agreed that slavery was of central importance in the Afro-American experience. The tendency in the past four decades has been to emphasize the long-range negative impact of that institution on black Americans. Since the 1930s students of contemporary race relations and black society, particularly in the fields of sociology and psychology, have used slavery to explain black deviation from white social norms. In the findings of these scholars, American slavery was such a totally oppressive system that it deeply scarred not only slaves but

Note. Footnotes for this chapter are located on pages 217-222.

their descendants. Slavery, they argue, undermined the
stability of the black family, emasculated the black male
and created a matriarchal society, and fostered feelings of
inferiority and self-hatred in blacks that produced serious
personality problems. In sum, slaves and their descendants,
denied participation in the dominant white culture and unable to develop their own culture, existed in a kind of cultural void, and by and large were unable to develop into
mature and well-adjusted persons.[1] This basically negative
view of Afro-American life and culture portrays the mass
of blacks as substandard and inferior members of the larger
society, due not to racial inheritance, but to the results of
slavery and oppression.

This interpretation of the impact of slavery appears reasonable and logical, partly because it reinforces in nonracial
terms the pejorative stereotypes of blacks held by most
white Americans. However, it is not solidly rooted historically. The scholars in question have not presented historical evidence giving insights into what it was like to be a
slave, evidence that might support their contention that
Afro-Americans were incapable of countering the total oppression of chattel slavery. Moreover, those who assume
that the slavery experience forced Afro-Americans into a
permanent groove in which they are still trapped have failed generally to consider the extent to which blacks helped
to shape their own destiny, both in slavery and in the years
since emancipation. The argument of this chapter that the
impact of slavery was by no means completely negative supports the position of the increasing number of scholars who
have come to maintain that the black historical experience
has been more affirmative and positive than was formerly
believed.

It is manifestly impossible for even the closest student
of black history and culture to comprehend fully what it
meant to be a slave in the American South. But if we are
to approach an understanding of the psychocultural dynamics of slavery, our investigation, while using the insights of
anthropology and sociology, must be essentially an historical inquiry. We cannot understand slavery and its impact

by observing contemporary black society or by relying on the use of psychological models such as that employed by Professor Elkins.[2]   An understanding of slavery and its effects can come only through a careful application of the historian's techniques of investigation and analysis. This does not mean that we should approach the study of slavery from a traditional viewpoint. On the contrary, we must make a persistent effort to view slavery from the perspective of the slave himself. It is imperative that the slave be seen as an active force in the history of slavery; hence, this chapter relies primarily on the historical sources left by slaves themselves—slave folklore, songs, religious traditions, and the varied records of slave responses to the "peculiar institution." As Eugene Genovese suggests, only if scholars maintain a studied openness to black culture and to the traditions and sensibilities of black people can we hope to sharpen our perception of the Afro-American experience. Even under these circumstances, our understanding of the psychocultural dynamics of slavery will remain imperfect.

We have seen above (Chapter 3, pp. 85-92) that in the culture contacts of Europeans and Africans in the New World, the dominant whites allowed only partial and incomplete acculturation to occur, resulting in the development of a new and unique Afro-American culture. In this chapter we will explore the nature and extent of culture contact and change in the American South. What were the dimensions of the distinctive subculture that emerged and to what extent did this subculture modify the impact of slavery on Afro-Americans? Our primary focus will be on the cultural aspects of antebellum black history, the ways and patterns of life of millions of black slaves instead of the selected activities or ideas of a few black leaders.

As noted previously, African culture was not applicable in the new circumstances in which enslaved Africans found themselves. Hence, if they were to survive, slaves had to make profound cultural adjustments. In contrast to the conclusions of folklorists, musicologists, and some anthropologists (see pp. 90-91), the consensus of most historians of slavery has been that the cultural adaptation required by the system of slavery in North America was so thorough that Africans lost essentially all their traditional culture. These scholars suggest that just as memories of Africa faded rapidly in the minds of black slaves, so, too, did African culture quickly die in their life patterns. Although scholars such as Melville J. Herskovits and John Hope Franklin have argued that African survivals in slavery were numerous and important, the common conclusion has been that slaves in North America, unlike their Latin American brothers, retained almost nothing of significance from African culture. According to historian Stanley Elkins, for instance, "few ethnic groups seem to have been so thoroughly and effectively detached from their prior cultural connections as was the case in the Negro's transit from Africa to North America." And historian Kenneth Stampp maintains "that by the antebellum period slaves everywhere in the South had lost most of their African culture." To such scholars, the cultural background of the North American slave is apparently irrelevant. Their implication is that slaves and slavery in the antebellum South, except for the genetic characteristics of those enslaved, would not have been essentially different if the slaves had been of Chinese or Malayan origin. In fact, historian Joel R. Williamson argues specifically that the Afro-American slave "saved little of Africa beyond his dark skin."

Under close scrutiny this view simply does not hold up. As we have seen in Chapter 1, culture is tenacious and persistent, and tends to maintain powerful continuity. One cannot shed his culture easily even when subjugated in an oppressive institution. Hence, the cultural heritage of the slaves was not only relevant, but highly significant in shaping the Afro-American experience. It did, indeed, matter in important ways that North American slaves had an African instead of a Chinese or some other cultural heritage.

Scholars in the past who have explored the question of the African impact on Afro-American life and culture—even a perceptive scholar such as Herskovits—have mistakenly sought to find that impact in behavioral patterns, social forms and institutions, or cultural objects that were specifically definable as African. This approach has caused them to overlook the process of cultural adjustment described in Chapter 3, by which the African heritage was adapted by Afro-Americans to meet the conditions they encountered in their new environment. African culture could not simply be transferred to the New World and planted in new soil. African institutions and forms, customs, and cultural patterns were inapplicable in the new environment, and African slaves were forbidden to take any material possessions with them. But Africa culture was not lost. Historian George P. Rawick argues cogently that the Afro-American slave could not lose or give up the essence of his culture because "he brought with him his past":

He brought with him the content of his mind, his memory; he recognized as socially significant that which he had been taught from childhood to see and comprehend as significant; he gestured, laughed, cried, and used his facial muscles in ways that he had learned as a child. He valued that which his previous life had taught him to value; he feared that which he had feared in Africa; his very motions were those of his people and he passed all of this on to his children.

As numerous scholars point out, Afro-Americans did retain in their life patterns a few cultural elements that were clearly African. But the influence of Africa on Afro-American life and culture was not limited to these specific retentions. Much more significant was what individual blacks retained of their African heritage in their innermost beings; retentions which were reflected in Afro-American thought patterns, beliefs, emotions, and mental attitudes and images. The most important Africanism by far was the continued use of African philosophical concepts by Afro-Americans, in their outlook on the world and life itself, and in the ways they thought, acted, and spoke in various life situations.

Afro-American religion, for example, while not African in institutional aspects, was profoundly influenced by the retention of African thought and outlook. As with Africans, religion permeated the lives of Afro-Americans to an extent that modern man has difficulty comprehending. Religion was a part of everyday life, and black slaves, like their African forebears, made no sharp distinction between the worldly and the sacred. Hence, the sacred songs of the slaves, the spirituals, were commonly sung not only during religious ceremonies but while the singers were rowing boats, milling grain, walking home from the fields, or relaxing and socializing in the quarters. Just as African gods and spirits were an immediate and intimate part of the world of man, so, too, were God and the other chief figures in Afro-American religion. Thus, in their spirituals blacks spoke on extraordinarily intimate and personal terms with God, and with Jesus, Mary, and the mythic Old Testament heroes. In numerous songs Afro-Americans casually indicated how, with redemption, they would walk with, talk with, and live with God and Jesus. The extent of the intimacy they assumed is well expressed in the spiritual "Hold the Wind:"

> When I get to heaven, gwine be at ease,
> Me and my God gonna do as we please.
> Gonna chatter with the Father, argue with the Son,
> Tell um 'bout the world I just come from.

In its underlying purposes and approaches, Afro-American religion was essentially an adaptation of traditional African religion to meet the needs of African descendants in the New World. Culture historian Lawrence W. Levine contends that Afro-Americans, denied meaningful participation in the temporal world of the slaveholders, fashioned their own special world, incorporating African conceptions of existence and being and fusing the secular and spiritual sides of life:

They extended the boundaries of their restrictive universe backward until it fused with the world of the Old Testament, and upward until it became one with the world beyond. The spirituals are the record of a people who found the status, the harmony, the values, the order they needed to survive by internally creating an expanded universe, by literally willing themselves reborn.

The self-generated world of the slaves, reflected in their

religious music, was characterized by a sense of affirmation and ultimate justice, and it held out to every man the certain prospect of spiritual rebirth within his lifetime. In Afro-American religion past time and future time were telescoped into the present. Blacks sang of events of the distant past, such as the crucifixion or the battle of Jericho, as if they themselves had been present and the events had just occurred. Likewise, salvation was always seen as imminent and the Kingdom of Heaven was described as vividly as if it were right around the corner. Salvation, for all practical purposes, was not in the future, but in the present-to-come. Afro-American religion, like its traditional African counterpart, was strongly oriented to the present, or, in other words, to the here and now. Writers who have viewed black religion as fundamentally otherworldly and escapist have simply failed to realize how the worlds of the slave—temporal and spiritual—were integrated in his mind and how the "New Jerusalem" was to be attained not in some distant future but within his lifetime.

In the process of cultural adjustment, then, Afro-Americans retained much of African culture, but altered it to meet the needs of their new lives. The result was the development of a new, distinct pattern of life for black people, an *Afro-American* product of combined African and Euro-American cultural elements.[3] Not all the important aspects of African culture were preserved in altered form in North America, however. As in the case of Afro-American religion, much of the institutional side of African life was lost, and the slavery regime proved to be infertile ground for the preservation and growth of the African plastic arts. Retention and development of African cultural elements depended on a number of factors, among them the strength of the tradition, its potential relevance for Afro-Americans, and the tolerance, at least, of the master class. Another very important factor was the degree of compatibility of African and Euro-American traditions. Where those traditions came into sharp conflict, as in the case of social and political structure, the African influence on the new subculture was small. Where the traditions were not alien or fundamentally dissimilar, as in the cases of music and the techniques of agricultural labor, they tended to reinforce one another. In these areas, therefore, African retentions gave a strong African flavor to the new Afro-American culture.

The cultural shock suffered by all Afro-Americans was profound but it was particularly severe for native Africans who were enslaved. Africans had extraordinary attachment to their native land and their kinship groups. We have seen in Chapter 2 that the African's very being, his "personness," depended on kinship, and kinship itself was deeply rooted in the land. African scholar John S. Mbiti points out that Africans in traditional societies "walk on the graves of their forefathers, and it is feared that anything separating them from these ties will bring disaster to family and community life." Hence, mere separation from their specific kinship groups, community religions, and native land areas was profoundly traumatic for Africans who were enslaved. Moreover, the enslaved African had to endure a series of physical and psychic shocks in the course of capture, transportation, and seasoning in the New World. And in his new environment, he found himself among strangers, some of them Afro-American slaves, who did not understand his language, habits, or customs.

Consequently, cultural adjustment was particularly difficult for the enslaved African. He not only had to make the psychological adjustment from the freedom he enjoyed in his native society to the chattel slavery required by an alien society, but he had to make cultural adjustments to the larger culture as well. He had to put aside African ways while he learned a new language, new work techniques, and new modes and styles of day-to-day living. The cultural adjustment achieved was often far from perfect. Unlike American born (or creole) slaves, native Africans had experienced freedom, and enslavement could and did produce bitterness, defiance, apathy, and despair. The response of noncreole slaves to their condition tended to be more extreme than that of slaves born into the system, and included obstinacy and uncooperativeness, self-mutilation and suicide, and organized violence. Throughout the Americas disgruntled native Africans contributed in highly disproportionate numbers to slave revolts.

Some Africans had greater difficulty in adjusting to New World conditions than others. Ibo slaves, for instance, had a reputation in the Caribbean and the United States for being extremely sensitive, with a marked tendency toward despondency, suicide, and high death rates. And Africans from Gabon made notoriously poor slaves; ". . . they generally die," the slave trader William Bosman noted, "either on the passage or soon after their arrival in the islands. The debility of their constitution is astonishing." Like the Amerindians, these Africans did not make good slaves, perhaps because, as George P. Rawick suggests, they came from "self-sufficient subsistence economies without elaborate social structures and state forms." Consequently, their internalized values and attitudes relating to work and, more importantly, to authority were antithetical to the situation they faced in the New World, where an authority unsanctioned in their traditions required highly organized, unvaried, and almost unrelieved labor. They were the products of folk societies in which work imperatives were imposed by some social organization of the folk such as the tribe or the kinship group, traditional groupings that had no real meaning in the altered circumstances of New World slavery.

On the other hand, in such complex African societies as the Ashanti, Akan, Mandingo, Fanti, Hausa, and Yoruba, more elaborate agricultural production techniques required a more rationalized organization of labor to increase the quantity of trade commodities. Africans from these societies were accustomed to systematic work and to serving as both subordinates and superiors in an established system of authority. Consequently, Afro-Americans with such traditions had greater adaptability in adjusting to chattel slavery. For example, the Coramantee, an English designation for Akan-Ashanti peoples, were considered excellent slaves and were used in the West Indies as a cadre to season slaves imported directly from Africa. Yet, Coramantee

slaves were also noted for leading slaves revolts. Slaves
from the more complex societies could accept authority,
thus preserving their lives, but at the same time they had
the ability to resist, usually covertly but sometimes overtly,
thus preserving their sanity.

There is evidence that the language barrier was especially difficult for some native Africans, and even their children, to overcome. In the early 1700s Virginia Governor
Alexander Spotswood commented on the "Stupidity" of
the colony's slaves and the "Babel of Languages" to be
heard among them. The colony's House of Burgesses made
clear the distinction between creole Negroes and "Negroes
Imported hither," noting of the latter that "the Gros [*sic.*]
Barbarity and rudeness of their manners, the variety and
strangeness of their Languages and the weakness and Shal-
lowness of their minds renders [*sic.*] it in a manner impossible to attain to any Progress in their Conversion." Runaway advertisements indicate that a considerable number of
slaves in the plantation colonies did not speak English, and
throughout the colonial period the language barrier was
considered a detriment to the conversion of African-born
slaves. The language problem apparently persisted well into the nineteenth century, with some slaves never learning
to communicate verbally with whites. Ex-slave Cass Stew-
art, recalling his contact in the late antebellum period with
"salt-water niggers" fresh from Africa, claimed that they
could not even understand each other.

There can be no question that transplanted Africans had
real difficulty making themselves understood, by their fellow slaves as well as by whites. But their supposed ignorance and slowness in learning to communicate were generally exaggerated by whites, who erroneously looked upon
the developing varieties of Afro-American language as ludi-
crously substandard dialects of English. Actually, from
the time they set foot on New World soil, black slaves began learning to communicate in new ways, a process that
led to the gradual development of the distinctly new system of creole languages described in Chapter 3 (pp. 87-88).
Although the developing creole languages would come to

influence the language of the slaveholding class, they were peculiarly Afro-American languages, created out of the black experience. They were nonwritten languages, but they were not substandard in any sense; they allowed Afro-Americans to express themselves freely, forcefully, and often with considerable beauty and grace. Anthropologist Sidney W. Mintz maintains that these languages were "surely one of the most significant cultural achievements of transplanted Africans, attesting both to the resourcefulness and creative genius of the slaves, and to the capacity of language systems to expand as necessary."

For creole slaves, the process of cultural adaptation was somewhat easier than for transplanted Africans, and the second, third, fourth, and succeeding generations of Afro-Americans were progressively better adjusted to their New World situations. Just as creoles were better able to communicate with each other and with whites than were native Africans, they were also better able to cope with slavery, the feature of Euro-American culture that had the greatest impact on their lives. Adjustment to slavery did not mean acquiescence by Afro-Americans in their enslavement. It did not mean complete subservience and submissiveness, because an integral feature of the adjustment process was schooling in resistance. Hence, the later generations of Afro-Americans, after years of experience under slavery, were well versed in opposition to the "system." The New Orleans *Courier* of February 15, 1839, writing in criticism of the internal slave trade, noted that there could "be no comparison between the ability and inclination to do mischief, possessed by the Virginia Negro, and that of the rude and ignorant African."

Just as it was inevitable that in the process of cultural change Afro-Americans would retain features of African culture in their life patterns, it was also inevitable that they would incorporate some elements of Euro-American culture into Afro-American life. White Americans encouraged limited acculturation for a variety of reasons. In the first place, if slavery was to be a viable economic institution, slaves had to learn to communicate with whites and with each other and to carry out at least rudimentary agricultural and mechanical tasks. Hence, whites promoted the education of Afro-Americans in the spoken English language, in crafts, in household and personal service, and in agricultural practices. Another factor that prompted whites to educate blacks in the ways of whites was white ethnocentrism. Whites looked on blacks as uncivilized barbarians and believed their Euro-American culture to be superior to any other civilization in the world. Some whites considered it proper to bring at least a degree of "civilization" to their slaves; some, particularly clergymen, thought it their humanitarian and Christian duty to instruct and convert slaves. Such whites encouraged black conformity to white ideals, encouraging blacks to adopt Euro-American religion, Euro-American concepts of marriage, the home, and the family, and Euro-American moral and ethical standards.

The deep and persistent white fear of black insurrection and retaliation also promoted limited acculturation as a method of slave control. The Christianizing and "civilizing" of black slaves would hopefully help to reduce slave discontent and unrest by encouraging a sense of contentment and belonging. Whites assumed that cultural borrowing, even to a limited degree, would promote slave satisfaction and lessen the likelihood of slave opposition to the established order. Slaves with special privileges, or even tolerable situations, would fear losing them, and would therefore tend to submerge feelings of discontent and ideas of resistance. White encouragement of pair-bond mating and childbearing likewise promoted cooperation and good behavior, as the presence of spouses and children discouraged running away and other types of resistance. Historian Joel Williamson suggests that "Southern whites had either to tame the tiger or be eaten by it." Partial acculturation was one way to tame the tiger.

Despite the difficulties that Afro-Americans faced in making cultural adjustments, they appear to have been generally responsive to the limited acculturation allowed by whites. West Africans had a long tradition of cultural borrowing. They tended, for instance, to adopt new gods readily, particularly the supposedly more powerful gods of a conquering tribe. Although most of the borrowing was from cultures very similar to their own, the tendency to take on new culture elements suggests a flexibility of mind that left West Africans open to external culture change. Although Afro-Americans retained important features of African philosophy and world view, they readily adopted the supernatural figures of the Euro-American and certain aspects of his religion. If black slaves could accept change in such a profoundly important area as religion, it is not difficult to understand their receptivity to cultural borrowing in such areas as language, social institutions, and modes and styles of day-to-day living.

Another reason for the openness of slaves to limited acculturation was practical necessity. As we have suggested above, enslaved Africans generally experienced a degree of culture shock and lived temporarily in a kind of cultural void in the New World. The influence of this cultural weightlessness was toward accommodation to the dominant culture. If African-born slaves and their descendants were to offset the disadvantages of being marginal or out-of-culture persons, they of necessity had to achieve some sense of cultural identity; one alternative was partial adaptation to Euro-American culture. Moreover, if they were to make the most of their practical situations, or to improve their material conditions to any significant degree, they had to acquire appropriate work skills, learn some English vocabulary, and conform to certain Euro-American customs and practices.

The acculturation process did not operate with great consistency. The requirements of slavery prevented the uniform borrowing of Euro-American cultural elements by Afro-Americans. Ordinarily whites allowed slaves to live in single-family units and practice a doctored form of Christianity, but they could not afford to allow slaves opportunities for education and for the full development of a sense of independence and worth as individual human beings. The pace of acculturation also varied considerably, ebbing and flowing in response to sundry circumstances.

The attitudes and fears of whites constituted perhaps the most important factor influencing the rate of culture change, because substantial acculturation could occur only with the approval or at least the acquiescence of whites. Generally, acculturation proceeded more rapidly when whites felt more secure.

In the colonial period, when large numbers of new slaves were introduced into the plantation colonies each year, planters sought to maintain control by preserving the distinct differences between blacks and whites and preventing solidarity among the blacks. Consequently, whites considered it dangerous to allow large-scale cultural borrowing by slaves. As late as the middle of the eighteenth century, for example, there was considerable opposition to the conversion of slaves to Christianity. In the words of a religious tract of the period, it was a general complaint of the slave-holding clan "that christianizing the Negroes makes them proud and saucy, and tempts them to imagine themselves upon an Equality with white People." The implication of conversion that all men were spiritual brothers was, of course, alarming. According to two Anglican ministers, many southern planters believed that conversion increased slave discontent and made slaves "more perverse and untractable"; some whites charged that conversion actually promoted slave rebellion instead of Christian obedience. Conversion also required instruction in English, and a common language would make it possible for slaves to discuss their grievances and organize resistance. Consequently, until the 1740s there was little effective conversion among the masses of slaves in the southern colonies, and most remained outside the Christian fold. Although the famed preacher, George Whitefield, was criticized for giving "great countenance" to the New York slave "conspiracy" of 1741 (see p. 114), there was comparatively little opposition to conversion in the northern colonies where blacks were not concentrated in large numbers and hence appeared less dangerous.

In the early colonial period even partial acculturation proceeded slowly and fitfully. The English had had little

previous experience with blacks, and the large-scale importation, particularly in the eighteenth century, of slaves
from Africa and non-English areas of the New World kept
the cultural gap between the two peoples quite wide. "To
the relatively lettered English colonists," Winthrop Jordan
writes, "Negroes must indeed have seemed ignorant and
often downright stupid."[4] To blacks, on the other hand,
the ways of whites must have appeared strange and bizarre.

However, from their first contact with white men in the
English mainland colonies, blacks began making cultural
adjustments to the dominant culture; they learned to communicate with whites and with each other, and they observed the daily lives of whites and sought in some respects
to imitate white ways. At least some slaves lived in very
close, if restricted, proximity to the white world. They
were, in Professor Rawick's words, in "constant interac-
tion" with whites. Thus they were able to acquire knowledge about various aspects of Euro-American culture and
to adjust their lives partially to the dominant culture. In
exceptional cases, slaves learned to read and write, sometimes with the help of whites, in spite of legal prohibitions
and the social pressure to keep slaves from learning such
skills. The small number of slaves who could read and
write were in a particularly advantageous position to learn
about and borrow from the dominant culture.

The limited evidence from historical sources indicates
that by the middle of the eighteenth century a number of developments were encouraging a more rapid acculturation process for larger numbers of blacks. The Great
Awakening, the momentous revival of the 1740s, which
emphasized emotional, highly personal religion and the
spiritual equality of all men, greatly stimulated black participation in Christian religions. Blacks attended camp
meetings, taking active part in the revival services, and
some black exhorters or preachers carried the Christian
message to audiences of blacks and whites, meeting sometimes in one body, sometimes in separate gatherings. Beginning with the Great Awakening and prompted by subsequent revivals in the years down to 1800, more and more

blacks joined Protestant churches, particularly the evangelical sects. Religious conversion in turn fostered adjustments in other aspects of Afro-American life. Thus, in 1749 the Reverend Thomas Bacon was able to praise his black audience for having their children baptized, for publishing the banns of marriage, and for "honestly joining in Marriage"—in sum, for "growing more regular" in the ways of Euro-America.

The spirit and ideals of the Age of the American Revolution further promoted cultural adjustment by blacks. The general humanitarianism of the era led to noticeable improvement in the physical treatment of slaves and encouraged whites to accept the idea that Afro-Americans, like themselves, were human beings with human feelings and aspirations. By the last quarter of the century, some slaveowners were beginning to discourage slave promiscuity and to promote the establishment of autonomous slave families patterned on the Euro-American concept of the family. They also increasingly attempted to prevent the breakup of slave families, although they were often unsuccessful. In addition to the growth of humanitarianism, the substantial decline of slave importations in the Revolutionary period was a factor promoting the acculturation of blacks. With the decline in the number of unseasoned blacks, the cultural gap between blacks and whites narrowed; just as blacks were growing more accustomed to whites, whites were becoming more accustomed to and less fearful of blacks. In the absence of large numbers of foreign-born blacks, whites felt more secure and were less apprehensive about blacks observing and borrowing from their way of life.

Consequently, some slaves in the plantation South, as well as free blacks generally, made substantial cultural adjustments in the late eighteenth century. In 1801, for example, George Tucker of Virginia wrote matter-of-factly about the "advance of knowledge" among Virginia slaves, noting that each year added "to the number of those who can read and write." Free blacks, particularly in Northern cities, borrowed heavily from Euro-American culture. In the decades after the Revolutionary War, middle-class blacks established a plethora of separate black fraternal, mutual aid, public service, and moral uplift societies, patterned after their white counterparts. Afro-Americans also set up independent schools and businesses, and under the leadership of such men as Richard Allen and Absalom Jones of Philadelphia they launched a movement for separate "African" churches. Black leaders founded the African Methodist Episcopal Church (A.M.E.) in Philadelphia in 1794 and the African Methodist Episcopal Zion Church (A.M.E.Z.) in New York in 1800, and after the turn of the century black Baptists began to organize all-black churches on a local basis. The movement for exclusively black churches made headway in the South as well as the North. The establishment of separate black organizations, given impetus by the rising hostility of whites after the mid-1790s to nonsegregated institutions, demonstrates the extent to which a small number of blacks made profound adjustments in the way of conforming to the dominant culture.

The acculturation process continued in the nineteenth century. The decline of post-Revolutionary abolition sentiment, the hardening of slavery in the early years of the new century, and especially the regularization and formalization of the institution in the late antebellum period worked toward acculturation. When white Southerners began to rationalize that slavery was a positive good and to believe that that institution would permanently subjugate blacks, they could proceed with little fear to Christianize and "civilize" them, to educate them to conform to white standards and ideals. As indicated in Chapter 5, the outlawing of the external slave trade in 1808 ended the large-scale importation of slaves and restricted the introduction of African culture elements. This, of course, facilitated enculturation, the process of adaptation to the dominant culture.

Historian Joel R. Williamson argues that in the decades immediately preceding the Civil War, southern whites pursued the task of Americanizing black slaves as never before. The success of whites in this endeavor varied widely across the South. The degree to which Afro-Americans made adjustments to white culture seems generally to have varied in inverse ratio to the proportion of blacks in the total local population. British scientist and author Sir Charles Lyell, observing slave life in the decade before Fort Sumter, suggested that acculturation could only proceed very slowly on the great plantations of the Deep South:

So long as they [slaves] herd together in large groups, and rarely come into contact with any whites, save their owner and overseer, they can profit little by their imitative faculty, and cannot even make much progress in mastering the English language . . . .

Generally, it was where the black population was relatively small and in circumstances where blacks had greater exposure to Euro-American culture that the acculturation process was most effective. Acculturation proceeded more rapidly and thoroughly on the smaller farms, in towns and cities, among slave artisans and domestics, and among free blacks. Blacks in these situations clearly made greater adjustments to white culture than did the field slaves on the larger plantations, particularly in the more isolated areas of the South. Nevertheless, even under optimum conditions, the antebellum Southern regime was hardly able to achieve signal success "in making blacks white-like," as one historian has claimed.

Actually, throughout the slavery experience Afro-Americans retained positive remembrances of Africa and their African past. While it may be true that some slaves looked at new slaves from Africa with contempt and misgivings, and showed little interest in specific "Africanisms" that lingered among noncreole slaves, historian Kenneth Stampp's conclusion that "most ante-bellum slaves showed a desire to forget their African past" is seriously misleading. Moreover, there is considerable evidence that Afro-Americans perceived, in a general way, the significance of their African heritage in their everyday lives. They knowingly used "doctorin'" remedies from "Africy," organized autonomous "African" churches, and sometimes entertained themselves on festive occasions with African songs and stories. Authors of antebellum slave narratives spoke without hesitation or apology of their African forebears, and pointedly denied the inferiority of the "African race." Indeed, Afro-Americans obviously admired the spirit, dignity, and courage displayed by some recently arrived slaves from the "fatherland" or by uncowered second-generation Afro-Americans.

But as we have seen in the preceding pages, Afro-Americans, uprooted from their African homeland and denied access to much of the dominant white culture, found neither African nor Euro-American culture adequate for their needs. Consequently, they were compelled to develop their own life-styles, their own life patterns, their own Afro-American subculture, utilizing elements of both the African and white American cultural traditions. The resultant subculture was more than simply a mixture or amalgam of the two older cultural patterns; it was essentially a new cultural system especially adapted to the needs of Afro-Americans and to the peculiar circumstances in which they lived in the United States.

All blacks shared in the black sub-culture. White racism prevented the entry of blacks, with few exceptions, into the dominant society, and guaranteed that all blacks would be influenced, to a greater or lesser degree, by the sanctions operating toward the development of a distinct subculture. Thus, free blacks in the North as well as the South, slaves on small farms, and urban slaves, however much they made adjustments to Euro-American culture, were products of the black subculture and participated in it, at least partially. However, the strongest impetus for the development of a unique Afro-American cultural system occurred on the great plantations where the slave population was large; consequently, the black subculture was shaped predominantly by the way of life of plantation slaves. In the following pages we will examine the nature and dimensions of the black subculture that developed in the plantation South.

In examining slave culture, it is essential to apply the concept of cultural relativity discussed in Chapter 1. Students of slavery have generally given little attention to

slave life, and when they have, they have often made clearly ethnocentric judgments. Thus, historian David B. Davis
has made the sweeping suggestion that it is "doubtful . . .
whether the mass of slaves in any country ever enjoyed a
meaningful religious life." Scholars generally have argued
that the slave family, lacking stability, cohesiveness, and
legal standing, served little economic or social purpose in
slave life. Historian Kenneth M. Stampp, in a 1956 publication, went so far as to maintain that "only incidentally"
was the slave woman "a wife, mother, and home-maker,"
and he concluded that "the male slave's only crucial function within the family was that of siring offspring." In the
past most students of slavery have agreed, at least tacitly,
with Stampp's conclusion that the "average bondsman . . .
lived more or less aimlessly in a bleak and narrow world."

Writers who have made such statements have taken white
Euro-American institutions, behavior, and values as normal
and desirable. The impossibility of a fair evaluation of
slave life from this perspective is pointedly demonstrated by
sociologist Jessie Bernard's gratuitous assertion that because slave marriages of any kind were "so uncommon,"
most slave children "were born out of wedlock"! Slave
culture must be judged on its own merits. Neither wed-
dings nor legal sanctions make marriages, and familial institutions and practices among the slaves must not be judged as ineffective and substandard simply because they differed from those in white culture. Nor may one conclude
that because slaves did not enjoy various benefits and advantages of the larger society they necessarily lived point-
less and miserable lives. Finally, it is highly presumptuous
and somewhat arrogant to denigrate the various life roles
of slaves on the assumption that slaves *must be* what their
masters wanted them to be. Afro-American slaves were
not made in the image and likeness of their masters.

Although the attitudes and actions of white Americans
operated to force blacks to develop an alternative cultural
system, the Afro-American subculture was basically the
creation of blacks. Whites, for all their authority and power, did not determine the development of black culture.

For example, the absence of Euro-American legal sanctions for slave marriages did not determine the structure and role of the slave family. Similarly, the fact that slaveowners permitted or encouraged conversion to Christianity did not give slave religion its central meaning or major characteristics. Afro-American slaves lived, in effect, in two worlds. One world was the white man's world, where slaves lived in close contact with whites, as on small farms, or when they worked under the relatively close scrutiny of whites, in the fields or in plantation households. Here white influence on slave behavior was most pronounced, but even here it was not deterministic. Theoretically slaves were under the control of their masters at all times, but on the large plantations and to some extent on the small farms there were often opportunities for slaves to escape into their own black world, beyond the effective exercise of close scrutiny. Northern journalist Frederick Law Olmsted reported that in the slave quarters and black settlements, slave life was "relatively unconstrained." Here slaves related to other slaves on their own terms; here other sanctions besides the slave codes and the overwhelming power of the whites influenced slave consciousness, slave behavior, and slave patterns of life. The slave quarters were the crucible in which slave culture was created.

It was largely in the slave quarters, for instance, that Afro-American slaves created the slave family, a familial system developed to meet the human desires and needs of the slaves themselves as well as the demands of the system of chattel slavery. Contrary to common opinion, the family did exist as a viable institution among slaves. As indicated in Chapter 5, slaveholders promoted pair-bond mating and childbearing by slave couples. With this encouragement, the decided trend in slave family organization was in the direction of the Euro-American standard, the single-family unit, with modifications produced by the exigencies of slave life. Historian Willie Lee Rose has suggested that "the most *typical* domestic picture [of slaves] is of a father and mother living together in a humble cabin with their children."

Moreover, the sense of family was strong. The trauma of family separation is a pervasive theme running through the slave narratives, indicating the extensiveness and strength of family ties among the slaves. As fugitive slave Alexander Hemsley put it, "the unwillingness to separate of husbands and wives, parents and children was so great, that to part them seemed to me a sin higher than the heavens,—it was dreadful to hear their outcries, as they were forced into the wagons of the drivers." The depth of a slave mother's love for her children is evident in the painfully touching remarks of ex-slave Mary Younger. "It almost kills me," she said, "that . . . . [my children] are there [in slavery], and that I can do them no good." The slaves' strong sense of family was expressed frequently and in various ways. Slaves mothers hid children, suffered severe punishment, and pleaded with sellers and buyers alike in attempts to prevent the breakup of their families. Parents risked punishment and sale in trying to protect their children from mistreatment, and many a runaway slave virtually sacrificed his freedom in fulfilling his desire to be near loved ones. Much of the resistance to "being sold South," which included self-mutilation and suicide, was due to the reluctance of slaves to be separated from their families and their kinsmen.

The evidence of a viable family life among slaves comes from both slave and planter sources.[5] Although slaveholders referred not infrequently to slave promiscuity and inconstancy, their attitudes and actions relative to the internal slave trade and to slave management indicate that they clearly understood that family attachments were very important to the slaves themselves.[6] If slave families were frequently broken up, it was not usually through the action of the slaves themselves, but through the operation of forces beyond their control, and with the demise of slavery thousands of blacks traveled across the South seeking reunion with loved ones and relatives. Recent research by historian Herbert Gutman shows that a very large majority of rural blacks, including adult men, lived in single-family units in the Reconstruction period, and studies by other scholars suggest that this situation was a continuation of family patterns established during slavery. The evidence clearly points to greater stability and cohesiveness in the slave family than students of slavery have traditionally recognized.[7]

The relatively high degree of family stability and cohesiveness achieved by slaves was possible only because both slave men and slave women carved out viable familial roles and worked together to accomplish the goals they set for their families. Too much has been made of the emasculation of the male slave and the dominance of women in slave society. Once again, evidence from both white and black sources, but particularly from the slave narratives, contradicts the traditional view. The slave husband and father generally performed important functions in the family. Although not the breadwinner in the usual sense of that term, he often played an important economic role by hunting and fishing to supplement the family diet, by constructing and repairing furniture and household items, by organizing the family garden if one were allowed, or, in some cases, earning cash to be spent for his family's benefit. But more important, the male slave also participated actively in the most significant task of slave parents, the preparation of their offspring for adult life in the world they knew. Slave fathers shared with slave mothers in disciplining and teaching their children, and in laying down rules and guidelines for family behavior. Former slave Jacob Stroyer noted that he was whipped by both his father and his mother, and ex-slave Joseph Sanford indicated that both parents took part in the teaching process: "My father always advised me to be tractable, and get along with the white people in the best manner I could, and not be saucy. My mother always taught me to serve the Lord—which has ever been my aim . . . ."

Slave men sometimes exercised dominant authority in the home, and apparently they frequently used physical coercion on both wives and children. But it is not necessary to prove that slave husbands generally were the primary source of family authority, or that they were highly successful in protecting their families. What should be established is that the male slave was not generally emasculated nor relegated to a position of secondary importance in the family. There is little indication from slave sources that slavery destroyed the manliness of slave men or undermined their status and prestige in slave society. There is little evidence that the slaves themselves considered women the primary source of authority in the family or the larger society. The slave family was a tenacious and vital institution because of the strength and energy infused into it by both slave men and women. The slave family survived because, in their own minds, slave men and slave women were first husbands and wives, fathers and mothers, providers and homemakers, and members of the black community, and only incidentally laborers for and the property of the master class.

Although the tendency in slave society was toward the establishment of family units similar to those in white society, the circumstances of slavery forced significant modifications. The slave family developed and existed in the face of continual, varied, and severe difficulties. Families were frequently disrupted through sale, separation, or divorce, often despite vigorous objection by family members. Sometimes the slave father or another member of the family was absent much of the time because he did not live or work where his family resided. And when all members of the family lived in the same household, both parents were normally away from the family for a large part of each working day. Even under optimum conditions, slaves were limited in their ability to perform the familial roles customary in the autonomous white family. Consequently, the slave family system developed a flexibility that contributed not only to the complexity of the system's structure, but also to its strength and vitality. Because the single-family unit was unable to carry out fully the functions required of an effective family system, Afro-American slaves created an extended family system in which the responsibilities of rearing children and caring for family members were shared to some extent by the larger community.

In the slave family the biological parents might well exercise duties and prerogatives similar to those exercised by parents in a autonomous white family, but slave society did not delineate sharply the roles of "father" and "mother" nor insist on the rigid fulfillment of these roles by slave fathers and mothers. George P. Rawick is essentially correct in suggesting that the "slave community acted like a generalized extended kinship system" in which there was community concern for the well-being of all individuals, especially children, in each slave family. In slave families children generally had considerable family responsibilities; older children, for instance, frequently cared for younger children. Relatives of the immediate family, including grandparents, uncles, aunts, step and half siblings, and close and distant cousins, sometimes lived with the family and performed important familial functions. In addition, other members of the slave community, especially older men and women who were highly respected or who had had wide experience in family affairs, were called on to help fulfill family purposes. In some instances, such as in the punishment of misbehaving children, the slave community as a whole exercised a collective responsibility. The extended family system operated effectively both on a day-to-day basis and in times of crisis, in the first case supporting the work of the actual slave parents and in the second instance providing parent surrogates or other family members. In short, the system provided a degree of security and stability by virtue of its insurance that complete deprival of kin and family was highly unlikely. Whatever the dispersal of the immediate family, it was almost certain that someone would be available to care for the members of the family wherever they came to live in the realm of slavery. Clearly, the flexible and improvisational extended family system fulfilled the deepest needs of Afro-American slaves far more adequately than a rigid nuclear family system could have.

The operation of the extended family system in slave society suggests that the role of community in slave life was more significant than most students have believed. Historians have generally assumed that the slaveholders were largely successful in their attempts to forestall the development of a sense of unity and common purpose among their bondsmen. In recent decades, some black writers and leaders, frustrated in their attempts to achieve black solidarity, have echoed this interpretation, at least to the point of emphasizing the presence on the plantations of a minority of slaves who identified with the ruling whites and served their purposes, sometimes even to the extent of betraying their fellow slaves. Yet the evidence is clear that despite the persistent efforts of whites to discourage group consciousness among the bondsmen, the slaves came to see themselves as a people quite distinct from whites, a people with common problems, common interests, and a common destiny. In short, blacks on southern plantations developed a strong sense of community, a form of incipient black nationalism. Professor Rawick argues that the "reality of community was the major adaptive process for the black man in America."

The slave sense of community, however, was far from perfect. By deftly playing on the desire of their slaves for recognition, prestige, and special favors, slaveholders deliberately fostered class consciousness and divisiveness in slave society. House servants, said the former slave Austin Steward, "are ever regarded as a privileged class; and are sometimes greatly envied, while others are bitterly hated." Some slave drivers were considered "vicious" by their fellow slaves; fugitive slave Jacob Stroyer even expressed pleasure at the death of a cruel driver, "Uncle Esan." Henry Bibb noted that there were marked distinctions in slave society, with some slaves "refusing to associate with others whom they deem beneath them in point of character, color, [or] condition . . . ." There was considerable distrust of house servants by other slaves, but the numbers of "despicable talebearers and mischiefmakers" who would betray fellow slaves were swelled by bondsmen from every rank.[8] The escape or resistance plans of numerous slaves were revealed by black brothers who hoped thereby to earn special favors from the whites. John Little, a runaway slave, was betrayed by a free black in return for a reward of $10, and another fugitive, Leonard Black, was turned in by his closest friend. There is little wonder, then, that slaves often distrusted fellow slaves, or that those who were planning escape or resistance moved with extreme caution. Some slaves did not even keep their brothers, wives, or parents informed of their plans.

There were numerous conflicts of a more petty nature in slave society. Field slaves as well as artisans and domestics vied among themselves for assignments that carried high prestige, and bondsmen from different plantations quarreled and fought over the relative merits of their masters. One ex-slave noted that he had heard slaves object to working in the field in small groups, lest "some passerby should think that they belonged to a poor man, who was unable to keep a large gang." Ex-slaves Austin Steward, Josiah Henson, and Frederick Douglass all commented that slaves commonly exhibited a "foolish pride" that prompted them to go to inordinate lengths to please their masters and, ultimately, to identify at least in part with their oppressors. "Often," wrote Josiah Henson, "was the encomium of 'smart nigger' bestowed upon me, to my immense gratification." Henson offers the extreme example of slave identification with the system of bondage in the almost incredible story of how, in accordance with his master's wishes, he led 21 slaves, including his wife and two children, from Maryland through a portion of the free state of Ohio to Kentucky.

But despite the betrayals, class divisions, and partial identification with the master class, the central loyalty of slaves was generally to the slave community. Slaves themselves sought to define and to enforce what was best for the slave community, and the value system that operated in slave society was oriented toward the promotion of black solidarity and mutual concern. Hence, tattling and informing were taboo in slave society, and slaves who betrayed fellow bondsmen risked ostracism or perhaps severe physical punishment. As Austin Steward noted, masters sometimes had to send their informants away, "for fear of the vengeance of the betrayed slaves." The attitude of the slave community was apparently well understood by whites; in commenting on a slave who had betrayed another, a Tennessee judge observed that the fact that a slave "should abandon the interests of his caste, and betray black folks to the white people, rendered him an object of general aversion."

The operation of the slaves' self-generated value system tended to encourage resistance to slavery and made the task of slaveholders infinitely more difficult. It made possible a situation in which thousands of slaves all over the South were able to escape temporarily from their plantations for periods varying from a few hours up to several years. The commitment of slaves to the common cause provided the protection of silence for those who stole from whites, resisted work, sabotaged plantation operations, tried to disrupt the system through violence, or simply engaged in "putting on" "ole massa." The sense of community also helped to make it possible for a relatively small number of slaves to make it to the North or to Canada and to escape altogether from slavery. The slave narratives are replete with examples of blacks, free and slave, who helped fellow blacks in need, whatever the nature of the need.[9] These black Good Samaritans were acting on the premise that they and their fellow sufferers were a different people from whites, a people unto themselves. The actions of these thousands of blacks speak louder than any words as proof that a real and tenacious sense of community bound together the black slaves of the plantation South.

In no other area of slave life was the role of community more significant than in the creation and development of black religion. Only a people with a strong sense of togetherness and a firm belief in their own destiny could have created a religious experience for themselves that reflected such a positive world view and which came so close to fulfilling satisfactorily their deepest temporal and spiritual needs. The clearest expression of slave religion, of course, are the sacred songs, the slave spirituals. Despite disagreements over the origins of the spirituals, almost all students of slavery and/or slave life have been profoundly impressed by these religious songs and have viewed them as creative expressions of great beauty and sensitivity. Musicologist Newman I. White has referred to them as "the most impressive religious folk songs in our language," and historian Vincent Harding has described them as "the most profound verbal expression of Afro-American religious experience." As early as the 1920s White suggested that the spirituals represented "the greatest single outlet for the expression of the Negro folkmind."

Yet scholars have generally failed to appreciate the significance of the spirituals and of slave religion in slave life and culture. They have not perceived that creations as beautiful and powerful as the spirituals could not have been the product of a hand-me-down Christianity that the slaves had accepted from their masters as they would have a bundle of old clothes. Students of slavery have usually exaggerated the role of whites in shaping the religious beliefs and practices of the slaves, suggesting that the mass of slaves meekly accepted the propagandistic preachings of white ministers on submission and obedience. The traditional view of slave religion all but denies the slaves any meaningful religious experience. Slave religion was, according to the traditional myth, a distorted, degraded version of Christianity, fashioned to meet the needs of ignorant and superstitious blacks. It was characterized by a primitive fundamentalism in belief and an unrestrained emotionalism in practice. It served primarily to provide release from the cares of this world and the promise of a better life to come, and its escapist orientation and focus on the hereafter prompted its adherents to accept unquestioningly their condition in this world. In the traditional view slave religion was truly the opium of the oppressed.

Actually, as we have noted previously (see Chapter 3, pp. 88-89 and Chapter 6, pp. 173-175), Afro-Americans did not adopt a bastard Christianity as their own; instead they combined aspects of traditional African religions and Christianity to produce a new black faith, a functioning, integrated religion especially suited to sustaining their religious needs. Religion cannot be dismissed lightly in any discussion of a people's life and culture; this is particularly true of North American slaves. The slaves were profoundly religious; their very existence and every department of their lives were intimately associated with religion. Moreover, in their sacred songs, the slaves have left a record of their religious experience that is remarkably useful for an inquiry into slave life and culture.

The single most important fact about slave religion is that it was largely created and defined by the slave community. Slaveholders had made little attempt to convert slaves to Christianity before 1750, and intensive and systematic efforts at conversion were not made until the last three and a half decades of slavery. As a result, Afro-American slaves had been able to retain important aspects of traditional African religions and to adapt Christianity to the imperatives of their peculiar condition. Uprooted from his African past, the North American slave needed what anthropologist Paul Radin calls a "fixed point," and he found that stability in the "Christian" God. But, Radin adds, "The ante-bellum Negro was not converted to God. He converted God to himself." Afro-Americans transformed Christianity to meet their needs, adding new practices and ceremonies, expanding the galaxy of supernatural beings, infusing new sensibilities, emphasizing different aspects of God's revelation, and even altering the traditional image of Christ the Savior.

The slaves clearly recognized the differences between their religion and their masters', between their God and the white man's God. "White folks can't pray to the black man's God," noted Henrietta Perry, a Virginia slave. The persistent efforts of white ministers and masters to induce slaves in the name of religion to submit and obey, to accept their status as one ordained by God, and not to lie or steal simply "turned off" many slaves. Moreover, most of the white churches did not sanction the shouting, moaning, handclapping, dancing, and exuberant singing—in short, the freedom of expression—that blacks felt were essential in the exercise of a fulfilling religion. Throughout the antebellum period, slaves continued to participate outwardly in the religion of their masters, sometimes attending the same services as the whites or, more often, meeting as a special group to hear a white minister or a slave preacher under white supervision. But white religion did not meet the needs of Afro-Americans, and the slaves turned to their own community to order their religious lives and to seek spiritual fulfillment.

Of all the areas of plantation life, slave religion was the one least influenced by white example. The slaves themselves determined the nature and types of expression, the content, the orientation, the tone, and the character of their religion. For this reason black religion differed significantly from traditional western Christianity. The slaves picked and chose, omitted and altered in order to fashion their own religion. They related very closely with the oppressed "Hebrew children," seeing themselves as God's special chosen people in eighteenth- and nineteenth- century America. The spirituals make repeated reference to the slaves as the people of God, and contain innumerable allusions to the deliverance of the Israelites and their leaders from situations of distress. It is little wonder, then, that black religion had a strong Old Testament flavor, and that the slaves found their religious heroes among the great figures of the Old Testament—Noah, Jonah, Samson, Daniel, David, Joshua, Moses, and the archangel Gabriel. Their God was a mighty God, their Jesus a powerful and protective warrior king.

Slave religion was essentially a communal, not a private affair. Individual religiosity was not curtailed, but the primary outlet for religious expression was through the community of slaves. In speaking of their religious experiences, slaves and ex-slaves almost always used the plural "we" and they invariably spoke of communal functions such as praise meetings, funerals, sings, ring shouts, and prayer-and-experience meetings. The very structure of the spirituals, based on a call and response pattern, demanded communal participation. It is very significant that the sacred songs of the blacks made almost no positive references to whites, but posited a black world peopled by parents, relatives, and friends, living and dead. Leadership in this world of the slaves was apparently dominated by those who were believed to possess special religious powers. The leadership roles of the black preachers, mystics, and oracles depended on their special relationships with their black brothers and sisters; their power resulted, Professor Rawick writes, from "their deep contact with the soul of the congregation and the community." The "amen" and "hallelujah" responses in black religious services were a means through which the congregation could verify the leader's mystic communion with his people.

In concentrating on the language of the spirituals as evidence of the travails of those held in bondage, scholars have generally failed to recognize that slave religion was emphatically a religion not only of hope but of *promise.* It is true that a man so sensitive to the nuances of the Afro-American experience as the great black leader, W. E. B. DuBois, called the spirituals the "sorrow songs," and that Frederick Douglass spoke of the "deep melancholy" and bitter "anguish" expressed in slave songs. The slaves, of course, did sing about their problems, sorrows, and sufferings in their spirituals. The emphasis of the spirituals, however, was not on the tribulations of the slaves, but on their deliverance from their troubles. Persistently the sacred songs emphasized transformation, triumph, salvation. The spirituals are filled with references to "Canaan," the "Kingdom," the "Holy City," the "mansions above," or, most significantly, simply "home." The slaves were certain that deliverance would come and that they would be going "home"; it was only a matter of time before they "would walk the golden streets of the New Jerusalem." Slave religion was characterized by the supreme confidence that is so evident in the spirituals.

In their sacred songs, the slaves expressed almost no sense of unworthiness and projected a decidedly positive self-image. They were God's people, a troubled but struggling, persevering, and righteous people, wholly worthy of salvation if only they followed the Lord. Indeed, many slaves felt morally superior to their white slaveowners. After seeing his sister whipped and her persecutor shortly afterward attend religious services, Austin Steward could hardly help feeling that whites were hypocrites: "Can any one wonder that I, and other slaves, often doubted the sincerity of every white man's religion?" Ex-slave David West noted that he loved his former master, since deceased, but he continued, ". . . I can read the Bible, and I do not see any thing there by which he could be justified in holding slaves: and I know not where he has gone to." Fugitive slave Henry Brant thought it would be "a hard case" for a man to "continue to do as the slaveholders do" and then to "obtain heaven." Henry Atkinson, another fugitive slave, was even more certain: "It appears to me that God cannot receive into the kingdom of heaven, those who deal in slaves." There seems little question that the slaves were alluding symbolically to a retributive justice for whites when they referred in the spirituals to such events as the drowning of Pharaoh's army or to Goliath's downfall. Ultimately God's justice would prevail and the slaves would wear crowns of glory while the slaveholders suffered punishment. In the words of abolitionist Moncure D. Conway, the slaves, ignorant and unlettered as they were, "had conceived a symbolism of their own, and burdens of prophecy, and had changed the fields on which they toiled into the pavements of the New Jerusalem, glorified with spirits arrayed in white."

However, the slaves were not concerned only with salvation after death. Their whole religious experience is a testament to their desire for and belief in deliverance in this world. It is significant that all of the Old Testament heroes of Afro-American slave religion faced difficulties and troubles that were analogous, in the minds of the slaves, to their own trials and tribulations; it is more significant that each of these great religious figures achieved deliverance in this world. If God had delivered Daniel from the lion's den, Jonah from the belly of the whale, and the Hebrew children from the fiery furnace, then, the slaves asked, "Why not every man?" In speaking of the sacred songs Frederick Douglass observed that "Every tone was a testimony against slavery, and a prayer to God for deliverance from chains." And Charles Ball, another ex-slave, observed that the religious faith of the slaves was premised on the firm belief that they would be delivered from their earthly bondage: "The idea of a revolution in the conditions of the whites and the blacks is the cornerstone of the religion of the latter." In essense, Afro-American slaves, who neither separated the sacred from the secular nor envisioned heaven as being far off in time or space (see pp. 173-175), simply fused the ideas of worldly and of spiritual deliverance.

Slave religion was inherently subversive of the institution of slavery. It not only held out the hope of radical improvement in the earthly condition of slaves, but it also fostered the development of slave communal autonomy and individual self-esteem. Moreover, the very fact that slaves adhered to and practiced a religion that was considered by whites pernicious and dangerous and that was usually prohibited tended to undermine a system of social control based on the exercise of absolute power and authority. In the practice of their religion, slaves generally had to defy their masters, covertly or overtly. In order to be able to express themselves freely, they held their prayer meetings or sings late at night, in slave cabins, in hollows or dugouts in the fields, in selected sites or constructed "hushharbors" in the woods or swamps. Detection meant punishment, and consequently the slaves became adept at carrying on their religious activities surreptitiously.

Because the slaveholders were unable to exercise the close supervision that would have cut off normal channels of communication in the slave community, the slaves generally had little need for an elaborate system of secret communication. Occasionally, however, they may have employed prearranged signals, including the words of such sacred songs as "Steal away, steal away, steal away to Jesus." Whether or not such songs were consciously composed to dupe slaveholders, they clearly came to have double meanings for some slaves. To Frederick Douglass and other slaves, for example, being "bound for the land of Canaan" connotated not only a hope of reaching heaven but also of escaping to the free states of the North. Douglass recalled that it was a spiritual, which included the line "I don't expect to stay much longer here," that first planted in his mind the idea of running for freedom, and many other fugitive slaves were sustained in their hopes of achieving freedom by their religious faith. For many of those in bondage, slave religion served to amplify, or even to induce, the ideas and feelings of protest. Slave protest cannot be separated from slave religion.

The discussion of slave religion brings up the question of slave morals and ethics, a subject that has been much misunderstood by whites. Whites have recognized that Afro-Americans have generally been zealously religious people, but it has also been their common opinion that blacks have usually not been very "moral." George Washington, expressing the typical views of a slaveholder, observed that his slaves stole and ruined his property, feigned illness to escape work, and were habitual liars and malingerers. Slave carpenters, Washington wrote, were notorious slackers, and he complained that he could not trust a single one of the domestic servants. It is clear from Washington's observations that the Protestant work ethic had little appeal for slaves, particularly for those like Betty Davis, who was "laid up" for two days for every one she worked.

Slave immorality, in the minds of white contemporaries, was most pronounced in the area of sexual behavior. Southern whites believed that most slaves took an easygoing attitude toward marriage, that relationships between slave mates were generally quite casual, and that marriage among slaves was actually a euphemism for sexual relations. Most whites, North and South, believed that slaves were generally and incurably promiscuous. A Mississippi planter, writing in *DeBow's Review*, knew of no means by which to regulate or restrain slave "habits of amalgamation and intercourse"; abolitionist Moncure D. Conway, born and reared in Virginia, spoke of "general licentiousness" and "wholesale prostitution" among the slaves, conditions that were often encouraged or even compelled, Conway charged, by the slaveholders. Gordon Chapman, a northern visitor to a southern plantation, after observing that "not one of the slaves attended church on the Sabbath," commented further on the sexual lives of the slaves. "The social relations were scarcely recognized among them, and they lived in a state of promiscuous concubinage."

Antebellum whites, of course, were judging slaves in terms of accepted white moral standards. They, like whites in the years since, failed to understand that the activities of Afro-American slaves were governed by an in-group moral code, incorporating moral values and standards that did not conform to white conceptions of "right" and "wrong". Of course, the moral and ethical precepts of Christianity and of western culture did have some influence, but the specific and unique circumstances of black bondage were of far greater significance in the emergence of a system of slave morality. It is not surprising, given their belief in the sinfulness of slavery and in white moral hypocrisy, that black slaves did not adopt unchanged the ethics and moral standards of whites; however, it is ironic that the slaves employed a type of situational ethics, adhering as a matter of course to Christian precepts, such as those concerning lying and stealing, only in their dealings with fellow slaves or other blacks.

There is overwhelming evidence in the slave narratives and in slave folklore, for example, of a black double standard in the appropriation of property belonging to another. The slaves commonly "liberated" their masters' corn, watermelons, sheep, young calves, and food of various sorts, but chickens and pigs seemed to be the most desired prizes. Invariably, slaves justified such actions; they reasoned among themselves, ex-slave Austin Steward noted, ". . . as slaves often do, that it can not be *stealing*, because 'it belongs to massa, and so do *we*, and we only use one part of his property to benefit another. Sure, 'tis all massa's.'" Mary Raines, recalling her days in slavery, took the same position: "I never call it stealin'. I just call it taking de jams, de jellies, de biscuits, de butter and de 'lasses . . . ." To whites such transgressions constituted stealing and were clearly immoral; to slaves these acts simply constituted "taking" and were necessary and legitimate. Josiah Henson was so convinced of the justice of stealing one of his master's chickens for a female friend that he felt "good, moral, heroic." Moreover, the slave community generally protected the transgressors against white authority; black brothers and sisters universally feigned ignorance or offered erroneous explanations, sometimes quite imaginative, of what happened to the property in question.

Standards governing relations among the slaves themselves were another matter. For instance, theft by one slave from another was *not* sanctioned or tolerated. The slave community had its own system of searching out guilty parties and of meting out justice to slaves who had violated the community's standards of conduct. A thief might be detected, Jacob Stroyer tells us, by any of three intriguing ways: "one with a Bible, one with a sieve, and another with graveyard dust." Once discovered, a slave who had transgressed against his fellow slaves might be ridiculed, isolated, or punished physically, even to the point of death in extreme cases. The degree to which slaves abided by their own moral standards varied widely, depending on numerous circumstances and individual personalities, but the evidence suggests that adversity strengthened the sense of community and the disposition of slaves to deal with their fellow bondsmen with sensitivity and fairness.

The conditions under which slaves lived necessarily influenced their attitudes about sexuality. Slaves were thrown together, regardless of sex, into crowded quarters where they ate, slept, and lived with a minimum of privacy. "In a single room", Josiah Henson recalled, "were huddled, like cattle, ten or a dozen persons, men, women, and children. All ideas of refinement and decency were, of course, out of the question." Slaves were provided skimpy clothing, and mature men and women often wore only a long cotton or linen shirt or frock in the summer. Thomas Hedgebeth, a free black, observed that some of the slaves

with whom he worked were "without clothing enough for
decency." Under such circumstances, with slaveholders
universally encouraging procreation, and in the absence of
significant institutional restraints on the sexual activity of
the bondsmen, there is little wonder that many a slave
woman bore numerous children by different fathers, that
many unmarried slaves became mothers and fathers, and
that, in the words of Moncure Conway, "an old maid is
utterly unknown among the women." In describing slave
marriage, fugitive slave Soloman Northup felt compelled
to add to his statement the qualifier, "if such an institution
may be said to exist among them." "Either party can," he
noted, "have as many husbands or wives as the owner will
permit, and either is at liberty to discard the other at
pleasure."[10]

Clearly, sexual attitudes and practices among the slaves
differed widely from those approved in white society. In
general, blacks were much less inhibited than whites in
sexual matters, and apparently they engaged in greater
heterosexual activity, particularly in the adolescent and
early adult years. But their nonadherence to the Victorian
morality espoused (but often not practiced) by southern
whites does not justify the assumption that sexual morality
was nonexistent among slaves. There were in the slave
community strong cultural sanctions for a basic fidelity in
marriage, once the couple involved felt they had contracted
a marriage.[11] Religious faith, concern about the care of
children and relatives, and real affection and love between
husband and wife operated to hold slave marriages together.
The devotion of many slave wives and husbands to each
other is strikingly demonstrated in historical records, both
from white and black sources. Like their white counterparts, black wives do not seem to have been very understanding of transgressing husbands, and vice versa. Fidelity
among slaves likely varied considerably from individual to
individual and from family to family. The Reverend William Ruth of Colchester, Canada, a former slave, believed
that his congregation of ex-slaves excelled whites in the
observance of the "laws of chastity." However, to imply

that slaves generally were more chaste than whites would not only be unwarranted but beside the point. What is important to understand is that blacks developed and generally adhered to their own standards of morality, in sexual as well as in other aspects of life. In this sense we can say of the entire slave community, as the Reverend Smith said of his small flock, ". . . as a general thing [they] are a moral people."

Because students of slavery have underestimated the role of community in slave life and have been so keenly interested in slave revolts, they have too often neglected the magnitude and variety of slave resistance to the system of bondage. But resistance to slavery was so pervasive and is such an important key to an understanding of slave life and culture that it would be virtually impossible to exaggerate its significance. Slave resistance took many forms, varying from the simple rejection by a single slave of the propagandistic teachings of his master to the bloody violence of a large-scale slave revolt. Without question, the most important form of slave resistance was that engaged in by the slaves on a habitual, day-to-day, often almost casual basis. There were numerous ways in which the slaves routinely resisted bondage. Day-to-day resistance was sometimes essentially passive, as when slaves feigned illnesses, pretended ignorance and ineptness, or utilized some type of dissimulation to escape work or to at least slow it down. Routine resistance might take the form of the verbal aggression contained in slave songs, tales, and anecdotes, which expressed variously slave protest, criticism, anger, and, in some instances, defiance. Routine resistance might take a more overt form and include activities specifically designed to disrupt the plantation routine. This type of active day-to-day resistance involved various kinds of sabotage, including breaking, misplacing, and losing tools, damaging crops and destroying other property, and abusing and mistreating work animals. Self-mutilation was not uncommon as a form of resistance, and suicide and killing, especially of slave children by their parents, were not unheard of.

Another common form of resistance was running away.
Although escape to the North or to Canada was very difficult and was achieved by only a relatively small number
of slaves, it was not at all unusual for slaves to take temporary "French leave" from their plantations. The evidence
from contemporary sources, including the newspapers,
leaves little question that at any given time hundreds of
slaves could be classified as temporary runaways. Slaves
showed such a propensity for running away that Dr.
Samuel Cartwright of Louisiana became convinced that
there was a disease unique to blacks, "Draptomania", which
caused its victims to run away.[12] Runaways, with the help
of family, relatives, or other sympathetic folk, often hid out
in the woods, swamps, or hills for weeks, months, or, in
some cases, even years. Sometimes they hid out individually,
sometimes in small groups. The slaveholders were often
able to catch runaways or to employ slave catchers who
used dogs to track them down. Severe punishment usually
awaited the runaway on his return to the plantation. On
the other hand, some fugitive slaves actually bargained with
their masters and escaped punishment in return for voluntarily returning to the plantation. As a matter of fact, a
surprising number of slaves became so adept at escape and
negotiation that they appear to have been able to go and
to come almost at will. Henry Bibb, for example, made
escape an art: "Among other good trades I learned the
art of running away to perfection. I made a regular business of it, and never gave it up, until I had broken the
bands of slavery . . . ."
Permanent escape from slavery was much more rare. The
slaves generally lacked knowledge of geography and understanding of the world outside the plantation, and the slaveholders took advantage of their ignorance and fear to discourage flight. Masters told their slaves horror stories
about northerners in general and abolitionists in particular.
This, of course, tended to increase the slaves' culturally engendered distrust and fear of all whites. Slaves were told
that they could not possibly escape, "that times were so . . .
[modern] with the telegraph and railway, that . . . [they]

couldn't get away." Former slave Isaac Williams believed
that the fear produced by such propaganda was "what
keeps the poor fellows there: that, and knowing that some
do set out, and get brought back, and knowing what is done
with them." Escape from the slave South was indeed a
formidable undertaking. A system of rewards and shared
antiblack sentiments encouraged whites, slaveholders and
nonslaveholders alike, to be active in the apprehension of
fugitive slaves. As a consequence, runaways often felt as
if they had small chance of success. "All the way along,"
observed William Grose, "I felt a dread—a heavy load on
me. . . . I would look up at the telegraph wire, and dread
that the news was going on ahead of me. At one time I
was on a canal boat—it did not seem to go fast enough
for me, and I felt very much cast down about it . . . ."

Perhaps an even more important deterrent to permanent
escape than fear and ignorance was the attachment of
slaves to their loved ones. Frederick Douglass thought
that "thousands would escape from slavery . . . but for the
strong cords of affection that bind them to their families,
relatives and friends." Separation from wives, children,
and husbands was indeed traumatic for many slaves. Henry
Bibb wrote that it had taken "all the moral courage that
I was master of to suppress my feeling while taking leave
of my little family." Another runaway slave, Henry Atkinson, noted that leaving his wife was "like taking my heart's
blood." "I never expect to see her again in this world—nor
our child," he added. Yet despite the difficulties and the
trauma involved, thousands of slaves did escape to the
North or to Canada, often through the use of clever ruses.
Most of the permanent fugitives were from the border
states and the states of the upper South; they escaped
singly, by twos or threes, or in groups of up to 16 or 18.
Generally, the number of escapees amounted to a slight
trickle, but at times the trickle became a flood. Francis
Henderson, who had been a slave in Washington, D.C., observed that in 1841 many slaves were fleeing to the free
states: ". . . it was two from here, three from there, etc.—
perhaps forty or fifty a week . . . . Men would disappear

all at once: a man who was working by me yesterday would be gone to-day,— how, I knew not. I really believed that they had some great flying machine to take them through the air."

Resistance by slaves also included direct defiance of slaveholders and their representatives. Slaves such as Francis Henderson, John Little, and Mrs. Christopher Hamilton refused to be whipped by their masters or overseers. John Holmes' narrative of his life as a slave is virtually a story of skirmishes and scraps with masters and overseers; Holmes bragged that he would not be whipped ("master sha'n't whip me, mistress sha'n't whip me, nobody sha'n't whip me") and he apparently got away with it. In relating how a "foolish, peevish" slave was whipped every day, Francis Henderson suggested that weakness invited punishment. Defiance, on the other hand, sometimes staved off whippings. Gilbert Dickey, a North Carolina slave, vowed after he had been badly abused to kill the next man who struck him: "I was never punished afterward, although I was sometimes threatened. If they find a man determined and resolute not to be whipped, they will sometimes let him alone: but in other places, they will do it at any rate."

Finally, resistance included violence of various types aimed at the master class. In their defiance of whites, slaves sometimes, in the heat of passion, engaged their masters or overseers in hand-to-hand struggles or flailed out at them with whatever weapons were available. In other instances, Afro-American slaves deliberately and clandestinely murdered whites with weapons such as knives, axes, or other tools, by the use of poison, or by burning their dwellings. Historian Joel R. Williamson suggests that fire was the foremost black weapon against whites; fire was quick, silent, and lethal, and it struck terror into the hearts of whites, especially in the dark of the night. In addition to dwellings, slaves burned barns and stables and their contents of livestock and crops. Some slave violence was the result of marauding bands of slave maroons who used guerrilla tactics to steal and pillage from plantations near their maroon hideaways.

The ultimate form of violent slave resistance, of course, was the slave revolt or insurrection. As we have seen in previous chapters, resistance to slavery had been manifested in the form of slave uprisings and revolts from the beginning of the African slave trade to the end of the eighteenth century. The nineteenth century would be no exception. Insurrections continued to occur, on slave ships, in slave coffles in the internal slave trade, in cities and towns, and on the plantations.

Scholars have long disagreed over what actually constituted a slave revolt, the number of such revolts, and the significance of the frequency or infrequency with which they occurred. It is not necessary here to set forth a narrow or carefully circumscribed definition of a slave revolt or to determine precisely how many revolts occurred that fit the prescribed definition. Stated simply, a slave revolt was a planned violent uprising by a number of slaves directed specifically against the whites. Its ultimate objective was to break the bonds of slavery, through escape from the land of bondage or a turnover in the organization of power. It is now clear that slave revolts were not uncommon or insignificant in the antebellum South. Despite the fact that they were generally unsuccessful, they demonstrate clearly the failure of the slaveholding class to break the wills of those enslaved.[13] The slave revolts were not the purposeless and nihilistic thrashing about of a psychotic people; they were the desperate but reasoned actions of those who had determined that they must strike out against slavery even if failure meant certain death. The slave revolts were the first radical blows for black freedom. As such, they helped to widen the existing cracks in the institution of slavery and they bequeathed to later generations of Afro-Americans a tradition of heroic resistance, hope, and determination, a tradition passed down in folklore and song:

> And your name it mought be Caesure sure,
> And got you cannon can shoot a mile or more,
> But you can't keep de world from moverin' round
> Nor Nat Turner from gaining ground.[14]

Within a single decade in the early nineteenth century, black slaves organized two of the most potentially destructive revolts in the history of Afro-America. Both were led by impressive men, strong, dedicated, and charismatic: Denmark Vesey, a free black who was a skilled carpenter and property owner, and Nat Turner, a slave mystic and preacher. Vesey had purchased his freedom in 1800, but his wife and children were held in bondage by a Charleston, South Carolina, slaveholder. A man of great pride, sensitivity, and courage, Vesey became obsessed with the idea of liberating his enslaved family and his black brethren, and he committed himself fully to accomplishing that purpose.

Recruiting a cadre of five other able and dedicated black liberators, including an ingenious organizer named Peter Poyas and a religious healer and conjurer called Gullah Jack (who was believed to possess supernatural powers), Vesey allegedly attracted to his support an army numbering in the thousands. Weapons were secured and elaborate plans were made to seize the city of Charleston in the summer of 1822 with six strike forces that would seize arsenals, armories, and guard houses. No white person was to be spared. Only the top leaders of the plot knew the crucial details of the insurrectionary plan, and for an organization so large, security was amazingly effective. In their recruiting, the insurgents, by and large, had carefully followed Peter Poyas' warning to be wary of domestic servants: "But take care and don't mention it to those waiting men who receive presents of old coats from their masters, or they'll betray us . . . ." Poyas' admonition was well taken, for ultimately it was a "favorite and confidential" slave who first leaked word of the plot to the whites.[15] Because the chief leaders were sworn to secrecy and because they played the role of falsely accused but innocent slaves so well, the authorities initially had great difficulty in determining if an insurrectionary plot really existed. Finally, however, after some of the rebels who had been arrested began to talk, charges were considered against 131 blacks, and 93 were put on trial; 35, including Vesey, Poyas, and Gullah

Jack, were executed and 43 were exiled from the state. Most of the conspirators were never discovered; the enrollment list of only one of the six leaders and that a small one—was ever found.[16]

Nine years later and many miles away in Southampton County, Virginia, the most famous slave insurrection in United States History and the one which had the greatest impact on the Afro-American experience occurred. From the standpoint of black vengeance being visited on whites, the Nat Turner revolt was also the most successful in North America, since at its conclusion 57 white men, women, and children lay dead. Yet ironically, the plans for Turner's insurrection were not made so far in advance nor were they nearly so elaborate as those conceived by Gabriel in 1800 and Denmark Vesey. Actually, the lack of a great deal of prior planning, recruitment, and organization helps to explain how the rebels were able to wreak such havoc. Turner knew that other slave plots had been discovered before they could get underway, and he was determined that the "march of destruction and murder should be the first news" of his war against the whites.

Nat Turner was the son of a father who later escaped from bondage and an African-born mother who so hated slavery that she attempted to kill her newborn baby. Turner possessed, in his own words, "uncommon intelligence for a child" and "learned to read and write . . . with the most perfect ease."[17] His father, mother, and acquaintances became convinced that he had special powers and impressed on him the idea that he "surely would be a prophet . . . ." Young Turner was quite close to his grandmother, who was "very religious," and religion became the matter that principally occupied his attention. As a young man, according to his own account, he "wrapped . . . [himself] in mystery, devoting . . . [his] time to fasting and prayer . . . and hearing the scriptures commented on at meetings . . . ." Revelations of the Holy Spirit confirmed Turner in the impression that he had been "ordained for some great purpose in the hands of the Almighty." By his twenty-fifth birthday, the great mission had taken on clearer implications:

And about this time I had a vision—and I saw white spirits and black spirits engaged in battle, and the sun was darkened—the thunder rolled in the Heavens, and blood flowed in streams—and I heard a voice saying, 'Such is your luck, such you are called to see, and let it come rough or smooth, you must surely bare it.'

In February 1831, after he had taken an eclipse of the sun as a sign to begin the "fight against the Serpent," Turner informed four trusted friends of the "great work laid out for me to do . . . ." He first set July 4 to begin the uprising, but postponed the date when he became ill. On Sunday, August 21, Turner met for dinner by a stream with six other slaves, including one named Will, who would later wield the "fatal axe" so effectively that Turner would dub him "the executioner." It was at this "feast" that the plan for the rebellion was worked out. Just after midnight on August 22 the small rebel group stealthily entered the home of Joseph Travis, for whom Turner worked, and speedily dispatched the family of five. During the night the Turner band, picking up followers along the way, worked its way across Southampton County, killing every white person encountered except the family of a poor farmer. The rebels were heading for the county seat, Jerusalem (a name with striking appropriateness in light of Turner's Messianic self-image). Ultimately the insurrectionist force numbered around 70, attracted not only by the idea of striking a blow for freedom but also by their faith in Turner as a religious leader. ". . . [T]hey believed and said," Turner noted, that "my wisdom came from God."

The insurrectionists never reached Jerusalem (now Courtland, Virginia). On Monday afternoon they were defeated in a short engagement at Parker's field, three miles from Jerusalem, and after a final skirmish the next morning, the revolt was over. Seventeen of the rebels were subsequently executed, and 12 were banished from the state.[18] Turner himself was not captured until October 30. From the time of his capture to the moment of execution, he maintained

a "calm, deliberate composure." He freely admitted his
part in the insurrection, but he never intimated feeling
even the slightest guilt or remorse for his actions. He had
taken up Christ's yoke to "fight against the Serpent," he
said, because the Spirit had informed him that "the time
was fast approaching when the first should be last and
the last should be first." Queried as to whether he did
not now find himself mistaken, he replied, "Was not Christ
crucified?"

What is implicit in the preceding pages is that slavery,
for all its elaborate system of regulation and control, never
developed to its logical conclusion; it never became a total
institution exacting total subservience and submissiveness.
Any system of absolute control requires the isolation of
individuals and the denial of meaningful interpersonal relationships. But the antebellum slaveholding class was unable
to exercise complete authority over their bondsmen, because their system of control did not provide for systematic
and thorough physical and psychological isolation of the
slaves as individuals. Consequently, slavery in the antebellum South could not and did not close off the opportunity for the generality of slaves to develop as individual
beings. It follows that the institution, contrary to the
claims of scholars such as Stanley Elkins, was simply not
"closed" enough to produce in large numbers the infantile,
irresponsible, servile, and happy-go-lucky Sambo personality
so common in white folklore and literature.

In the antebellum South the slaves' sense of community
was a buffer for most Afro-Americans, operating to preclude their individual isolation and thus to prevent their
complete degradation and dehumanization. The system of
slavery taught submissiveness and servility and indoctrinated
the slave with a feeling of deep inferiority and self-hatred.
However, the slave community covertly countered the message of slavery, making it extremely difficult for the slaveholders to enslave the minds of their slaves as they had
their bodies. The slave community provided "significant

others," which reduced slave identification with the master class, and offered an alternative cultural system geared to the everyday needs and desires of the slaves themselves. It was as members of the slave community that Afro-American slaves developed friendships and other interpersonal relationships and experienced, however imperfectly, an affirmation of self. Bolstered by the community, they clung tenaciously to a degree of self-pride and a sense of their worth as individuals. As members of the slave community, black bondsmen were more than chattels; they were—and they knew it—human beings with all the attributes that set men apart from the other animals.[19] "I was black," John Little recalled, "but I had the feelings of a man as well as any man."

Without question, the growth of the black community and the creation of an essentially autonomous black subculture were the most important developments of the Afro-American experience to 1865, and these developments would have a profound effect on the subsequent course of black history. Because Afro-American slaves retained a positive self-image and continued to see themselves as a "moral people" they were able not only to survive in slavery, but to transcend the institution that bound them, bequeathing to their posterity and to the world a unique example of survival and creativity in the face of extreme adversity. They "made it."

NOTES

[1] The ultimate statement of the negative impact of slavery on the slaves as individuals is in historian Stanley Elkins' *Slavery: A Problem in American Institutional and Intellectual Life.* Elkins assumes "that there were elements in the very structure of the plantation system—its 'closed' character—that could sustain infantilism as a *normal feature of behavior."* (Emphasis added.) Elkins further assumes "that the sanctions of the system were in themselves sufficient to produce a recognizable personality type," a type, he suggests, that has appeared widely in Southern lore as "Sambo." Elkins accepts the "major outlines" of the "Sambo" personality type as set forth in Southern literature and folk belief:

> Sambo . . . was docile but irresponsible, loyal but lazy, humble but chronically given to lying and stealing; his behavior was full of infantile silliness and his talk inflated with childish exaggeration. His relationship with his master was one of utter dependence and childlike attachment: it was indeed this childlike quality that was the very key to his being.

In identifying "Sambo" as a "plantation type" and in noting that a large majority of slaves lived on plantations, Elkins strongly implies that large numbers of slaves became "Samboes" in adjusting to the system of "absolute power" under which they lived.

[2] Some scholars, however, have tried to employ these methods. Sociologist Daniel P. Moynihan, for instance, uses his interpretation of the modern black family (however ethnocentric and patronizing it may be) as grounds for the conclusion that "American slavery was profoundly different from, and in its lasting effects on individuals and their children, indescribably worse than, any recorded servitude,

ancient or modern." See the so-called "Moynihan Report," U. S. Department of Labor, *The Negro Family: The Case for Federal Action* (Washington, D.C.: 1965). Stanley Elkins, on the other hand, attempts to assess the impact of slavery on its subjects through the use of modern personality theory and an analogy between slavery and the German concentration camps as systems of "absolute power." Data from the concentration camps indicate to Elkins "that infantile personality features . . . [can] be induced in a relatively short time among large numbers of adult human beings coming from very diverse backgrounds." Elkins simply assumes that such a process took place among black slaves in the antebellum South to produce the "Sambo" type discussed in footnote 1 above. Significantly, neither Elkins nor Moynihan provides substantial *historical evidence* to support his position.

[3] Historian Eugene Genovese comments as follows on the process of culture exchange between Afro-Americans and Euro-Americans:

. . . blacks, with their own traditions which extend back through such Afro-American forms as the slave songs, reach back to Africa itself. Blacks in America cannot avoid being Europeans too, just as to a lesser extent whites, especially Southern whites, cannot avoid being Africans too, however much they may howl at the thought; but the locus in each case has clearly been different. They share many things, and perhaps everything, but they combine them in entirely different ways to form distinct cultural configurations.

[4] Note, however, that only a small percentage of the white colonists were literate. In comparing the cultural heritage of Africans and Europeans, Professor George Rawick points out that there "was a thin veneer of literacy, in Latin in Europe and in Arabic in West Africa, but all but a small number of religious specialists were illiterate."

[5] After long neglecting the historical evidence left by slaves and their descendants, historians are increasingly using such material, including the narratives of fugitive slaves published prior to emancipation as well as recollections of former slaves such as those collected by the WPA (Works Projects Administration) during the 1930s. Like all primary materials, especially autobiographies and personal recollections, these sources must be used with careful and critical restraint, with due consideration to the circumstances under which they were produced. It is significant to note that for years historians have used similar material from white sources that have no greater claim to historical reliability. Recollections by former slaves and the slave narratives of the antebellum period cannot give us a complete picture

of slavery, or even of slave life, but used properly they are an indispensable source of firsthand information about, and useful insights into, what it meant to be a slave. As such, they come as close as possible to putting us in touch with the reality of slavery, as perceived by those who felt the impact of that institution most profoundly.

[6] We have already noted that slaveholders promoted pair-bond mating and the development of single-family units among the slaves *because* they believed that family ties made it easier to control their bondsmen. The imperatives of control also prompted masters and overseers to require slaves to participate in, or at least witness, the punishment of their spouses or other loved ones. "Sometimes, to cramp down the mind of the husband," ex-slave Henry Gowens noted, "he [the overseer] would compel him [the slave husband] to assist in the punishment of his wife." Another indication that slaveholders were aware of the affection that existed in slave families was their common use of subterfuge, trickery, and dissimulation in concealing their plans to sell particular slaves; not only were the slave owners reluctant to face the slaves to be sold and their families and relatives, and to listen to their entreaties, but they also knew that prospective separation from loved ones often prompted slaves to run away. The experience of David West was apparently typical:

> My mistress told me that I was not to be sold, and my master's brother told me the same, —but I had seen him carry away my father, sister, and aunt to Alabama to be sold .... Of course, I could not believe him, when he said I was not to be sold: for he had fooled my father with the story that he was going to remove to Alabama himself.

For the whole matter discussed in this footnote, see the essay by Eugene Genovese on "American Slaves and Their History" (p. 112), cited in the suggested readings for this chapter.

[7] Forthcoming independent studies by historians Eugene Genovese and Herbert Gutman will, in Genovese's words, "... argue forcefully that a sufficient degree of family cohesion existed among slaves to have laid the foundations for greater stability under freedom and that, in fact, considerable family cohesion was in evidence during and after Reconstruction." Genovese's study is on slave life, Gutman's on the black family in the period from the Civil War to World War I. Bobby F. Jones, "A Cultural Middle Passage," unpublished doctoral dissertation, University of North Carolina, Chapel Hill, N. C., 1965, and Willie Lee Rose, "Childhood in Bondage," a paper presented at the annual meeting of the Organization of American Historians (Los Angeles, April 1970), challenge the traditional view that the slave

family was particularly weak, unstable, and ineffectual as a social institution.

[8] In recent years the house slave has been the victim of pejorative stereotyping in most historical accounts. He is generally pictured as a privileged, selfish sycophant, the precursor of the modern-day "Uncle Tom." Once again, evidence from both white and black sources indicates that although some house servants considered themselves members of a privileged caste and some served as informers who betrayed their fellow slaves, house slaves frequently ran away, participated in conspiracies and revolts, and worked with the rest of the black community to resist, on a broad front, the degradation of chattel slavery.

[9] Jacob Stroyer, for instance, noted that "runaway slaves generally had fathers, brothers, cousins, or confidential friends who met them at certain appointed places, and brought them such things . . ." as food and clothing.

[10] In some cases slaves did not have so much discretion in choosing and discarding mates. Some masters attempted to promote stable marriages, and some went to considerable lengths to establish and enforce rigid regulations governing marriage, the behavior of married slaves, and divorce.

[11] Henry Bibb noted that he and his wife promised each other "that after marriage we would change our former course and live a pious life: . . . Clasping each other by the hand, pledging our sacred honor that we would be true, we called on high heaven to witness the rectitude of our purpose. There was nothing that could be more binding upon us as slaves than this . . . ." Bibb pointed out that many fugitive slaves were anxious to have their marriages made official and legal once they reached the North: "But as soon as they get free from slavery they go before some anti-slavery clergyman, and have the solemn ceremony of marriage performed according to the laws of the country."

[12] Cartwright attributed the slovenliness and carelessness with which some slaves performed their tasks to another alleged disease, *Dysaethesia Aethiopica*, also peculiar to blacks. When a slave labored "in a headlong, careless manner, treading down with his feet or cutting with his hoe the plants" he was supposedly tending, it was due, the doctor wrote, not to malicious intention, but rather to "the stupidness of mind and insensibility of the nerves induced by the disease."

[13] The only slave revolts that might have been successful were those in which the objective, or at least one objective, was escape from slavery, and only in the Texas uprising of 1851 is there firm evidence that this objective was achieved. The controversy over the frequency

of slave revolts and their meaning in the Afro-American experience is caught up in semantics and definitions. Historian Herbert Aptheker, using a broad definition that includes unconsummated conspiracies and accepts unconfirmed reports and rumors, maintains that there were some 250 revolts in the antebellum South. Historian John Blassingame employs a narrow, carefully worded designation and concludes that there were "at least nine slave revolts in [North] America between 1691 and 1865." Stanley Elkins, arguing that uprisings in Brazil were much more numerous and serious, suggests that only three revolts in the United States "emerge as worthy of any note"; Carl Degler agrees that rebellions were "not frequent" in the antebellum South, but in a well-informed discussion maintains that "the contrast with Brazil is not as sharp as the usual comparisons often assert."

[14] A recent book, Henry Irving Tragle, *The Southampton Slave Revolt of 1831: A Compilation of Source Material* (Amherst, Massachusetts: University of Massachusetts Press, 1971), presents evidence that the tradition of Nat Turner (see above, pp. 213-215) did indeed live on, at least for some black Americans. "I believe it possible," Tragle writes in his introduction, "to say with certainty that Nat Turner did exist as a folkhero to several generations of black men and women who have lived and died in Southampton County [Virginia] since 1831."

[15] But see the comments on house servants in footnote 8 above. Furthermore, Robert S. Starobin, ed., *Denmark Vesey: The Slave Conspiracy of 1822* (Englewood Cliffs, N. J.: Prentice-Hall, 1970), points out that the evidence on the Denmark Vesey case ". . . reveals some surprising information about those blacks who informed against conspiracies. Popular mythology holds that the so-called 'house nigger' group usually betrayed revolts; but in this case the informers came from various backgrounds."

[16] In 1964 historian Richard Wade, in an essay entitled "The Vesey Plot: A Reconsideration," *Journal of Southern History*, 30:148-161 (1964), startled students of slave revolts with the assertion that "no conspiracy in fact existed." Pointing to increasing racial tension, white fear and hysteria, and errors and inconsistencies in the records concerning the matter, Wade concluded that the "'plot' was probably never more than loose talk by aggrieved and embittered men." "Thus," he argues, "Charleston stumbled into tragedy." Despite Wade's well-reasoned argument and the *possibility* that it could be essentially correct, we believe that the weight of evidence points to the contrary, to the existence, in other words, of a well-conceived and serious conspiracy.

[17] Thomas Gray, the white lawyer who recorded Turner's *Confessions* (published in Baltimore in 1831), made the following observation relative to Turner's intelligence: "As to his ignorance, he certainly never had the advantages of education, but he can read and write, (it was taught him by his parents,) and for natural intelligence and quickness of apprehension, is surpassed by few men I have ever seen."

[18] The wave of white hysteria that generally followed black slave revolts resulted in the indiscriminate massacre of scores of blacks in Southampton and surrounding counties in the days immediately after the Turner insurrection. Editor John Hampden Pleasants of the Richmond *Whig* witnessed "the sanguinary temper of the [white] population, who evinced a strong disposition to inflict immediate death, upon every prisoner." Pleasants wrote "with pain" of "the slaughter of many blacks, without trial, and under circumstances of great barbarity . . . ." Most of those summarily lynched, perhaps more than 100, had taken no part whatever in the uprising. The dissection of Nat Turner's body and the final disposition of his remains further demonstrate the extent to which the imperatives of slavery and racism brutalized the minds of whites and prompted them to irrational behavior.

[19] A brief word of warning may be in order at this point. In emphasizing the development of the black community and the evolution of a distinct Afro-American subculture, we are by no means arguing that the slavery era was a golden age for Afro-Americans. What we *are* saying is that these occurrences made it possible for Afro-Americans to develop the resilience and the perseverance necessary to withstand the deeply searing experience of slavery and to resist the dehumanizing effects of that institution.

SUGGESTIONS FOR FURTHER READING

The scholarly literature pertinent to this chapter has grown tremendously in recent years. The best full-length treatment of the subject matter of the chapter is George P. Rawick's remarkably fresh and provocative *From Sundown to Sunup: The Making of the Black Community* (Westport, Conn.: Greenwood Publishing, 1972), Vol. I of the projected multivolume *The American Slave: A Composite Autobiography.* In addition to Rawick, Eugene D. Genovese, Sterling Stuckey, John W. Blassingame, Lerone Bennett, Jr., and Lawrence W. Levine have been keenly interested in the nature of the cultural processes involved in the Afro-American experience in slavery and have provided the most perceptive treatments of the development of an Afro-American subculture. Levine's cogently argued "Slave Songs and Slave Consciousness" first appeared in Tamara K. Hareven, ed., *Anonymous Americans: Explorations in Nineteenth-Century Social History* (Englewood Cliffs, N.J.: Prentice-Hall, 1971). Stuckey draws on the same kinds of materials in "Through the Prism of Folklore: The Black Ethos in Slavery," first published in *The Massachusetts Review,* 9:417-437 (1968), and reprinted in an excellent collection by Eric Foner, *America's Black Past: A Reader in Afro-American History* (New York: Harper & Row, 1970). Several of the essays in Genovese's *In Red and Black: Marxian Explorations in Southern and Afro-American History* (New York: Pantheon Books, 1971) contain ideas pertinent to this chapter, but the most important of the selections is "American Slaves and Their History," an essay that apparently may be taken as a short preview of Genovese's forthcoming book on slave life. Blassingame's *The Slave Community: Plantation Life in the Antebellum South* (New York: Oxford University

Press, 1972) is an excellent study of slave life and the development of the slave community; Bennett's "The World of the Slave," *Ebony*, 35:44-56 (February, 1971), is an outstanding capsule treatment of these same topics. Winthrop Jordan's *White Over Black* contains much useful information on the cultural processes at work in the seventeenth and eighteenth centuries, but Jordan's view of the extent to which the generality of blacks made cultural adjustments to the dominant culture should be weighed against the interpretations of the scholars cited above. John S. Mbiti, *African Religions and Philosophy* (Garden City, New York: Doubleday & Company, 1970), is helpful in exploring the matter of the continuing influence of the African heritage on Afro-Americans. On the same subject, see Melville J. Herskovits, *The Myth of the Negro Past* and *The New World Negro*. Both are cited in Chapter 3.

Two studies based on pre-Civil War slave narratives and a number of the published recollections of ex-slaves interviewed in the 1930s may be consulted with profit in connection with this chapter. They include Charles H. Nichols, *Many Thousand Gone: The Ex-Slaves' Account of Their Bondage and Freedom* (Leiden, Netherlands: E. J. Brill, 1963); Stanley Feldstein, *Once a Slave: The Slaves' View of Slavery* (New York: William Morrow, 1971); Norman R. Yetman, ed., *Life Under the "Peculiar Institution": Selections from the Slave Narrative Collection* (New York: Holt, Rinehart and Winston, 1971); Norman Yetman, ed., *Voices from Slavery* (New York: Holt, Rinehart, and Winston, 1970); and Benjamin A. Botkin, *Lay My Burden Down: A Folk History of Slavery* (Chicago: The University of Chicago Press, 1945). The collections of slave narratives cited in the suggested readings for Chapter 5 are particularly important for this chapter, as are the works of Olmsted *(The Cotton Kingdom)*, Weld *(American Slavery As It Is)*, and Conway *(Testimonies Concerning Slavery)*, also cited in previous pages. The pre-Civil War collection of slave narratives by Benjamin Drew, *The Refugee: Or The Narratives of Fugitive Slaves in Canada: A Northside View of Slavery* (Boston: John P. Jewett, 1856), reprinted in 1969 by Addison-Wesley Publishing, Reading, Massachusetts (ed., Tilden G. Edelstein), contains a wealth of information and insights. The student should also consult the classic autobiographies of Frederick Douglass: *A Narrative of the Life of Frederick Douglass, an American Slave, Written by Himself* (Boston: Anti-Slavery Office, 1845); *My Bondage and My Freedom* (New York: Miller, Orton, and Mulligan, 1855); and *Life and Times of Frederick Douglass* (Hartford, Conn.: Park Publishing, 1882). Two other works previously cited contain useful material, Carl Degler's *Neither Black Nor White* and Kenneth Stampp's

The Peculiar Institution. A excellent collection of readings with pertinent selections (particularly E. Franklin Frazier's discussion of "Motherhood in Bondage") is Melvin Drimmer, ed., *Black History: A Reappraisal* (New York: Doubleday & Company, 1969).

The most provocative and coherent treatment of slave religion is in Levine, "Slave Songs and Slave Consciousness," (cited above); Stuckey, "Through the Prism of Folklore," (cited above), and Vincent Harding, "Religion and Resistance Among Antebellum Negroes, 1800-1860", in the useful collection by August Meier and Elliott Rudwick, *The Making of Black America: Essays in Negro Life & History,* Vol. I, (New York: Atheneum, 1969), also contain valuable insights into specific aspects of slave religion. For slave songs and music see the essays by Levine and Stuckey, Eileen Southern's *The Music of Black Americans: A History* (New York: W. W. Norton, 1971), and Leroi Jones, *Blues People: Negro Music in White America* (New York: William Morrow, 1963). The significant subject of slave folklore is explored in Stuckey's essay, in the introduction to Osofsky's *Puttin On Ole Massa* (cited in Chapter 5), and in Bernard Wolfe's intriguing "Uncle Remus and the Malevolent Rabbit," *Commentary,* 8:31-41 (1949). For the development of Afro-American language, see Sidney W. Mintz, "Toward an Afro-American History," (cited in Chapter 3). David Brion Davis, "The Comparative Approach to American History: Slavery," in Foner and Genovese, eds., *Slavery in the New World* (cited in Chapter 3) and Jessie Bernard, *Marriage and Family Among Negroes* (Englewood Cliffs, N. J.: Prentice-Hall, 1966), present interpretations of specific aspects of slave life with which we disagree.

In recent years scholars have been particularly interested in the subjects of slave resistance and slave personality. A classic on "Day-to-Day Resistance to Slavery" is Raymond A. and Alice H. Bauer's essay in the *Journal of Negro History,* 27:388-419 (1942), which is reprinted in a number of anthologies. An excellent general treatment is William F. Cheek, *Black Resistance Before the Civil War* (Beverly Hills, Calif.: Glencoe Press, 1970), and there is much useful material in Herbert Aptheker, "Slave Resistance in the United States," and Joel R. Williamson, "Black Self-Assertion Before and After Emancipation," both in Huggins, Kilson, and Fox, ed., *Key Issues in the Afro-American Experience* (cited in Chapter 5). On slave revolts, see, in addition to the titles cited in the footnotes, Herbert Aptheker, *American Negro Slave Revolts* (New York: Columbia University Press, 1943); Eric Foner, ed., *Nat Turner* (Englewood Cliffs, N. J.: Prentice-Hall, 1971); John B. Duff and Peter M. Mitchell, eds., *The Nat Turner Rebellion: The Historical Event and the Modern Con-*

troversy (New York: Harper & Row, 1971); John Oliver Killens, ed., *The Trial Record of Denmark Vesey* (Boston: Beacon Press, 1970); Harvey Wish, "American Slave Insurrections Before 1861," *Journal of Negro History*, 22:299-320 (1937); and Marion D. DeB. Kilson, "Towards Freedom: An Analysis of Slave Revolts in the United States," *Phylon*, 25:175-187 (1964), reprinted in Meier and Rudwick, eds., *The Making of Black America*, Vol. I. (cited above). On the controversial issue of slave personality see Stanley Elkins, *Slavery* (cited in Chapter 5), and Ann J. Lane, ed., *The Debate over SLAVERY: Stanley Elkins and His Critics* (Chicago: University of Illinois Press, 1971), especially the essays by Earl E. Thrope, "Chattel Slavery and Concentration Camps"; Mary Agnes Lewis, "Slavery and Personality"; Eugene D. Genovese, "Rebelliousness and Docility in the Negro Slave: A Critique of the Elkins Thesis" and "American Slaves and Their History"; George M. Fredrickson and Christopher Lasch, "Resistance to Slavery"; and Elkins' reply, "Slavery and Ideology." Perhaps the best general treatment of the subject is Kenneth M. Stampp's well-informed and reasoned essay, "Rebels and Samboes: The Search for the Negro's Personality in Slavery," *The Journal of Southern History*, 37:367-392 (1971).

Chapter 7

ABOLITION AND EMANCIPATION: An Interpretation

If the institution of slavery was of central significance in the concurrent histories of Euro-America and Afro-America, as it clearly was, then it should be obvious that its abolition would also have tremendous influence on the course of the total national history. Aside from the establishment of chattel slavery, probably no single event has exercised a greater shaping force on American affairs than the abolition of that institution. Recently most historians have come to recognize more clearly than ever that the slavery question lay at the heart of the regional antipathy that produced the American Civil War. Certainly emancipation of the slaves was a direct result of the war, and emancipation marked a clear turning point in Afro-American history. However, what is not entirely clear even now is just how slavery caused the war, and how the war ended slavery. Historians generally agree that the kind of emancipation that came as a result of the war was limited in scope, and that the abolition of slavery did not entirely free the blacks nor make them the equals of whites. Somehow emancipation with all its cost in human lives did not live up to its promise, and those who had fought so hard to abolish slavery had to accept something less than freedom for the black population of the United States. The question still unanswered is *why* this was so?

Chapter 7 attempts to answer these difficult questions, these "hows" and "whys" of abolition and emancipation.

Note. Footnotes for this chapter are located on pages 260-263.

To do so, we turn again to culture considerations, and especially to the consideration of the nature and meaning of slavery and racism in the total structure of American culture. The key to the thorniest problems relating to emancipation lies in establishing just how deeply embedded slavery and racism were in the American cultural interstices. Our conclusion is that slavery was *not* well integrated in the total national culture and was thus "culturally vulnerable," while white racism was perfectly integrated into the dominant American value system and therefore persisted as a determinant of black status in the United States long after slavery had been technically abolished.

Antislavery attitudes existed in America from the very beginning of chattel servitude. Most blacks, slave and free, opposed the existence of racial slavery. However, as we observed in Chapter 4, antislavery feelings were not limited to blacks. White Quakers and many white Methodists opposed the institution from the outset, and the spokesmen for eighteenth-century enlightment rationalism also argued against it. The American Revolutionary philosophy and black participation in the Revolutionary War brought antislavery to such an intensity that slavery was actually abolished over a period of years in all of the northern states. Despite their sincerity, efforts at abolition in the South failed as the "necessary but evil" argument prevailed, and thus slavery came to be an essentially regional institution. The same argument prevailed in the Federal Constitutional Convention at Philadelphia, and as a consequence slavery was written into the Constitution of the United States.

But even in the nineteenth-century South there were substantial numbers of whites who fully realized that chattel slavery was diametrically opposed to the libertarian-humanitarian principles on which the United States was supposedly founded as a nation, and that American national purpose was compromised by the continued existence of the institution. Moreover, despite the religious sanctions for slavery, many white Americans had come to agree with the new Protestant evangelical preachments that slavery, because it was anti-humanitarian and anti-equalitarian, was sinful and that slaveowners were sinning by owning slaves. In two important ways, then, the continued existence of slavery produced serious doubts in the minds of Americans. Such doubts furnished the basis of the vulnerability of the institution. As long as these doubts prevailed, slavery could not become completely integrated into the mainstream of American culture. And indeed the doubts persisted and actually intensified (at least in the free states) right up to the moment of emancipation. This is not to say that most white Americans of the antebellum period were openly opposed to slavery, but only that many of them did harbor serious doubts as to its acceptibility in a Christian nation professing to believe in the promise of the Declaration of Independence.

There were, of course, some whites and many blacks who *were* overtly opposed to the institution of slavery and who acted accordingly. At no time in the nation's history did overt antislavery activity cease. In the early nineteenth century antislavery societies operated in most northern and southern states. But white antislavery elements prior to 1830 generally tied their antislavery activity to firm colonizationist principles. They wanted to abolish slavery, gradually and painlessly, and at the same time eliminate all the blacks by "colonizing" them somewhere in Africa or Latin America or the American West; colonization anywhere would suffice, as long as it did not permit blacks to remain in white America as a permanently unassimilable element in the total population. Such opponents of slavery, for all the sincerity of their feelings about the institution, were clearly what we would now term racists. Blacks and whites, they believed, could not live together. The American Colonization Society, founded in 1816 by a group of white antislavery activists, was the agency through which the forces of gradualist emancipation and colonization would operate until the coming of the Civil War.

The great majority of black antislavery spokesmen, however, and a significant minority of the whites, were not in favor of colonization in principle, and favored rapid rather than gradual emancipation.[1] This element of American antislavery opinion came to be termed "abolitionist," and was believed by the majority of white Americans to be quite "radical" in its proposals, especially after 1830, when abolitionism took an "immediatist" turn.[2]

The rise of immediatism in American abolitionism has been the subject of considerable historical controversy. Several reasons have been advanced to explain the sudden emergence of the "new abolitionism." First, the late 1820s saw a significant increase in militance among the *black* abolitionists. Many black antislavery leaders began to speak out openly against colonization, and early in the decade the Denmark Vesey conspiracy (see Chapter 6) had provided a dramatic example of antislavery activity at its most militant. In 1828 two black antislavery spokesmen, John B. Russwurm and Samuel E. Cornish, began publication of the first black abolitionist newspaper, *Freedom's Journal*, proclaiming in the first issue that "Too long have others spoken for us. Too long has the public been deceived by misrepresentations." During its existence, *Freedom's Journal* remained outspoken in its abolitionism and in its insistence that blacks must speak out for themselves.

One of the agents representing the paper was a young black man, a clothing dealer from Boston by the name of David Walker. In 1829 Walker published a militant statement calling for the immediate emancipation of all slaves, and urging bondsmen to rise in violent revolt against their masters should emancipation not be forthcoming. The 76-page pamphlet entitled *Walker's Appeal, in Four Articles ...* was addressed to the "coloured citizens" of the world, but its message was clearly intended for both black and white Americans. Walker claimed that Afro-Americans were "the most degraded, wretched, and abject set of beings that ever lived since the world began." He contended that four things were responsible for their condition. Slavery was most important, followed by ignorance, the colonization movement, and "the preachers of Jesus Christ." Walker urged blacks to resist all four forces of oppression to the end, and he served notice to whites that "America is as much our country, as it is yours." Finally, he called on the slaves to revolt and overthrow their masters if the conditions of blacks were not immediately improved. Once this violent strike for freedom had commenced, it should be quick and deadly: ". . . do not trifle," Walker admonished the slaves, "for they will not trifle with you—they want us for their slaves, and think nothing of murdering us in order to subject us to that wretched condition—therefore, if there is an attempt made by us, kill or be killed." ". . . We must and shall be free I say . . . ." "And," he warned the whites, "wo, wo will be to you if we have to obtain our freedom by fighting."

It would be difficult to overstate the effect produced by this militant call for liberty. Southern state legislatures quickly acted to ban it in their respective states and even to make possession of a copy a felony. The more conservative elements in the abolitionist movement condemned it as inflammatory and dangerous. But *Walker's Appeal* provides yet another example of black militance that had a profound influence on the rise of antislavery immediatism.

American abolitionists who moved toward immediatism were also under the influence of their foreign counterparts. The year 1829 saw the official end of slavery in Mexico (a fact that proved deeply disturbing to American slaveholders in Mexican Texas), and by 1831 the British immediatists had procured a law requiring emancipation in the British West Indies. The Americans were thus encouraged to increase their efforts. They had to do so to stay in step with the worldwide abolitionist crusade of the 1820s and 1830s.

Finally, evangelical revivalism played a significant role in the rise of immediatism, particularly among the white abolitionists. In 1820s the rise of Protestant revival preaching captured the popular imagination with its fervor and sincerity. Thousands flocked to hear and to participate in revival meetings characterized by an emphasis on enthusiastic preaching and emotional responses from the assembled congregations, who were taught that all humankind was a product of God's work and that holding human beings in bondage was thus immoral and sinful. The revival movement emphasized man's responsibility to eliminate evil institutions in his quest for perfection on earth. Such preachers as Charles Grandison Finney in New York and Lyman Beecher in New England converted countless hundreds to immediatism, and their influence spread westward to Ohio, Indiana, and Illinois through the work of their converts. Many active abolitionists were themselves preachers, and Theodore Dwight Weld, a major figure and a key leader in western abolitionist circles, was a Finney convert. On the basis of conscience and morality, then, increasing numbers of abolitionists argued for the immediate abolition of slavery. Their influence was of incalculable but unquestionable significance.

It was a combination of circumstances and events, however, that gave the rise of immediatism its enormous impact and made the abolitionists a real force in national affairs. *Walker's Appeal* may be thought of as the initial step in the direction of notoriety, but in 1831 two occurrences actually launched American abolitionism into its militant phase and commenced abolitionism's role in the process that would culminate in Civil War and emancipation. On January 1, 1831, a Boston reformer by the name of William Lloyd Garrison began publication of a radical, militant, immediatist newspaper, the *Liberator*. In straightforward language Garrison specifically renounced gradualism and called for immediate, total, uncompensated emancipation of all slaves in the United States. His language was as uncompromising as his principles: "Let Southern oppressors tremble—let their secret abettors tremble—let their Northern apologists tremble—let all the enemies of the persecuted blacks tremble." And if Garrison's words were not adequate to evoke the old southern fear, Nat Turner's revolt in Southampton County, Virginia, coming six months after the birth of the *Liberator*, assuredly was. (see Chapter 6).

There is considerable evidence that Garrison's rise to fame and to the leadership of the abolitionist movement came at least partly from a certain confusion in the public mind. Somehow *Walker's Appeal*, Turner's revolt, and the appearance of the *Liberator* came to be related in the reports of antislavery activity, especially in the South. And so Garrison's militance, real though it was, was given added impact by its association with one clear call for violence and one terrifying instance of violence. White Southerners were never able to separate their image of Garrison from their fear of slave insurrection, and Garrison and abolitionism quickly came to be the symbols of that great fear in their minds.[3]

One year following the appearance of the first issue of the *Liberator*, on January 6, 1832, the Garrisonian wing of American abolitionism was institutionalized when 12 men meeting in a small room beneath the African Baptist Church in Boston founded the New England Anti-Slavery Society. Their stated principles included not only immediate abolition but also the general improvement of the lot of black people in all the states. The Garrisonians dedicated themselves to the principle of equality, a principle they would hold at least theoretically until after the Civil War. Garrison was, of course, the leader of this group and its most vocal spokesman throughout its long history.

The "new spirit of abolitionism" (as historian Benjamin Quarles has called it) received further institutional support with the founding of the American Anti-Slavery Society in December 1833. Sixty-three delegates to the first convention, representing 11 states, met in Philadelphia, and despite considerable disagreement as to means and ends, the group managed to agree on the statement of two overriding principles: "the entire abolition of slavery" and the general improvement of "the character and condition of people of color" in the United States. The establishment of a national organization gave some focus to the abolitionist crusade, even though the most important work of the American abolitionists would remain largely local and grass roots in nature.[4] In 1840 Garrison would take control of the American Anti-Slavery Society, providing leadership and additional focus through his emphasis on immediatism and his unrelenting opposition to colonization.

When the newly formed American Anti-Slavery Society resolved to better the conditions of black people in the North as well as the South, it was undertaking a reform of monumental proportions. In the Jacksonian era, the "Age of the Common Man," few if any blacks had achieved anything resembling equality in any phase of American life. Only the tiniest minority of the northern black population had the right to vote, and only in Maine, Vermont, New Hampshire, and Massachusetts could even that minority vote without special restrictions based on color. Some 93% of the northern free blacks had no vote at all, and every state admitted to the Union after 1819 restricted the vote to whites. Economic opportunity was similarly restricted. The vast majority of free blacks worked in low-paying menial jobs or as servants of whites. Moreover, white laborers were determined to maintain this situation, for blacks represented potential competition in the job market, and whites totally rejected the idea that blacks should serve in the same employment capacity as themselves. Working with blacks would mean associating with them, and white workers simply would not tolerate the loss in social status they believed would result from such association. Even the Irish immigrants, next to the bottom on the socio-economic ladder, quickly assumed the racist notions of other Euro-Americans and behaved accordingly. Segregation in education and in most public facilities was the common practice long before the day of systematic "Jim Crow" law. Black Americans were despised, feared, resented, and treated with utter contempt by the vast majority of whites in the North.

Accordingly, the abolitionists' announced decision to attack discrimination in the North as well as slavery in the South met with warm reception among the black population. The few blacks who had managed to overcome the disadvantages confronting them and achieve some measure of material success developed a renewed enthusiasm for the abolitionist cause that resulted in another active, verbal wing of the abolitionist movement. The black abolitionists were to become an effective goad, prodding their white counterparts and insisting that the "Civil Rights" aspect of the movement be given its due in the double-edged assault on white racism and its institutions, black slavery and antiblack discrimination.[5]

The militant abolitionists, white and black, pursued essentially similar tactics in support of their cause. Although there were various opinions as to the most effective means of attacking slavery and discrimination, abolitionists employed two fundamental means of assault. First and oldest was the tactic of "moral suasion," the effort to play on the conscience of white America to achieve the abolition of slavery by convincing the nation of its sinful and immoral nature. The moral suasionists were trying to generate a kind of "affective change" (see Chapter 1) in the basic American value system in order to induce a substantial alteration in mainstream American culture. In pursuit of this goal the moral suasionists maintained an active press, created a large antislavery literature, and used lectures and sermons to persuade the public of the justice of their cause. They waged a true propaganda campaign in the modern sense of the term and employed the techniques of propaganda with considerable effect.

Not only did they preach and lecture and write in their crusade. "Moral suasion . . .," writes one historian of American abolition, "was not a collection of naive sermons on brotherhood. The abolitionists were tough." Employing the tactics that have come to be associated with the twentieth-century Civil Rights Movement, "they sat-in, prayed-in, and spoke-in to break the barriers of caste . . . ." They used civil disobedience and direct action protest in their cause, even at the risk of mob violence and arrest. William Lloyd Garrison publically burned a copy of the United States Constitution, declaring it to be a proslavery document. Ordinarily, the moral suasionists did not operate through traditionally established political or social institutions. They tended instead to avoid the uses of politics in their quest, leaving the employment of that approach to the second type of abolitionist.

The "political abolitionists" were those who were convinced that slavery could best be eliminated by the operation of the political system; they believed that the institution could be attacked most effectively through the courts and the legislatures of the states and the federal government, and most especially through political parties. Initially they had little success in convincing the major parties of the day to accept antislavery as party policy, so they proceeded to organize their own parties: first the Liberty Party in 1839, then the Free Soil Party, which was formed in 1848 and soon after absorbed the Liberty Party, only to be itself absorbed by the Republicans on the eve of the Civil War. This is a story, however, that will require greater elaboration later. For now it is enough to say that the "moral suasionists," in renouncing all traditional political avenues of change, were the more "radical" of the abolitionist elements.

To some degree all abolitionist activities were racially "integrated"; that is, the various groups contained both black and white members who acted more or less in concert. But in some important ways the blacks, operating individually or through all-black organizations, pursued policies that differed somewhat from those of the white-dominated abolitionist groups. Frederick Douglass, a former slave from Maryland and the greatest of the black abolitionist leaders, declared in 1855: "OUR ELEVATION AS A RACE IS ALMOST WHOLLY DEPENDENT UPON OUR OWN EXERTIONS .... The history of other oppressed nations will confirm us in this assertion .... The oppressed nation itself has always taken a prominent part in the conflict." He was, of course, correct in the latter assertion, and black Americans exerted themselves independently in ways that have only recently been closely studied.

The primary, although by no means exclusive, thrust of the independent black abolitionists was the promotion of the anti-discrimination goal of the abolition crusade. Many northern blacks feared, often justifiably, that their white counterparts were at best lukewarm in their support

of black equality. In 1839 one black abolitionist noted
that the white abolitionists, in their campaign against plantation slavery in the South, "overlooked slavery in the
North . . . ." A second major distinction between black
and white abolitionism was the result of the more direct
personal contact that the blacks had had with slavery.
White abolitionists were often theoretical and given to abstraction as they pursued their ideological ends. Black
abolitionists, as Benjamin Quarles has observed, "had no
fondness for abstraction. Their interest was more personal.
A Negro could scarcely muster enough detachment to live
in the realms of pure principle . . . ." For the blacks there
was, quite simply, much more at stake.

We have already noted in passing one of the important
weapons employed by the blacks against slavery and oppression: the black abolitionist press. The black press was
of vital significance to the abolitionist movement, particularly in that it provided a black voice directed toward black
people, a voice that served to heighten abolitionist sentiment and conviction among the black population. Calling
consistently for freedom and equality, such publications
as *Freedom's Journal, Rights of All, The North Star* (later
Frederick Douglass' Weekly), the *Colored American*, and
the *Anglo-African* retained a singleness of purpose that the
white press could not match. Many of the most talented
black antislavery leaders were newspaper editors or frequent
contributors to the press, and their words played a key
role in creating a sense of solidarity among the black population.

A second source of leadership among the black abolitionists was the black church. In a culture that afforded
few paths of advancement for Afro-Americans, the ministry
provided one profession open to talented and ambitious
blacks, and it attracted many potential leaders. It is significant that all eight of the blacks who organized the
American and Foreign Anti-Slavery Society in 1840 were
clergymen. Included in the group were men who would
become key spokesmen of the abolitionist cause in the
years to follow, such men as Samuel E. Cornish, Theodore

S. Wright, and young Henry Highland Garnet. The church itself played a considerable role in the abolitionist movement, as historian Leon Litwack has noted: "In addition to being a center of religious devotion and ceremony, it was a school, a political meeting hall, a community recreation and social center, and, not too infrequently, a haven for fugitive slaves." As was the case with the black church of the plantation South, the northern black church served a function that went far beyond spiritual comfort and moral guidance.[6]

Black solidarity and commitment to the elevation of the status of blacks were clearly manifested in what has come to be termed the "Negro Convention Movement." From September 1830 through the next five years—the "crisis" years of American abolitionism—blacks held conventions to discuss their goals and to state their demands publicly. Meeting usually in Philadelphia, these conventions directed their attention to three or four central concerns in addition to the abolition of slavery. They demanded the general economic advancement of blacks through increased job opportunities, and the end to discrimination, particularly the antiblack legal statutes existing in many northern states. They regularly denounced the American Colonization Society and stressed the need for black organization in the quest for equality and abolition. There is no quantitative means of assessing the actual impact of the Convention Movement, but its existence and functions tell us a good bit about the nature and goals of black protest in the middle of the nineteenth century. There *was* a black protest movement, its demands were specific and concrete, and it had sufficient support to continue its operations right up to the Civil War.

Black participation in the so-called "Underground Railroad" provided an example of direct action protest of an even more dramatic nature. Fugitive slaves attempting to escape from bondage needed all the help they could get on their incredibly difficult journey through slave territory, and even after reaching "free" country. Although it has been clearly demonstrated that no set system of escape routes from the South actually existed, there were many individuals who aided the "fugitives," sometimes at considerable danger to themselves. Most notable of these "conductors" on the metaphorical railroad was the indomitable Harriet Tubman, a woman of unbelievable courage and dedication who, after her own escape from bondage, made as many as 15 "raids" into slave states to escort over 200 slaves to free soil. Other less notable participants in the Underground Railroad served the fugitives by providing shelter, clothing, food, and "cover." In a somewhat more organized fashion, "vigilance committees" in the free states often afforded similar aid and provided money and legal advice to fugitives once they arrived in the North.[7]

But if the fugitive slaves needed the help of the abolitionists, they themselves also made important contributions to the cause of abolition. Although the actual number of escapees was relatively small, many of those who did make it proved invaluable, for they could speak and write of slavery from firsthand experience. On the platform and in the press, these former slaves could attack slavery by striking at the two basic (and faulty) premises that bolstered the institution: first, that the slave system was characterized by benevolent paternalism and contented, happy slaves; and second, that blacks were innately inferior to whites, that they were indeed something less than human and predetermined by nature to belong to a slave caste. The more articulate fugitives could readily counter both arguments, and this they did with great effect. Douglass himself was the greatest of the fugitive slave spokesmen, but William Wells Brown, Lewis and Milton Clarke, Henry Bibb, and others also contributed their talents to the cause. Many of them published accounts of their slave experiences. Douglass' *Narrative of My Life*, first published in 1845, went through many editions and revisions. Soloman Northup's account of his capture as a free black and his sale into slavery in Louisiana (one of the best of the slave narratives) sold at least 27,000 copies and was read by many times that number of people. Bibb and Brown also produced important slave narratives. As speakers and as writers, then, the former slaves could provide something that no others could hope to offer: an idea of what slavery was like from the point of view of the slaves themselves. Perhaps no other single element in the abolitionist movement was as effective as these firsthand accounts of slavery in bringing on the change in northern white attitudes that would be essential to abolitionist success.

The assault on slavery following the events of 1831 produced a powerful reaction in the slave South. Convinced that slavery was an essential integrative element in southern culture (including the southern economy), proslavery forces in the South began a defense of the institution that would ultimately contend that slavery was not really a "necessary evil" at all, but rather a "positive good." Hence it was an institution that must be protected and defended against all assault. Moreover, many proslavery Southerners came to view all abolitionist principles as characteristically *northern* principles, and to consider "the North" as a monolithic antislavery monster. Thus, white Southerners in their paranoic defense of slavery based their antipathy to "the North" on their confusion of "northern" and "abolitionist" sentiments and attitudes.

Ironically, the militant abolitionists constituted only a tiny minority in the North, and, in fact, they confronted some major disadvantages in their reform efforts there. Foremost among the disadvantages was antiblack prejudice in the North and West. So long as the abolitionists' goals were exclusively antislavery, gradualist, and colonizationist, they were on safe ground north of Dixie. But as we have already noted, with the emergence of Garrisonian immediatism, the abolitionist crusade took on the dual goals of abolition *and* equality for blacks in the North. It was because of this second objective as well as their increased militancy and radicalism that the abolitionists ran into serious trouble.

Alexis de Tocqueville, one of the more perceptive analysts of American culture in the Jacksonian era, was struck by the antiblack prejudice prevalent in the free states. In his famous *Democracy in America* he wrote: "The prejudice of race appears to be stronger in the states that have abolished slavery than in those where it still exists; and nowhere is it so intolerant as in those states where servitude has never been known." Doubtless Tocqueville's statement was somewhat exaggerated, but in its claim that antiblack racism was pervasive in the free states, the assertion is essentially valid. The evidence on this point is clear-cut. We have already noted the segregation and discrimination practiced against blacks in the North. Such discrimination was for the most part viewed as natural and normal by whites, who accepted white supremacy as part of the nation's cultural fabric. Leon Litwack, whose book *North of Slavery* closely examines the status of blacks in the antebellum North, suggests that to most white northerners, "segregation constituted not a departure from democratic principles . . . but simply the working out of natural laws, the inevitable consequence of the racial inferiority of the Negro." The white majority never accepted the idea that blacks could ever be peacefully "integrated" or assimilated into the dominant culture; indeed, one of the greatest white fears was "amalgamation." Any sizable increase in the free black population, the sort of increase certain to result from unrestricted emancipation of the slaves, was consistently opposed by practically all northern and western whites.

Northern white opposition to blacks frequently boiled over into violent race riots. In Philadelphia alone five antiblack riots were set off by white mobs between 1830 and 1845, most of them during periods of economic dislocation when blacks represented a potential threat to the white labor market. Blacks were beaten and stoned, their homes and churches burned, and their families forced to leave the city to escape the white fury. Robert Purvis, a black leader in Philadelphia, described the white mob of 1842 as "one of the most ferocious and bloody spirited . . . that ever cursed a Christian (?) community . . . ." A grand jury investigation of the affair concluded that the attack was brought on by the "provocative nature" of a black parade commemorating the abolition of slavery in the West Indies. Purvis, in a despairing response to this finding, lamented, "I am convinced of our utter and complete nothingness in public estimation." The first great obstacle confronting the abolitionists, then, was white racism, personal and institutionalized, pervasive and intensely emotional.

A second major obstacle, although not as visible as the first, was of almost equal importance. The abolitionists, in their attack on slavery, represented a threat to certain deeply entrenched economic and social interests. Northern textile manufacturers were dependent on the South for most of their raw cotton. In addition, the slave states served as a primary market for crude cotton goods. Northern financial interests, deeply involved in the capitalization of the burgeoning textile industry, were also threatened by the prospect of emancipation. The simple fact is that black slavery was so deeply enmeshed in the whole economic structure of the nation that its abolition, many believed, would cause serious dislocation. Moreover, the attack on slavery *did* represent an attack on one form of private property, and private property, in the American value system, was sacrosanct and inviolable.

Yet another American trait created problems for the abolitionists. Mainstream Americans have traditionally exhibited a tendency to reject "extremism" of any sort; they have looked askance at any group demanding what Martin Duberman has called "large-scale readjustment," even in the direction of clearly needed reform. The liberal consensus in the United States has traditionally rejected the quick way, the total solution, the utopian answer, and accepted the gradual and the partial in the way of reform. The abolitionists seemed to represent the radical and the extreme. They were, in fact, both, and as such, they clearly cut against the American grain.

Moreover, as a recent and provocative study of anti-abolitionist mobs demonstrates, the abolitionists represented still another kind of threat: a threat to the sense of order, community, and propriety held by the members of the old, established elite, seemingly under attack on several fronts in this period of flux and change. In some respects the abolitionists even served as a symbol of all the disruptive forces threatening the old regime. The more extreme abolitionists were anti-tradionalist, frequently anti-institutional (particularly in their rejection of normal political channels and their condemnation of the conservative churches for their failure to join the antislavery cause), and generally unwilling to work with or through the old community power structure. They by-passed the mayors and sheriffs and city fathers and influential white clergy, and went directly to the people—all the people, including blacks, women, and young people—with their message, a message frequently translated by the old elite as equalitarian leveling and race-destructive amalgamation. Little wonder that "Gentlemen of Property and Standing" frequently participated in the violent attacks on abolitionists.

Finally, the abolitionists stirred up enormous opposition in the North because their goals and methods seemed to threaten the Union itself. Southern proslavery spokesmen, many of them in positions of power and prestige in the federal government, constantly and vociferously reminded the nation that the southern states would secede from the Union should any serious threat to slavery ever develop. Should the abolitionists gain any visible successes, the continued existence of the nation seemed in doubt. And to most white Americans, north and south, the dissolution of the union would be the ultimate disaster. Consequently, anti-abolition and prounion stances came to be synonymous in the minds of many American nationalists.

Benjamin Quarles has neatly summed up the opinions mainstream America held of the abolitionists:

By most of their countrymen, the abolitionists were looked upon as sappers of the social order who incited the slaves to rebel and the free Negro to seek intermarriage. And almost as bad, they endangered property rights, enfeebled the church, and subverted the Constitution.

It is little wonder that the opposition to abolitionism was

as fierce as it was in the North, at least during the first decade or so of immediatist domination of the movement. Fierce is the appropriate adjective to describe the anti-abolitionist resistance. The more "respectable" members of American society utilized social ostracism, economic sanctions and reprisals, individual assault and, as we have seen, mob violence against the objects of their wrath. Every leading abolitionist spokesman was attacked physically and often brutally in the course of his career. William Lloyd Garrison was marched through the streets of Boston with a rope around his neck and was seriously threatened with lynching. Elijah Lovejoy was murdered by an anti-abolitionist mob in Alton, Illinois, while trying to protect his press from the mob's assault. Such vigilante activity, tendered against these public menaces who threatened in a variety of ways to destroy the national cultural fabric, was considered appropriate by the majority whites.

But despite all the obstacles, the abolitionists did have *one* real advantage, one solid foundation from which to support their position and pursue their crusade. They were able to attack a culturally vulnerable institution, one *not* deeply embedded in the total culture pattern. For slavery was, after all, an institution peculiar to the South; despite its influence on national history, slavery was clearly a southern regional institution, one without strong cultural supports in other major regions of the nation. And in a period of intense regional identification and competition, the anti-southern prejudices of Northerners tended to encourage the development of antislavery attitudes. Moreover, the abolitionists were able to mount and focus their attack in a region in which the institution did not exist and where there were few to defend it on the basis of firm commitment and firsthand knowledge. Whenever the abolitionists were able to employ the symbols of the "anti-Americanness" of slavery—the slave-catchers, the auction block, the whips and shackles—they were able to win attention and, increasingly, even respect from many who had formerly been indifferent to the institution. Over the years the abolitionists also came to win the attention of some rather cynical, opportunistic politicians of the traditional stripe.

Yet if the cultural vulnerability of slavery was the sole major advantage of the antislavery forces, it was an advantage filled with danger and the threat of civil war, for the institution under assault was one that the slave South deemed of *central integrative* significance to its regional culture. To permit the destruction of slavery was to permit the destruction of the slave-plantation complex on which the southern subculture rested. Moreover, the politically verbal elements of the slave South had come over the years to realize that they were on the defensive in the continuing struggle for regional interest group power; in fact, they had come to see that they were more and more in a minority in national affairs. It was this reality that John C. Calhoun was trying to offset when he developed the theory of nullification in the late 1820s, and that the South Carolina Nullificationists were seeking to counter in the crisis of 1832 to 1833. Partly because of the efforts of the abolitionists, the institution of slavery became the focal point of regional power manipulation by the nation's dominant political forces.

The course of the abolitionist movement between 1840 and 1860 was shaped by (even as it helped to shape) national political affairs. Ironically, the abolitionists would experience a split in their ranks before they began to exercise effective political power. The split occurred in the spring of 1840. A significant number of abolitionists had come to object to several aspects of Garrison's position, particularly his espousal of more than one reform cause, his intransigent opposition to the clergy and to institutionalized religion in general, and, most important, his continuing refusal to pursue political channels as a method of attacking slavery. In May 1840 the anti-Garrisonian group met to form the new American and Foreign Anti-Slavery Society, the support for which came largely from outside Massachusetts and Pennsylvania, chiefly from New York and the Northwest. Its leaders included James Gillespie Birney, the Tappan brothers, and Gerrit Smith, all wealthy

New Yorkers, Judge William Jay, Joshua Leavitt, and Henry B. Stanton, as well as the eight black clergymen noted above. However, despite the support given the new organization by such men as Henry Highland Garnet, most blacks remained loyal Garrisonians and maintained their ties with the old American Antislavery Society.[8]

The commitment of the anti-Garrisonians to political action was manifested by the activities of the new Liberty Party, founded in 1840, the central purpose of which was to make slavery the focal issue in American politics. With both major parties desperately attempting to keep the slavery issue buried, however, the Liberty Party people could have done little to dramatize their singleness of purpose if other historical forces had not intervened. The major force was the regional fury unleashed by the acquisition of additional American territory as a result of the Mexican War. The question of slavery extension—a matter that had been temporarily settled by the Missouri Compromise of 1820—was back with a vengeance. The proslavery interests insisted on the necessity of slavery expansion if the institution and thus the Southern regional culture were to survive. By now, however, the politicians of the free states had become convinced that slavery must not be permitted to expand beyond its current limits. In the breach of this essentially irreconcilable confrontation, the movement known as "Free Soil" was born.

To understand the Free Soil Movement one must go back to the year 1846—to the Mexican War and to the congressional debate of that year over the disposition of territory acquired by that war—and to a Pennsylvania congressman named David Wilmot. In his famous "Proviso," an amendment to a war appropriation bill, Wilmot asserted that no territory acquired as a result of the war should ever be open to slavery. The Wilmot Proviso was killed in the Senate, but it reopened the furious debate between proslavery and free state representatives and aroused all the old rancor associated with that debate. Aside from its divisive nature, the most significant thing about the Proviso was the argument used in its support by Wilmot himself. His position was not that slavery was evil and should therefore be restricted, but that the newly acquired territories should be kept free of slavery *and* of black people so that the states carved from those territories might be populated solely by whites. "I plead the cause and the rights of white freemen," proclaimed Wilmot in 1847. "I would preserve to free white labor a fair country, a rich inheritance, where the sons of toil, of my own race and own color, can live without the disgrace which association with negro slavery brings upon free labor." Free soil maintained as a special preserve of free whites, such was Wilmot's position, and it quickly proved to be one on which many northern and western whites could take a stand. The Free Soil stance overcame the greatest objection to out-and-out abolitionism, because under the broad cover of Free Soil one could oppose slavery and its extension without commiting himself to equality for blacks or even to association with them. Under Free Soil, not only would slavery be circumscribed and limited to the states where it already existed; so would the great majority of black people.

The Free Soil position also overcame certain other objections to abolition. It did not represent an attack on property, its adherents claimed, since they did not propose to take slaves away from slaveowners; they wanted only to prevent slaveholders from taking that special variety of property into the territories. Moreover, the economic interests of the North, dependent on plantation produce for their own operations, would not be deprived of essential commodities. Cotton in particular would continue to be produced by slave labor on southern plantations. Free soil was a far less "radical" position than abolitionism and was thus considerably more acceptable to the basic American value system. Finally, there were many in the free states who favored some type of gradual abolition and believed that limiting slavery to the states in which it already existed would mean the eventual extinction of the institution over an extended period of time. Such people were able to salve their uneasy consciences by taking a position they felt to be in the *ultimate* sense, antislavery. Abraham Lincoln was one of these people. So perhaps were the majority of northern whites.

The Free Soil point of view acquired institutional form with the creation of the Free Soil Party in 1848, a party that proved quite attractive to dissident elements from the old-line Whig and Democratic parties, both of which were in a state of near fragmentation. But now the true abolitionists were in a quandary. The Free Soil Party was *not* an abolitionist party in any sense that would appeal to an immediatist. On the other hand the Liberty Party was itself seriously damaged by Free Soil co-optation and fragmentation in 1848, so that the political abolitionists had little real choice. Most of them chose to support the Free Soilers, reluctantly perhaps, but with the hope that they might ultimately influence the party in the direction of more militant abolitionism, or that events might permit the abolitionist use of the Free Soil political framework. The widening sectional rift and the growth of regional antipathy in the years immediately following the Mexican War would provide the abolitionists with the leverage for which they were hoping.

The Treaty of Guadaloupe-Hidalgo ending the Mexican War had barely been ratified when the struggle over slavery expansion broke out again. The raging controversy was temporarily settled by the famous "Compromise of 1850." By admitting California as a free state and leaving the status of slavery in the rest of the newly acquired territory undetermined, by promising the South a new, strict federal Fugitive Slave Law, and by abolishing the slave trade (but not slavery) in the District of Columbia, the compromisers managed to avert civil war over the slavery extension question. But the compromise was a patchwork job at best, one that contained within its own provisions the seeds of its eventual failure.

Be defining a large geographical area in which the status of slavery was left undetermined, the compromisers expanded the battleground in the war of slavery *versus* Free Soil. The new Fugitive Slave Law of 1850, one of the most viciously repressive pieces of legislation ever passed by Congress, subjected every free black in the North and West to potential capture by "slave catchers," who had only to swear to a local justice of the peace that their captives were fugitive slaves in order to obtain legal permission to to take them South into bondage. With slavery again as its focal point, the regional controversy grew more and more heated. Every matter relating to slavery or to the pro-slavery-Free Soil struggle for political domination came to be tremendously emotion-charged. As we have observed earlier, proslavery Southerners had come to view all "Yankees" as abolitionists and enemies. Now most Northerners came to see proslavery as a conspiracy to spread the institution over the entire nation, and as a threat to the personal liberties of whites as well as of blacks.[9] Proslavery Southerners even seemed willing to destroy the union over the issue of slavery, putting an end to the great experiment in republican government.

All of this is a familiar enough story to students of American history. Its pertinence to the Afro-American experience is indirect, but enormously significant. Black slavery and black people were at the base of the great regional contention, and thus represented a vast, although at times impersonal, historical force. But in one specific sequence of episodes, the black role in the great controversy was direct and determinative in bringing on the ultimate break. The passage and enforcement of the new Fugitive Slave Law offered the abolitionists an opportunity to dramatize the anti-libertarian aspects of American slavery and the plight of northern free blacks as well as of slaves. Despite several dramatic (and widely publicized) rescues or attempted rescues of blacks who were being returned to slavery, and despite the passage of so-called "Personal Liberty Laws" by several states, depriving federal officials of the aid of state law-enforcement machinery, the Fugitive Slave Law was generally well enforced. In the first few years of the act's existence, over 200 blacks were taken by slave catchers, and only a dozen or so were able to regain their freedom. So real was the threat posed by this law that hundreds of blacks left the northern cities in what Benjamin Quarles has called a "black exodus." From Pittsburg alone about 200 blacks departed for Canada even before the law was signed, arming themselves and vowing to die before returning to slavery.

It is important to note that northern blacks were infuriated by, and publically denounced, this federal assault on their constitutionally guaranteed rights. The usually mild-mannered pacifist Robert Purvis declared to the annual meeting of the Pennsylvania Anti-Slavery Society in 1850: ". . . should any wretch enter my dwelling, any pale-faced spectre among ye, to execute this law on me or mine, I'll seek his life, I'll shed his blood." Frederick Douglass was of the same opinion. More important, so were a great many northern whites, perhaps even a majority of them. For the capture or attempted capture of blacks under the authority of a dangerous law seemed to them as wrong and as "un-American" as anything they could imagine. Even though most whites were racists, and many did not like blacks and did not want them as equals, they could see and resent an obvious injustice and transfer their indignation against such injustice from the law and its enforcers to the slave South. As this process in social psychology occurred over and over again, the abolitionists found that their message was receiving a more sympathetic hearing. In fact, by the middle of the 1850s they actually achieved a certain element of respectability in the mainstream white community. When abolitionist Harriet Beecher Stowe published *Uncle Tom's Cabin* in 1852 (written partly as a protest against the Fugitive Slave Law), she gained not only respect but adulation. Northern whites were ready for her message, as the incredible sale of the book proved, and the North-South regional furor grew ever more heated.

However, in the continuing battle over the injustice (and unAmericanness) of slavery, the black man somehow got lost. Even as the first of the abolitionists' goals seemed to be achieving some success, the second—the equalitarian one—was being sidetracked. In 1857 black Americans were devastated by an unprecedented blow. They were informed that in the opinion of the Supreme Court of the United States, they were not Americans at all. In the case of *Dred Scott* v. *Sanford*, Chief Justice Roger B. Taney (a Maryland slaveowner) declared for the majority of the court that Afro-Americans were not citizens of the United States: ". . . they are not included, and were not intended to be included under the word 'citizens' in the Constitution, and can, therefore, claim none of the rights and privileges which that instrument provides for and secures to citizens of the United States." The court further declared that no legislative act could deprive slaveowners of the right to take their "property" into whatever United States territorial possession they pleased, compromise or no compromise. Thus, the only recognized relationship the federal government had with black Americans was in the enforcement of the Fugitive Slave Law. As a Columbus, Ohio, newspaper editor observed, the United States government was now dedicated to the principles of "Life, Liberty and the 'Pursuit of Niggers.'"

Deprived of any semblance of recognition by their own government and seeing little or no practical advance in status or opportunity for equality, the black spokesmen of the 1850s took a distinct turn toward a more militant stance. Their rhetoric grew angrier. Nonviolence was advocated less and less often, and violence and bloodshed came to be viewed as a very real possibility, perhaps a necessity. But there was a clear element of despair even in the angry rhetoric. Douglass voiced this despair and anguish late in the 1850s:

I can hate this Government [the United States] without being disloyal because it has stricken down my manhood, and treated me as a saleable commodity. I can join a foreign enemy and fight against it, without being a traitor, because it treats me as an ALIEN and a STRANGER, and I am free to avow that should such a contingency arise I should not hesitate to take any advantage in order to procure such indemnity for the future.

Martin R. Delany, prominent physician-journalist and a

notable black leader, had written Garrison somewhat earlier: "I must admit, . . . I have no hopes in this country—no confidence in the American people." Yet the two black leaders took different courses of action based on their similar conclusions. Delany undertook to lead an emigrationist movement based on black nationalist principles, and found a considerable following among those convinced of the hopelessness of the black man's plight in white America. Douglass chose to make his fight in the United States and continued to push for abolition and black equality. But by the late 1850s, the fight was getting noticeably rougher. A group of genuinely militant abolitionists known as the "Secret Six" were conspiring even as Douglass spoke to mount a direct assault on slavery in the South, an assault to be led by the veteran antislavery warrior, John Brown.[10]

Some years after the Civil War, Douglass, in reflecting on the significance of John Brown's attack on Harper's Ferry, expressed the opinion that the raid "began the war that ended slavery." "Until this blow was struck," Douglass claimed, "the prospect for freedom was dim, shadowy, and uncertain . . . . When John Brown stretched forth his arm the sky was cleared." Douglass was not overstating the case. No single episode in the long sequence of disagreements between North and South had as much impact on the future course of history as this attempt to foment slave insurrection in the area that had for so long feared slave revolt above all else. The ultimate threat to the white South became an active reality in this abortive attack by a man soon to become another martyr to the abolitionist cause. The emotional break between hostile regions was now complete. In retrospect it seems clear that the John Brown raid made the approaching conflict truly "irrepressible."

But the question remains, what was the role of the abolitionists in the coming of "the war that ended slavery"? The answer, as is so often the case with big historical questions, is not readily apparent. The precise role of abolitionism simply cannot be ascertained, but two functions of the abolitionists are clear enough. First, the abolitionists, as we have seen, served as goads to the national conscience, a conscience that would likely have continued to rest in satisfied torpor without such a prod. Americans were forced, whether they liked it or not, to recognize the inherent wrongness and "un-Americanness" of chattel slavery. Second, the abolitionists were instrumental in creating regional antipathy and hostility that were necessary preconditions of civil war. That the proslavery South felt threatened in the security of its socioeconomic system was largely the work of the abolitionists. Moreover, the abolitionists were successful in keeping the specific focus of the regional struggle on slavery at a time when most whites, in both the North and South, would have preferred to bury that divisive issue altogether or to render it harmless by ignoring it. Abolitionist successes in this respect were largely responsible for one major political party, the Republican, advocating freesoil principles in its campaigns of 1856 and 1860. Freesoil was, of course, not a truly abolitionist position, but it did provide the ultimate threat of circumscribing the slave South with free states. That threat, as historian Eugene Genovese has argued, was sufficient to generate an attempt at territorial-national insurrection by proslavery politicians in the South. This attempt may be said to have "caused" the Civil War, the war that ended slavery.

Although the war resulted in the abolition of slavery, emancipation was not an original war aim of the Union side. Abraham Lincoln resisted secession because he believed the Union to be "indivisible"; hence, in his view, the southern secessionists were committing treason. It was to preserve the Union, not to abolish slavery, that the North went to war.

And yet somehow slavery and emancipation were involved even from the outset, as the abolitionists insisted and as many whites and virtually all blacks believed. But the abolitionists had to convince President Lincoln that the advantages of emancipation would offset the disadvantages: the possible secession of the southern border states and the opposition of northern white racists. Convincing the President took considerable time, for Lincoln was not, at the outset of the conflict, committed to immediate abolition or to black equality. Strategic imperatives were far more important to this eminently practical man than were abstract antislavery principles. Indeed, it was only when Lincoln decided that emancipation was a strategic wartime necessity that he determined to issue the Emancipation Proclamation. By reducing the availability of black labor to the Confederates, by generating the fear of slave insurrection in the South, and by sanctifying the war as a moral crusade, the Emancipation Proclamation served vital strategic ends. The Proclamation itself was an almost totally dispassionate statement issued "as a fit and necessary war measure, . . . upon military necessity . . . ." Its provisions applied only to areas over which the United States Army exercised no control, that is, to areas still "in rebellion against the United States." Blacks freed by the advancing armies were advised to "abstain from all violence, unless in necessary self-defense," and to continue to "labor faithfully for reasonable wages." But near the end of the Proclamation, Lincoln included an enormously important statement: the new freedmen, he declared, if they were "of suitable condition," would be "received into the armed service of the United States . . . ."

If the Emancipation Proclamation provided only for a kind of "strategic" emancipation in the minds of Lincoln and most whites, it afforded Afro-Americans the real cause for which they had long hoped to fight. Frederick Douglass, for example, had fully appreciated the importance of black participation in the struggle for freedom. "Once let the black man get upon his person the brass letters, U. S., " he argued, "let him get an eagle on his button, and a musket on his shoulder and bullets in his pocket, and there is no power on earth which can deny that he has earned the right to citizenship in the United States." But initially blacks had been refused the right to participate in the war effort, partly because many whites sensed the validity of Douglass' statement and partly because most whites believed blacks genetically incapable of military service. In either case, white racism was involved. When in 1862 black abolitionist John Mercer Langston of Ohio suggested to Governor David Tod that black volunteers could be enlisted to fill part of Ohio's quota, Tod curtly refused. "Do you know, Mr. Langston," said the governor, "that this is a *white man's* government; that white men are able to defend and protect it? . . . When we want you colored men we will notify you." Within a matter of months after Tod's revealing dismissal of Langston's suggestion, United States policy changed. Lincoln and his Secretary of War, Edwin M. Stanton, determined that the potential military resource afforded by the black population could no longer be ignored. Late in 1862 the active enlistment of black troops began, and in March 1863 Stanton dispatched General Lorenzo Thomas to the lower Mississippi Valley to recruit and organize the freedmen into effective military units. On May 22, 1863, Stanton established the Bureau of Colored Troops within the War Department to serve as the administrative agency of black recruitment and training throughout the United States. (In June 1863, Governor Tod contacted Langston, authorizing him to recruit black troops, and by November 1863 a black Ohio regiment was in training.)

Contrary to the expectations of most white Americans, black Americans quickly proved themselves good soldiers. In two major engagements during the summer of 1863, at Port Hudson and at Milliken's Bend on the Mississippi River, black troops served capably. Later that summer the 54th Massachusetts Regiment, the best-known black unit of the Civil War, performed heroically in the assault on Fort Wagner in Charleston harbor. These three engagements served to convince former skeptics of the potential of black troops, and removed virtually all doubt as to the wisdom of arming the blacks. In all, as the official records indicate, almost 180,000 enlisted men fought in black regiments in the war. They participated in some 449 engagements, 39 of them major battles. Another 29,000 Afro-Americans served in the Union Navy. Approximately

37,300 blacks died fighting for the United States, and 21 Congressional Medals of Honor were bestowed on black servicemen. As one historian has concluded, "More than any other single factor the performance of Negro soldiers earned their race the respect of the North, made emancipation secure, and helped pave the way for the gains made by the Negro during Reconstruction."[11] The black military contribution to Union success, historians now agree, was crucial. James M. McPherson, perhaps the closest student of black participation in the Union war effort, has argued that without the help of black Americans from both North and South, "the North could not have won the war as soon as it did, and perhaps it could not have won at all."

Although it would be impossible to determine precisely the extent to which black participation in the war paved the way to permanent emancipation, it assuredly helped the cause. At approximately the same time that the successes of black regiments in the field became matters of record (late in 1863), a movement was launched to extend the limits of "strategic emancipation." Certain spokesmen for the freedmen realized that when the war ended slavery would remain an established, legal institution unless steps were taken to eliminate it completely by constitutional amendment. Accordingly, in December 1863 a number of abolitionist groups began to organize efforts to secure the passage of an emancipation amendment. They launched a petition campaign that resulted in the introduction and consideration of a proposed amendment in the House of Representatives. It passed the House January 31, 1865. "Neither slavery nor involuntary servitude," it stated, "except as a punishment for crime whereof the party shall have been duly convicted, shall exist within the United States, or any place subject to their jurisdiction." The necessary three fourths of the states ratified the Thirteenth Amendment before the end of the year. "Strategic emancipation" had been replaced by something more thorough and more permanent.

The permanent abolition of slavery had been achieved

with relative ease, once its proponents had made the decision to push for it. In the North, as we have noted, slavery was a vulnerable institution. Within a short time after emancipation, the abolitionists, formerly the object of such rancor and hatred, became heroes. Even in the South the fall of slavery produced something of a sigh of relief on the part of many whites. Despite the former feelings of white Southerners that the "peculiar institution" was of central integrative significance to their "way of life," they never made any serious attempt to reinstitute the slave system. They adjusted rather quickly to a new life devoid of the tension-laden practice of owning outright that "troublesome property."

The abolition of slavery was achieved within the lifetime of most of those who dedicated themselves to emancipation, and many of them believed that the ratification of the Thirteenth Amendment marked the end of their crusade. But other abolitionists saw that the amendment did little more than provide a kind of "technical emancipation." As Wendell Phillips had said of the Emancipation Proclamation, the amendment freed the slave but ignored the Negro. Abolition assuredly produced a sense of psychological liberation in the freedmen that matched their satisfaction in physical liberation. But any real change in the material and social status of black Americans would have to be based on attitudinal changes in white Americans. Whites represented an overwhelming majority of the population, and thus would have to control their antiblack prejudice before blacks could achieve much more than technical emancipation. Whites could not do this, as they had demonstrated throughout the course of the war. Even as northern whites had fought and died in a war partly dedicated to the abolition of slavery in the South, other whites had fought against black equality in the North and West.[12] The question of what to do with the freedmen once emancipation came had caused no end of difficulty even as the war progressed. Senator Ben Wade, later to play an important role in "Radical Reconstruction," stated the problem with startling lucidity: "If we are to have no more slave states," he asked, "what the devil are we to do with the surplus niggers?" The answer throughout the free states was similar. "We" keep them out altogether by law, or "we" make it impossibly uncomfortable for them by implementing discriminatory policies and practices. "We" continue to segregate blacks from whites in all possible areas, and "we" deprive blacks of any semblance of political or economic power. Ultimately "we" turn the whole matter of "what to do with the surplus niggers" over to the white South to settle in the manner it thinks best.

White racism was to limit the actual gains of blacks in both the North and South to the technical emancipation of the Thirteenth Amendment, despite the efforts of the old-line abolitionists to realize the second of their goals. In 1860 a British traveler commented on the nature of race relations in the North: "We see, in effect, two nations — one white and another black— growing up together within the same political circle, but never mingling on a principle of equality." Had he returned in 1865 following the ratification of the Thirteenth Amendment his observations would likely have been little changed. The white South would require considerable time to work out the nature of race relations in the former slave states; the process would culminate in the Jim Crow system written into law in the late 1890s. In the meantime, hundreds of blacks would die at the hands of white "vigilante" groups as the politicians occupied themselves with other matters.

In terms of culture analysis, the reasons for the failure of emancipation to "free" black Americans seem clear. While slavery had been neither central nor integrative in the American culture system, white racism was both. It was also pervasive and thoroughly embedded in the very fabric of the mainstream American culture pattern. Again, for meaningful change to have occurred in the status of blacks, whites would have had to have undergone psychic and attitudinal changes of inordinate complexity, and they would have had to have done so in such a manner as to create a new value system with regard to Afro-America. Such a change had not occurred by 1865. Consequently, the efforts of the so-called "radical" Republicans during Reconstruction were doomed to failure. Jim Crow practices would continue in the North and would be systematically instituted in the South. The continuing centrality of racism in American culture would account for the popularity of Booker T. Washington among whites (who misunderstood him), the grim phenomenon of lynching, the persistence of an Afro-American subculture, and the continued existence of the "two nations" that the famous Kerner Report would find still in existence in the middle of the 1960s.[13]

There is grim irony in the fact that the persistence of a black subculture, and its present-day expression in black in-group solidarity and increasing self-regard and identity recognition, are the products of a dominant culture that continues to deny Afro-Americans entry into the mainstream. Euro-American racism necessitated the development of Afro-America. Afro-America now exists as a viable and enormously important subculture element. It is the strangely healthy side effect of a chronic illness, and will continue to exist at least as long as the illness persists. What are the chances of complete recovery? Prognosis is poor. Afro-America seems assured of a continued and increasingly autonomous existence for the foreseeable future.

NOTES

[1] Black opposition to colonization was nearly unanimous, at least in the early years of the existence of the American Colonization Society. Blacks were deeply suspicious of any policy directly concerning their lives about which they had not been consulted. They argued further that colonization would only serve to reinforce the institution of slavery by removing free blacks who might be expected to serve the antislavery cause. Free blacks in Africa could hardly fight slavery in America. Finally, they saw colonization as a form of exile, and they believed that they had the right of any American to remain in the land of his birth.

[2] The term "immediatism" was used with something less than precision throughout the antebellum period. To some the term meant immediate emancipation of all slaves. To others it meant gradual emancipation begun immediately. To still others it meant something in between these positions. But one thing all immediatists shared was the determination that slavery be put on the path to extinction in the United States, beginning right away.

[3] Garrison's rise to fame proved nearly fatal to southern abolitionism. Although never completely dead, antislavery in the South would never again be permitted free overt expression. The supporters of slavery were able to associate *all* antislavery with Garrisonianism and to anathematize both.

[4] Several fundamental differences in the attitudes of abolitionists surfaced in 1833 that would later lead to the fragmentation of the movement's leadership. Two major differences are apparent. Garrison and his followers (which included *most* black abolitionists) believed that no gradualist reform movement would ever eliminate

slavery and the racism on which it was based, and that only a complete and immediate (although nonviolent) uprooting of the institution of slavery would ever prove effective. They were true radicals, who opposed constitutional and political means and rejected any form of "moderation." Garrison's opponents, however, were more traditional American reformers who wanted to operate within the system: to be "realistic," to avoid extremism, and to effect change slowly through the "moderate" means afforded by existing American institutions.

[5] Some controversy still rages over the degree to which white abolitionists were able to divest themselves of their own antiblack prejudices. Doubtless some abolitionists did harbor the common racist assumptions of most white Americans. But relatively speaking they were far less virulent in their prejudices and were usually able to hold their feelings in check. Some believed sincerely in the inherent equality of all races. The vast majority, despite frequent signs of paternalism and condescension, *did* uphold the principles of economic, political, and civil equality for Afro-Americans.

[6] In some instances, however, the black church served a conservative instead of a militant role in the black community. Some tradition-bound ministers continued to preach acceptance of this-worldly ugliness and pain as a means to other worldly beauty and happiness. Remember, David Walker blamed "the preachers of Jesus Christ" for much of the black man's trouble.

[7] A list of other black abolitionist leaders who served the fugitive cause at one time or another would include Frederick Douglass (in Rochester, New York), Samuel Ringgold Ward (in Syracuse), Robert Purvis and William Still (in Philadelphia), and Lewis Hayden (in Boston).

[8] Frederick Douglass was among the black leaders who remained with Garrison, at least for a considerable time. In 1849 Douglass still proclaimed himself loyal to the Garrisonian principles. However, in 1847 he had moved to Rochester, New York, where he came under the influence of the New York group, and having already begun publication of the *North Star*, he began using it as an instrument of documenting his shifting position. It was a position that ultimately called for the use of political action, appeals to the United States Constitution as potentially useful to antislavery interests, and the admission that violence might be necessary to achieve emancipation. In May 1851 he tacitly admitted his heresy to the annual convention of the American Anti-Slavery Society. The break with Garrison was complete.

[9] Wrote James Russell Lowell in the first series of his famous "Bigelow Papers:"

Wy, its jest as clear ez figgers,
Clear ez one an' one make two,
Chaps thet make black slaves o' niggers
Want to make wite slaves o' you.

[10] The group included Theodore Parker, Gerrit Smith, George L. Stearns, Samuel Gridley Howe, Thomas Wentworth Higginson, and Frank Sanborn. All were from Massachusetts. Although Douglass was not actively involved in the conspiracy he was closely associated with several members of the "Secret Six" and had been favorably impressed with Brown since their first meeting in 1847.

[11] For all the success of the black regiments in the field, and for all their contribution to a Union victory in the war, black troops served in a distinctly second-class status throughout the war. They fought in segregated units, usually under white officers (few blacks were commissioned during the war), they were ordinarily paid substantially less than whites, and they suffered from white discrimination and disdain in the North, frequently even while in uniform. Confederate troops frequently refused to treat them as soldiers at all, showing them no mercy in battle, refusing to take black prisoners, and perpetrating such atrocities on black troops as the infamous "Fort Pillow Massacre" of 1864. Only in the United States Navy were there no official Jim Crow policies, but of course black sailors were also subjected to individual acts of discrimination.

[12] Many black spokesmen saw clearly that white racism would hinder any efforts toward complete emancipation. The editor of the *Anglo-African* published an incredible statement of this viewpoint on March 29, 1862. He began his editorial by commenting that "the prejudice of the North" continued to form a "strong impediment" to any elevation of black status. Then he continued:

We may as well look this prejudice in the face as a disturbing element in the way of emancipation. Its manifest expression is, that setting black men free to be the equals of white men in the slave states is something more dreadful than rebellion or secession, or even a dismembered union .... The other form in which this prejudice is pronounced, is, in the fear expressed that the retaining of colored free laborers in the South will interfere with the domain of white laborers .... Poor, chicken-hearted, semi-barbarous Caucasians, when will you learn that 'the earth was made for MAN?' You have arts and arms, and culture, and an overwhelming majority in numbers .... Must you die and give no sign that you have been able to surmount the prejudice of race, or your dread of the Negro?

The editor had actually understated the potential for trouble from such prejudice. Northern antiblack sentiment exploded into the riots and lynchings of 1862 and 1863 that culminated with the vicious New York Draft Riots of July 13-16, 1863, in which undetermined scores of blacks were killed by a rampant mob largely composed of Irish immigrants.

[13] The nature of the subculture would, of course, come under powerful influence of *urban* imperatives following the "great migration" of the late nineteenth and early twentieth centuries. Whereas the plantation had been the crucible of black subculture developments prior to 1865, the urban black community would provide the dominant subculture determinants of the twentieth century.

SUGGESTIONS FOR FURTHER READING

Many of the titles recommended in connection with earlier chapters also apply to this one, especially to the background of nineteenth-century antislavery and emancipation. Most notable among them are Winthrop Jordan's *White Over Black*, David Brion Davis' *The Problem of Slavery in Western Culture*, and Arthur Zilversmit's *The First Emancipation: The Abolition of Slavery in the North*. The standard work on the abolitionist movement is still Louis Filler, *The Crusade Against Slavery, 1830-1860* (New York: Harper, 1960), but much important work has been done on the subject since 1960, some of which has modified Filler's analysis in one way or another. Two other older studies worthy of note are Gilbert Hobbs Barnes, *The Antislavery Impulse* (New York: Harcourt Brace and World, 1964), and Dwight Lowell Dumond, *Antislavery: The Crusade for Freedom in America* (Ann Arbor: University of Michigan Press, 1961).

One weakness of all the older studies of abolitionism is their failure to give sufficient credit to the work of black abolitionists. Benjamin Quarles has written an excellent monograph correcting this failure in his *Black Abolitionists* (New York: Oxford University Press, 1969). Leon Litwack's *North of Slavery: The Negro in the Free States, 1790-1860* (Chicago: University of Chicago Press, 1961) has a fine chapter entitled "Abolitionism: White and Black," and Quarles has done a full-length biography of the most important black abolitionist in his *Frederick Douglass* (Washington: Associated Publishers, 1948). Douglass may also be studied through his own collected writings in Philip Foner, ed., *The Life and Writings of Frederick Douglass*, 4 volumes (New York: International Publishers,

1950-1955). Other important blacks who participated in the anti-slavery crusade are treated in the following journal articles: Henry N. Sherwood, "Paul Cuffe," *Journal of Negro History*, *8*:153-229 (1923); Ray Allen Billington, "James Forten: Forgotten Abolitionist," *Negro History Bulletin*, *13*:31-36, 45 (1949); William M. Brewster, "Henry Highland Garnet," *Journal of Negro History*, *13*:36-52 (1928); William M. Brewster, "John B. Russwurm," *Journal of Negro History*, *13*:413-422 (1928); and Dorothy B. Porter, "David Ruggles, An Apostle of Human Rights," *Journal of Negro History*, *28*:23-50 (1943). A good synthesis of the entire abolitionist movement that incorporates recent scholarship on all participants is Gerald Sorin, *Abolitionism. A New Perspective* (New York: Praeger, 1972).

Racial attitudes and their significance are capably and imaginatively assessed in George M. Fredrickson, *The Black Image in the White Mind* (New York: Harper and Row, 1971). Northern and western antiblack prejudice and white racism have been clearly documented in an important series of monographs beginning with Litwack's *North of Slavery* in 1961. Lorman Ratner, *Powder Keg: Northern Opposition to the Antislavery Movement, 1831-1840* (New York: Basic Books, 1968) expands on a theme treated more briefly in Litwack, as does Leonard L. Richards, *Gentlemen of Property and Standing: Anti-Abolitionist Mobs in Jacksonian America* (New York: Oxford University Press, 1970), although Richards' argument is more sophisticated and complex. Eugene H. Berwanger, *The Frontier Against Slavery: Western Anti-Negro Prejudice and the Slavery Extension Controversy* (Urbana: University of Illinois Press, 1967) documents western attitudes toward blacks and slavery (the white westerners tended to hate both). Eric Foner, *Free Soil, Free Labor, Free Men: The Ideology of the Republican Party Before the Civil War* (New York: Oxford University Press, 1970) treats the abiding racism of the Freesoilers on the eve of the war, and V. Jacque Voegeli, *Free But Not Equal: The Midwest and the Negro During the Civil War* (Chicago: University of Chicago Press, 1967) extends the same basic idea into the war itself.

Some other important monographs treating a variety of related matters include Aileen S. Kraditor, *Means and Ends in American Abolitionism: Garrison and His Critics on Strategy and Tactics, 1834-1850* (New York: Pantheon Books, 1969); P. J. Staudenraus, *The African Colonization Movement* (New York: Columbia University Press, 1961); Larry Gara, *The Liberty Line: The Legend of the Underground Railroad* (Lexington: University of Kentucky Press, 1967); James M. McPherson, *The Struggle for Equality: Abolitionists and the Negro in the Civil War and Reconstruction* (Princeton:

Princeton University Press, 1962); and Dudley Taylor Cornish, *The Sable Arm. Negro Troops in the Union Army, 1861-1865* (New York: W.W. Norton, 1966). McPherson has also compiled a beautifully edited sequence of firsthand accounts together with fine transitional material in *The Negro's Civil War: How American Negroes Felt and Acted During the War for the Union* (New York: Pantheon Books, 1965).

Among the many journal articles treating abolition and emancipation and related matters, a few merit special mention. One useful historiographical guide is Merton L. Dillon, "The Abolitionists: A Decade of Historiography," *Journal of Southern History*, 35:500-522 (1969). Three other specialized articles important to the argument of this chapter are Eric Foner, "The Wilmot Proviso Revisited," *Journal of American History*, 56:62-79 (1969), Larry Gara, "Slavery and the Slave Power; A Crucial Distinction," *Civil War History*, 15:5-18 (1969), and Howard H. Bell, "Expressions of Negro Militancy in the North, 1840-1860," *Journal of Negro History*, 42:247-261 (1957).

Finally there are several good readers dealing with antislavery, all of which contain valuable essay-length articles on the subject. See Richard O. Curry, ed., *The Abolitionists: Reformers or Fanatics?* (New York: Holt, Rinehart and Winston, 1965), Martin Duberman, ed., *The Antislavery Vanguard* (Princeton: Princeton University Press, 1965), a group of mostly original essays by outstanding authorities in the field, and Hugh Hawkins, ed., *The Abolitionists: Means, Ends, and Motivations*, 2nd edition (Lexington, Massachusetts: D.C. Heath, 1972), which contains both primary and secondary sources, both well selected.

INDEX

267